PREFACE

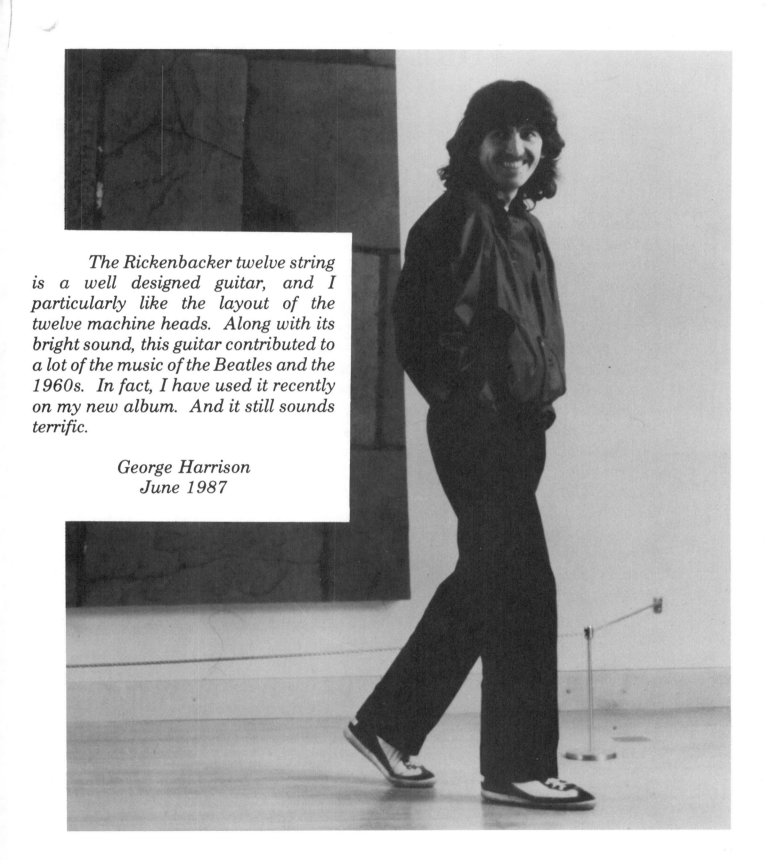

The Rickenbacker twelve string is a well designed guitar, and I particularly like the layout of the twelve machine heads. Along with its bright sound, this guitar contributed to a lot of the music of the Beatles and the 1960s. In fact, I have used it recently on my new album. And it still sounds terrific.

George Harrison
June 1987

FOREWORD

The History of Rickenbacker Guitars is fascinating reading for anyone interested in guitars, whether a beginner or a serious collector. It provides a wealth of information for determining the value on any Rickenbacker from the 1930s to the present.

Richard R. Smith has used his years of experience as a writer for Guitar Player Magazine to trace with exacting detail the development of the amplified guitar, from its inception in a mechanical form, through the electric Hawaiian, to the modern Spanish electric. He has also shown the human element behind the making of an instrument that revolutionized modern music.

In my opinion, the Byrds' sound would have been impossible without the invention of the Rickenbacker twelve string electric guitar. Indeed without Rickenbacker inventing the first electric guitar, there could never have been Rock 'n' Roll as we know it.

Reading this book reminded me of a book that I have on Mercedes Benz cars. The Rickenbacker is the Mercedes of guitars, with its elegant lines, its hand-built precision, and its excellent performance.

I hope you find this book as interesting and valuable as I do.

Roger McGuinn
June 1987

Acknowledgements

Many people helped to make this book possible. First on the list is John Hall. He understands the genuine interest people have in the Rickenbacker story, and he gave me invaluable and complete support trying to tell it accurately. Although retired, F.C. Hall freely answered many questions and helped me sort out many interesting facts about Rickenbacker. Everyone at the Rickenbacker office and factories helped in ways too numerous to list. Certainly without the help of the whole Rickenbacker organization, this book would have never been.

William H. Koon proofread and edited the manuscript as only an English professor with a collection of fine musical instruments could do. Bob Mytkowicz gave me valuable help tallying production totals and researching the Beatles' guitars. Marty Chodas helped set up my computer. Charles Chase at the Folk Music Center in Claremont, California, Cliff Archer at Archer's Music in Fresno, California, and Bob Ellefson at Valley Music Center in Hemet, California let me take photos at their stores during business hours. Jeffrey and Cindi Foskett let me take pictures of guitars in their living room.

George Harrison, Roger McGuinn, Pete Townshend, David Lindley, Alan Rogan, Nicola Joss, Jerry Byrd, Jeffrey Foskett, Alan Weidel, Carla Olson, and Derek Davis all helped with information about Rickenbacker artists.

Many other people helped put together details on guitar models, helped tie together facts, read the manuscript, and/or supplied photographs: Nolan Beauchamp, Jesse Beauchamp, Al Frost, Steve Soest (Soest Guitar Repair, Orange California), Tracy Sands, Dick Burke, Tom Wheeler (Guitar Player Magazine), R.C. Allen, Mary Patterson, Sharon Seal, Cindi Foskett, Greg Glass, John Quarterman, Gary Nichamin, John Peden (Guitar World Magazine), Robb Lawrence, Dirk P. Vogel, Naida Osline, Mike Newton, Michael Lee Allen, Bob Christopher (Screaming Strings, Decatur, Alabama), Jimmy Distefano (Sam Ash Music, New York, New York), Forrest White, Bob Rissi, Pat V. Conte, Bob Guida, Greg Henline, Kenny Blackwell, Dave Pivar for his help with the computer typesetting, and last, but not least, Ron Middlebrook. Thanks to everyone.

Introduction

Rickenbacker emerged as the first company formed for the sole purpose of providing fully electric instruments to musicians: Its 1931 start heralded the world of amplified music. Though the company developed a full line of electric stringed instruments in the 1930s, most players knew Rickenbacker for its fine steel guitars. Later, musicians knew the company for its wide variety of fretted electric guitars and basses played worldwide by some of the most famous people in music.

This book describes the Rickenbacker company's history and the development of Rickenbacker instruments including information about many of the Rickenbacker artists and their instruments. During the last fifty years, entire styles of music have evolved around electric guitars, and often Rickenbacker was at the center of change. This story shows how Rickenbacker helped shape the modern music culture with its novel instruments and timely innovations.

In addition to the history, this book provides accurate information for the Rickenbacker collectors scattered all over the world. While Rickenbacker's story is one of innovation and change weaved into the dynamic progression of twentieth century music, it is also one of nostalgia. Today many old Rickenbacker instruments are collector items because of their historical significance and/or because of their unique construction and tone. This book helps collectors date their instruments and determine their instrument's originality. Also, contained herein lies all of the available production records for collectible Rickenbacker instruments.

The company manufacturing and selling Rickenbackers has had several names, the first being Ro-Pat-In Corporation, Makers of Electro String Instruments. The owners changed the name to Electro String Instrument Corporation in 1934. Electro String made Rickenbacher Electro instruments with *Rickenbacher* spelled as it was in German. By the mid 1930s Rickenbacker usually had its current spelling, which for simplicity's sake this book will use throughout.

When F.C. Hall bought Electro String in 1953, the Radio and Television Equipment Co. took over the distribution of Rickenbacker instruments. In 1965 Mr. Hall dropped the Radio and Television and Equipment Co. name, and his sales distribution company became known as Rickenbacker, Inc. He still called his manufacturing company the Electro String Instrument Corporation. In September 1984 F.C. Hall retired and his son John Hall became the sole owner of the company and combined the distribution and manufacturing of Rickenbacker guitars into one company called Rickenbacker International Corporation (RIC).

Certainly, many facts in this book contradict earlier published accounts of Rickenbacker's history. The main reason for these discrepancies is the recent discovery of new information in original documents previously unavailable to researchers. The company put many original Rickenbacker files into storage years ago and virtually forgot them. I used these records as a basis for much of my original research.

I divided the book into two parts. Part One relates the events before George Beauchamp (pronounced Beechum), Adolph Rickenbacker, and the others formed an electric guitar company. This section includes the history of the National String Instrument Corporation, but only as it concerned Rickenbacker's founders. (This account does not attempt to tell the complete National story; that history had enough controversies to fill another book.) Part One also tells the story of Rickenbacker's early years up to the time Adolph retired from the instrument business. In addition, Part One contains details about the instruments made between 1931 and 1953.

I based the information in the first half on original files, catalogs, and correspondence from the period of 1928 through 1953. Nolan Beauchamp, George Beauchamp's son, was a significant source of additional information. Besides having grown up with guitars and music, Nolan was an engineer and worked for Electro String in the 1940s. We had many lengthy conversations, and he was kind to provide detailed historical notes and several photos of his father.

Another source for information in Part One was Doc Kauffman, the venerable Southern California inventor. He was a friend and associate of George Beauchamp and Adolph Rickenbacker for several years. Doc, who lives in Santa Ana, California, was always free to answer my questions and relate his experiences with the company.

Additional information in Part One comes from Al Frost, who went to work making National guitars in 1934. He stuck with the business through its transition into National-Dobro and its move to Chicago. Soon Frost was a partner in the Valco Manufacturing, Co., formed in 1943. Valco owned the National trademark and carried on the National tradition of quality guitars for years. Al Frost provided original National documents, photographs, and important patent information. Equally important and valuable to me were his insights from a manufacturer's perspective into those early days of the electric guitar.

The second part of this book deals with Rickenbacker's modern history under the ownership of F.C. and John Hall. Sections in the second half describe the details of the modern standard guitars and basses made from 1954 to 1986.

I based Part Two on information gathered from original files, catalogs, and price lists at the Rickenbacker office. The company's extensive photograph collection from over the years could be a book in itself. I used all of the Rickenbacker company's information freely thanks to the full cooperation of John Hall. I received additional invaluable information in many conversations with John Hall and F.C. Hall.

There are two conspicuous omissions in the story: steel guitars made after 1954 and Rickenbacker amplifiers. I included steel guitars for the 1930s and 1940s because of their historical significance and because of their appeal to collectors. Rickenbacker amps have a marked historical significance and deserve serious study beyond the scope of this book. If someone writes an accurate history of the electric guitar amplifier, it will have to include a detailed account of Rickenbacker's contributions.

After reading this book, you will see that it is easy to fall into traps trying to generalize about Rickenbacker guitars. The rich variety of Rickenbacker features and models are among the most interesting of all American electric guitar makers. I am sure this work will not answer all the questions about Rickenbacker guitars; however, it should be a good start. I welcome any questions or information readers care to send. Please contact me through Centerstream Publications, Box 5450 Fullerton, CA 92635 USA.

Richard R. Smith

Table of Contents

The Early History

Part One

The "MIDGETS" of the Tonal World Attain to GIANTS Stature!

A miracle has come to pass in the realm of beautiful tone.

The soft, fairy-voiced Hawaiian guitar, the tinkling mandolin, the ethereal Spanish guitar—all have been liberated, dignified, and given their rightful place among orchestral instruments.

HOW?

Touched with the magic wand of electrical genius the quality they lacked has been conferred upon them—

VOLUME!

Controlled volume—more than sufficient for the largest orchestra.

As much or as little as you want. You can start the tone softly and build up a tremendous crescendo, or execute a musicianly swell, without stroking the strings again. You can follow every dynamic effect of wind or percussion with no trouble at all. Marvellous, isn't it? Hardly believable till you hear it.

In addition to the added volume, the tonal qualities of each instrument have been vastly improved. The building of the instruments and the adjustment of the sound magnifying device have all been pointed to that end. There are no dissonances, or *noises* picked up to mar pure tone or damp vibration.

What would you say of a Hawaiian guitar you could hear a quarter of a mile on a clear day, or a Spanish Guitar louder than any piano? That's what we have in the new

RICKENBACHER ELECTRO INSTRUMENTS

Rickenbacker brochure circa 1934.

1

The National String Instrument Corporation_____

The story of Rickenbacker guitars began with a Texas born musician named George Beauchamp and his search for a louder, improved guitar. Beauchamp was the central figure in the founding of two important guitar manufacturing companies: National and Electro String (Rickenbacker). These companies did not set out to change music instrument history; they set out to change the lot of guitarists. Still, the people in these companies invented several unique musical instruments that left indelible imprints on the American music culture.

Beyond the musical importance of the instruments these two companies introduced, National and Electro String influenced the music industry by using new economical manufacturing techniques and untried materials to make guitars. Some of their ideas were failures while others were successes. In either case, Beauchamp and his associates made a headstrong entrance into the traditional realm of old-world craftsmanship and redefined it with modern new-world attitudes. Beauchamp's most significant individual contribution to the world of musical instruments was the first commercially sold practical electric guitar--the Electro. This development was just part of a story filled with quarrels, controversies, and achievements. It began in Los Angeles, California.

George Beauchamp was a vaudeville performer, a trained violinist, and a steel guitarist. His booking agent was the prestigious William Morris Agency. George called one of his music trios with his brother Al and a friend named Slim Hopper *The Boys from Dixie*. When Slim and George performed as a duo, they called the act *Grasshopper and George*. In the mid 1920s Hawaiian music was popular, so, George usually played steel guitar in vaudeville. His instrument was a flat top steel string acoustic with a high nut.

Like many of his frustrated guitarist contemporaries, Beauchamp was seeking a louder guitar. Guitarists wanted to stand out like the brass and reed instruments and become effective soloists in all situations. To be truly effective, the guitar needed a tone and volume potential that could cut through an orchestra. At least, guitarists wanted an instrument that could stand its own ground against a banjo, the loudest of the acoustic stringed instruments.

One plausible solution to the guitarist's problem, an idea that started in the late Nineteenth century, was to apply the principles of nonelectric phonographs to instruments. Good examples of phonograph influenced instruments came from the English company Strohviol which had jerry-built several bizarre looking styles. Beauchamp had seen a violin with a phonograph-like horn coming out of its body used by a fellow show performer. He thought someone could build a guitar with a similar amplifying horn. (Perhaps George did not know that Strohviol had already made such a steel guitar.) George's search for a craftsman to do this work led him to John Dopyera.

John Dopyera was a violin repairman and inventor with a shop fairly close to Beauchamp's Los Angeles home. His earlier work included a patented shipping crate and a patented machine for making picture frames. By the mid 1920s John and his brother Rudy had spent a lot of time designing improved banjos that they built in John's shop. Their efforts eventually led to several banjo related patents. (Besides John and Rudy, the Dopyera brothers included Emil, Robert, and Louis. Over the years each became involved to some degree, either in instrument manufacturing or in financing these ventures.)

John realized that as the popularity of banjos began to decrease in the mid 1920s, he needed a new direction. He had already considered making guitars as the natural progression of his business by the time Beauchamp came to him. The Dopyeras built a guitar for George following his suggestions. It sat on a stand and had a wild-looking walnut body with a Victrola horn attached to the bottom. According to one report, Beauchamp played this instrument in vaudeville for a short period, although it was a disappointing failure.

The Tri-Cone Guitar

After John built the first guitar, there was another idea inspired by a phonograph. Nolan Beauchamp recalls that his father took the reproduction head off their Victrola. The head had a small mica disc attached to a needle; when the needle vibrated playing a record, the disc mechanically amplified the sound through the horn. (The mica disc acted like the tissue paper in a kazoo.) George gave the disc to Dopyera and suggested he apply the same principle to a guitar.

Dopyera has usually insisted that the idea for a disc or diaphragm type resonator was his alone, something he had thought about long before he met Beauchamp. Regardless of where the idea came from, John started to experiment with discs made out of a variety of materials.

George Beauchamp as he looked in the National catalog from about 1930. George was National's general manager from 1928 through 1931.

Adolph Rickenbacker as he looked in the same catalog from 1930. Adolph's title at National was engineer.

Rickenbacker's shop around 1929. This picture appeared in the blue National catalog circa 1930.

These included paper, pressed fibre, glass, tin, and other sheet metals.

John found that conical shaped 98% aluminum resonators, with the proper thickness and hardness, worked the best.[1] John says that he turned a lathe originally used to make banjos hoops into a spinning lathe. His nephews, Paul and Carl Barth, spun the resonator discs. (Paul Barth later told Nolan Beauchamp that they had learned the metal spinning technique working for an L.A. jewelry concern.)

The resonators were wafer-thin, like the mica discs in the Victrola reproduction heads. John attached his resonators to a cast aluminum bridge that had an inserted wooden saddle. He installed this assembly into a metal guitar body. Dopyera tried using from one to four resonators in his tests, concluding that the best combination was three. The aluminum resonators amplified the bridge's vibrations the same way the small mica disc in a Victrola reproducing head amplified the needle's vibration. After some tinkering and adjustments, the prototype was ready. It got the nickname tri-cone or triplate.

Research into Dopyera's early work shows that he first sought to patent a tri-cone resonator guitar design on October 12, 1926.[2] This design, which must have represented the early prototype made for Beauchamp, had the three resonators concentrically arranged with respect to the bridge. The three legs of the bridge were the same length. Beauchamp loved the new guitar so much, he told John that they should go into business together to manufacture it.

Since the original prototype design apparently did not meet John's exacting standards, he perfected another design--the one they would manufacture. This guitar still used three resonators, but Dopyera positioned them in the guitar differently. Like the first version, the bridge on the new design had three legs. Each leg attached to the top of a cone, but one leg was longer. It had an orangewood saddle inserted directly into it to contact the strings. John applied for a patent on the improved tri-cone April 9, 1927.[3]

Once they were satisfied with the design, the Dopyeras started to make the tri-cone guitars in their shop. The brothers called the new guitars Nationals, the name they used for their banjos. John Dopyera once estimated that they built about twenty-five before a big-

ger factory was a reality. Meanwhile, George began a search for investors and capital to build that factory.

Forming the National Corporation

Beauchamp took a National prototype and the Sol Hoopii Trio to a wild, lavish party being held by George's cousin-in-law, millionaire Ted E. Kleinmeyer. The group played and impressed everyone with the wonderful sound of the new guitar. Kleinmeyer, excited about the guitar and the prospects for an investment in a new company, gave Beauchamp a check that night. Nolan Beauchamp reports that it was for $12,000--more than enough money to start organizing a new company to begin substantial production of the new metal body guitars.

No one knows the exact date factory production of the National guitars began, but almost without a doubt, the tri-cone Silver Guitars started rolling out sometime in 1927.[4] Soon after this the inventors and investors decided to form a corporation since a corporation could issue stock to raise capital to expand the factory further.

The State of California certified the National String Instrument Corporation on January 26, 1928. The Dopyera brothers sold the trademark National name (they had registered it August 16, 1926) to the corporation in exchange for common stock. Besides Ted Kleinmeyer, Paul Barth, George Beauchamp, and John Dopyera, the original members of the new organization included Murray Ferguson. Ted Kleinmeyer was president and George Beauchamp was secretary/treasurer. George signed the minutes for the board of director's first meeting on February 29, 1928.

At a July 16, 1928 meeting, the directors unanimously resolved to divide the executive management end of the company into three departments. The first department's head was the general manager. His job covered business relations, the sales force, and the office employees. In addition, the board granted him "General Supervisory power of the complete business." The second department's head was the factory superintendent. His job was to oversee all work of manufacture and raw material and to supervise all factory workmen. The third department's head was the assistant factory superintendent. His responsibility was to supervise the stockroom and the shipping department.

At the same July 1928 meeting John Dopyera moved and Paul Barth seconded that the directors appoint George Beauchamp general manager. The board vote was unanimous. Likewise, the directors unanimously appointed John Dopyera as factory superintendent and Paul Barth as assistant factory superintendent. George's salary was $55. per week, John's was $50, and Paul's was $48.

The new company, still fueled for the most part by Teddy's cash, got off the ground in a big way. Acting as general manager, George hired some of the most experienced and competent craftsmen available, including several members of his own family and several members of the Dopyera family. He purchased expensive new equipment for the factory they had located near Adolph Rickenbacker's metal stamping shop. The address was 1855 West 64th Street, Los Angeles, California.

The original National instrument line included Spanish and Hawaiian style tri-cones. The different models ranged from the plain, non-engraved Style 1 to the top-of-the-line Style 4. Beauchamp designed the engraving pattern for the ornate Style 4 Artist's Model. Today collectors call this the Chrysanthemum pattern. Dopyera and his wife designed the Style 3, called the Lily of the Valley. The company also made four string tenor guitars, a mandolin, and a ukulele. All of these employed Dopyera's three diaphragm amplification system.

Adolph Rickenbacker

Adolph Rickenbacker was born in Switzerland in 1892. Apparently, as a child his parents died and other relatives brought him to America. One of his distant cousins was World War I flying ace Eddie Rickenbacker. Before moving to Los Angeles in 1918, Adolph lived first in Columbus, Ohio and then in Chicago, Illinois. He and two partners formed the Rickenbacker Manufacturing Company in 1925 and two years later incorporated the business. Beauchamp met Rickenbacker through Ted Kleinmeyer, who knew him from another manufacturing venture. Adolph was a likeable and generous guy from most reports. His friends called him Rick.

By the time he had met Beauchamp and

Local residents remember this house to be Adolph Rickenbacker's birthplace.

had joined forces with the guitar operation, Rick was a highly skilled production engineer and machinist. He was proficient in a wide variety of manufacturing techniques using both metals and plastics. In addition, Rick had business experience and money to invest. He owned thirty-four shares of National's preferred stock and seventeen shares of its common stock from June 1928 to July 1933. The company gave him the title of engineer on the back of an early catalog.

Rickenbacker Mfg. manufactured the metal bodies for the Nationals with one of the largest deep drawing presses on the West Coast. The shop was able to produce as many as fifty guitars a day. That was enough production capacity to challenge the major Eastern and Midwestern guitar manufacturing companies.

The Single Cone National Guitars

Despite National's ability by 1928 to turn out hundreds of guitars, if not thousands, the company did not have a well diversified line of instruments. The elaborate tri-cone guitars were expensive and soon demand for them dropped. It was obvious that the West Coast firm needed new guitar models with lower production costs to increase sales and to create a better cash flow. In his experiments John Dopyera had either ruled out a single cone design or could not make one that worked well. He stated in a patent application for the tri-cone: "It is preferable to use three and never less than three resonators."

Seemingly, a single resonator guitar with a simple bridge setup was the answer to the company's money problem. According to Nolan Beauchamp, his father perfected and patented the economical and highly popular single resonator design. It is likely the single cone National ukulele, which followed the earlier tri-cone uke, was their first instrument with the single cone. Beauchamp equipped the Triolian models, originally introduced in late 1928 as wooden body tri-cones, with his single cone resonator. Several other later models used Beauchamp's system too. Their sales gave the company a much needed boost.

Disagreements at National

Late in 1928 John Dopyera became disgruntled with what he felt was mismanagement

The first Triolians had wood bodies and three resonators like this example photographed in 1928.

6

The Grasshopper and George, circa 1924.
George Beauchamp (left) was a talented musician on the vaudeville circuit before he met John Dopyera.

7

National Style O circa 1931. This model and several other National models used the single cone diaphragm perfected by Beauchamp.

of the company's money and resources. Ironically, inventor Dopyera thought Beauchamp was wasting money spending time experimenting with new ideas. For one thing, they argued about the single cone resonator. John also said that Beauchamp tried to develop a new economical neck that failed.

John Dopyera, as brilliant as he was devising new instruments, was rather egocentric remembering National. He stated in 1973 that he was the "main spoke of the wheel" and had all the good ideas at the company. For whatever reason, John did not respect his boss George and as a consequence quit in January 1929. He resigned as an officer, director, and stockholder in the National on February 19, 1929. John assigned his stock interest to Kleinmeyer; Harry Watson took on John's responsibilities as shop superintendent. Dopyera formed the Dobro Manufacturing Co., later called the Dobro Corporation, Ltd., in collaboration with his brothers, and they introduced their own novel line of Dobro resonator instruments.

Beauchamp's reaction to the Dopyeras' new company, whether right or wrong, caused the brothers problems. National and Dobro had many of the same customers. As alleged in court later, George told many of these firms that the Dobro instruments infringed on the National patents. (Of course, the courts never resolved that issue.) When told that the Dobro product had patent problems, many of the distributors either cancelled orders or avoided Dobro products. The Dopyeras' reaction to Beauchamp was predictable. On January 1, 1931 a newspaper in Los Angeles announced that Dobro was suing National for $2,000,000 in damages.

Another problem within National was Ted Kleinmeyer, characterized by Nolan Beauchamp as a "spendthrift and playboy." He had inherited a million dollars at age twenty-one and was trying to spend it all before age thirty. Kleinmeyer would inherit another million then. Eventually he squandered all of his inheritance and died an alcoholic. Before that, Ted was both trouble and a lot of fun.

Likeable Teddy was a Roaring '20s version of the consummate party animal. His connections at City Hall gave him a police siren for his Lincoln so he could speed around L.A. with impunity. He bought expensive gifts like automobiles, radios, and phonographs for his relatives and friends. Being successful at losing money faster than he made it, Ted started to hound Beauchamp for cash advances from National's till. Nolan Beauchamp says that George's fault was that he could not turn people down--especially his friends. However, when business conditions got bad, George had no choice.

With the depression slowing business and with the pressure of a major lawsuit against the corporation, the company started cutting back on expenses. In July 1930 Harry Watson resigned as the factory superintendent and no one replaced him for two years. Apparently, a split developed within National's Board of Directors over company management. In the Fall of 1931, Beauchamp, Paul Barth, Adolph Rickenbacker, and C.L. Farr (National's attorney) started organizing support for a new project: George's development of a fully electric guitar.

Inventing a Practical Electric Guitar

In the twenties the idea for electric string instruments had been around for some time--at least thirty years. People had experimented with microphones and pickups for the banjo, guitar, and violin, not to mention the related efforts that went towards developing electric pianos and organs. Unfortunately, except for the works that reached the Patent Office, no one recorded most of those early efforts. However, by piecing together information from various sources, we do know that by the late 1920s, primitive, inefficient electric guitars did exist.

George Beauchamp thought about the possibility of an electric guitar even before he worked at National. Although not schooled in electronics, he started experimenting with electric amplification as early as 1925. First, George put together a small P.A. system with a microphone for his guitar. Second, he took the microphone apart and tried attaching the carbon button directly to the top of the instrument. Because the microhones did not work well, George looked for another solution. Another unsatisfactory, but enlightening attempt was a one string test guitar made out of a 2X4 piece of lumber. George attached a Brunswick electric phonograph pickup--a small coil of wire and a permanent magnet--to the board. He removed the phono needle from the

pickup and in its place, ran a metal guitar string.[5] This experiment shaped Beauchamp's thinking and put his efforts onto the right track.

Presumably when the problems at National were evident, George began his home experiments in earnest. He attended night school classes in electronics. By 1930, students of electronics knew that a magnetically sensitive metal moving through a magnetic field caused a disturbance. An adjacent coil of wire translated this disturbance into an electrical current. Electric generators, telephones, and electric phonograph pickups used this phenomenon. Beauchamp realized the problem was to create a practical way of translating a guitar string's vibration directly into an electrical signal.[6]

Nolan Beauchamp remembers that his dad often worked all night on the family dining room table trying to develop his electric guitar. George experimented with many different combinations of coils and magnets. He wound the first coils using the not-so-delicate motor out of the family washing machine. Paul Barth helped Beauchamp and said they eventually used a sewing machine motor. Their experiments lasted for several months. No one knows what every one of George's prototypes looked like or how many different versions there were. Although its full history remains a mystery, a technical drawing of one attempt is in the Rickenbacker files.

The strings on this early design did not go through the magnets, rather, they went between the two coils. George was working on this battery operated design as late as January 1932. The drawing of the early pickup shows that the magnets, instead of acting as a hand rest, interfered with the player's hands. It was obviously not practical, as Beauchamp must have realized.

The other known Beauchamp prototype design became familiar. It was the Frying Pan electric guitar. (Perhaps, George worked on both designs simultaneously, despite the Frying Pan's advanced features.) The pickup consisted of two horseshoe shaped magnets and one coil, hence the nickname horseshoe pickup. The guitar strings went through the magnets and over the coil. On the first horseshoe pickup there was a single core plate or blade in the center of the coil. (This was like a modern Bill Lawrence Pickup.) On later versions there were six pole pieces in the coil that concentrated the magnetic field under each string.

Nolan Beauchamp remembers his dad tested the first horseshoe pickup unceremoniously on a 2X4. When it was working correctly, Beauchamp asked former National craftsman Harry Watson to make a proper wooden neck and body for it. He set up shop in the Beauchamp's garage. In several hours, working with small hand tools, a rasp and a file, Harry completed the frame. George installed the electronics. It was nicknamed the Frying Pan or Panhandle because that was what it looked like. Adolph Rickenbacker and others close to Beauchamp liked to call it the Pancake. Several people contributed to George's effort. Besides Paul Barth and Harry Watson, there was Paul's father, Martin, and Adolph Rickenbacker. They were Beauchamp's friends and his support group. Nearly all the ideas came from George D. Beauchamp--a musician who wanted a better guitar.

The Early Rickenbacker Company Ro-Pat-In Corporation

George and his supporters formed a company called the Ro-Pat-In Corporation on October 15, 1931. (No one remembers the significance of the name.) Then on November 10, 1931, the National board of directors removed Beauchamp and Barth from their positions at National.

Unfortunately, the minutes from the November meeting did not spell out reasons for removing Beauchamp and Barth. The minutes do indicate that Kleinmeyer, Ferguson, and a newer member, Glenn E. Harger, voted against George and Paul. C.L. Farr and Beauchamp abstained. The minutes further stated that Barth and Beauchamp were given their checks in full, to and including November 14, 1931.

Perhaps the board fired George and Paul in response to the new electric guitar venture; however, it was probably the result of earlier differences in opinion about the National company's management. Undoubtedly, National was in the midst of several different power plays between stockholders that would last for the next two years. Curiously, at the January 4, 1932 board meeting, the company gave George a chrome plated Style O guitar engraved with the #3 Silver Guitar pattern and the name Geo. D. Beauchamp.

The National board changed characters in 1932 as three members left and new members stepped in to take their places. C. L. Farr resigned on March 31st and Paul Barth replaced him. In June 1932 Ted Kleinmeyer drove up to Taft, CA, and sold his controlling interest in National stock to Louis Dopyera. The National minutes indicated that Louis had owned stock earlier, but with the June stock transaction he became a member of the National board of directors. The other corporate directors elected Dopyera president. On July 11, 1932 Murray Ferguson resigned to make room on the board for Jack Levy.

After Kleinmeyer was out of the picture in the summer of 1932, the directors hired Paul Barth to fill the vacant factory superintendent position. George no longer had a position in National's management, but he continued to participate on the board until January 1934. For sure, Ro-Pat-In and National had business connections and overlaps for several years. For example, National's sales representative Jack Levy was one of Ro-Pat-In's first reps. Also, Rickenbacker Mfg. continued to make dies and stamped parts for National.

Getting Started

While the National company wrestled with its problems and infighting, Ro-Pat-In Corporation arranged to produce electric guitars in a small rented shop at 6071 South Western Avenue. The building was next to Rickenbacker's main tool and die plant.[7] It took until August 1932 to start production, to open the corporate books, and to choose corporate officers. The shareholders elected Adolph Rickenbacker president, Paul Barth vice president, and George Beauchamp secretary-treasurer. C.W. "Billie" Lane, who helped with an early preamplifier design, and C. L. Farr, both had financial interests in the company.[8]

George ran the instrument manufacturing operation and Adolph oversaw the metal shop. Only a couple of employees assembled guitars on Western Ave. in the beginning. Roy Van Nest's radio shop did electrical work on some of the first amps; Johnson Cabinet Works did most of the necessary wood working. Rick's other company still made metal parts and Bakelite plastic products such as Klee-B-Tween toothbrushes, fountain pens, and candle holders. (Bakelite was one of the first plastics; it was the material used to make bowling balls, although not by the Rickenbacker Mfg. Co.)

The company called the first guitars, "Electro String Instruments, Manufactured by the Ro-Pat-In Corporation." There were aluminum body Frying Pan steels and wood body electric Spanish models. However, Ro-Pat-In did not build their own bodies. The Aluminum Alloy Casting Company made the steel guitar frames while Harmony made the Spanish ones. Adolph Rickenbacker kept precise production figures, and he recorded all sales for the company's first six months: They sold thirteen Hawaiian guitars and four Spanish guitars in 1932. Obviously, the new electric instruments did not take the country by storm.

The new company faced several obstacles before finding success. Meanwhile, Adolph kept it alive with advances from his personal checking account and manufacturing business.[9] Timing was a major problem. There were few customers with extra money to buy guitars in the Depression years. (There were few customers with extra money for anything.) Another important factor often overlooked talking about electric instruments in the 1930s is electricity--many rural areas and some urban households did not have it yet.

Adolph once illustrated the setbacks they had just trying to get musicians to play the new electric guitars: "We were finally allowed to demonstrate one on a stage show--that was our big moment! After setting it up and the player began to play, all at once the speaker of our amplifier announced 'KHJ Los Angeles.' The manager pulled the cord and practically threw us out!"

Adolph told another story about a setback of a different nature: "In our darkest moments we received a call from a group of Hawaiian musicians that were ready to order a complete line of electrical instruments--steel and Spanish guitars, mandolin and bass. So we were back in business! We only had the steel guitar at this time, but we took the order. After about sixty days the order was complete and we called our good customers and informed them everything was ready for them the following morning. That evening we checked everything to be sure it was all okay and ready for them to pick up in the shipping department in the morning. But someone beat us to it--the whole outfit was stolen that night, and our whole two months of hard work went out the window!

"We started all over again, and we finally delivered the order, but it might as well have been stolen, as we never received the money for the instruments anyway. Poor George always tried to keep the bad news from me as he was afraid I would have a heart attack."[10]

The first professional artist to use one of the Electro guitars was a friend of George Beauchamp's named Jack Miller. Apparently, for a period of time he was also a Ro-Pat-In employee. Miller wrote articles about the "new amplifying guitar" for Down Beat Magazine in 1936. He told the readers his first job playing the instrument was at the Hollywood Grauman's Chinese Theater in 1932. The big break for Miller and the new steel guitar came shortly after this job.

Band leader Orville Knapp was looking for a stringed instrument for his orchestra when Miller approached him to demonstrate the Frying Pan. After several months of careful arranging and rehearsing, Miller found himself working with Knapp at the Beverly Wilshire Hotel. Subsequent national tours with this well received band led to national notoriety for Jack Miller. The tours also brought attention to the electric steel guitar he was playing. With tasteful arrangements Miller established the electric guitar in a popular music orchestra. It was exactly the kind of exposure the new guitar needed.

One of the unsung pioneering electric guitar artists was Alvino Rey. If Jack Miller was the first professional to use a Rickenbacker, Rey was a close second while playing with Horace Heidt's band in the 1930s. Rey still owns two of the early Electro steels and a variety of other manufacturer's electrics like the Gibsons he helped to develop.

Another professional guitarist who used the Frying Pan in the early years was Andrew Iona Long. He was a burly Hawaiian who had lost his right thumb in a bar fight. Andy picked the steel with two fingers. Because of his handicap he used his own unconventional tuning with three heavy gauge plain strings and three heavy gauge wound strings. The tuning and the heavy strings caused a terrific amount of tension on the aluminum neck.

One night the inevitable occurred at a

Andy Iona Long (second from right) pictured in 1951.

Top-Sol K. Bright (sitting center) and the Holly-waiians at the Brass Rail in San Francisco in 1934.

Far right-Jack Miller wrote several short articles for <u>Down Beat</u> magazine in 1936 explaining his electric guitar.

Right-This late 1935 catalog was the first to feature the Rickenbacker Bakelite instruments.

BROTHER MUSICIAN LISTEN TO A MIRACLE

DOWN BEAT

The First to Play Electric Guitar

Jack Miller

(Ed
know
Orvill
Astor
writte
many
chest
on th
to Ja
Beat,

Mr.
ing
answ
strun

Ne
many
tric
this
give
Have
about
a rou
Guita
ago,
and
ment
idea.
was
elimi
playe
of th
could
touch
a sn
has
I o

12

Los Angeles club where Long played a floor show--Andy's guitar buckled up like a jack knife. The Hawaiian with the folding guitar got the biggest laugh of the act. When he took the broken guitar back to the factory, he asked Beauchamp if he could make it do that every night. George laughed, but never intentionally added a collapsible lap steel to the Rickenbacker guitar line.

The Electro String Instrument Corporation

On May 21, 1934 Adolph approached the National board of directors and proposed selling them the rights to manufacture the Electro guitars. He offered them a ten per cent royalty. National deferred a decision on the matter, and Adolph probably soon withdrew the offer. At least, this episode was the first indication of Adolph's reluctance to pursue the manufacture of electric instruments. This period was a turning point for his company.

In 1934 the Ro-Pat-In shareholders changed the company's name to Electro String Instrument Corporation. They began to call the instruments "Rickenbacker Electros" in the ads and literature. Rickenbacker was already a famous name because of Adolph's cousin Eddie, and there is no doubt they wished to capitalize on that connection.

There were other reasons to name the guitars after Adolph. He and his wife Charlotte were the major stockholders and financial backers of the operation while it struggled to turn a profit. Considering Adolph's technical contributions to the company, naming the guitars Rickenbackers was the obvious thing to do. Also, it probably helped to re-energize Adolph's waning enthusiasm. What was the Rickenbacker name's biggest advantage? When they spelled it with a *K*, it was easier than the Beauchamp name to pronounce correctly.[11]

Despite the slow business, George was relentless experimenting with new ideas that would become additional trademark products for Rickenbacker. The first project after the Pancake steel was a fully electric violin. Work on this began in 1932. Beauchamp planned to make this violin and a new style of guitar out of molded Bakelite. Work on the Bakelite electric violin carried through into early 1935. The Electro String attorney made an inquiry to the Bakelite Corporation in New York City about the use of their product for musical instruments.[12]

Beauchamp's lawyer found out that a British inventor named Arthur Primrose Young had a patent on the manufacture of molded resin musical instruments.[13] The attorney also found out that Electro String was not the first company to make Bakelite musical instruments: The Fred Gretsch Manufacturing Co. had made banjo-ukes out of it while several companies used it to make clarinets. Electro got a license from Young and he received a royalty for all Rickenbacker Bakelite instruments.

Electro String produced their first Bakelite instruments for sale in July of 1935. On August 26 Adolph wrote to England: "We are just getting our molds completed for the Bakelite musical instruments and enclosing our statement showing sales for the month of July. We have had quite a little trouble with Bakelite being brittle. Do you happen to know of anything which would be stronger?"

Electro String's research and development paid off. Adolph solved most of the problems with Bakelite--they eventually used a different formula. (However, it was never ideal for musical instruments.) They expanded the instrument line in 1935 and 1936, creating a family of Rickenbacker stringed instruments. Each new Electro instrument used a variation of the horseshoe pickup. Besides guitars, there were mandolins, bass viols, violins, cellos, and violas. A prototype electric piano sat in the Electro front office for years.

One spinoff of the Electro family of instruments was the electric orchestra. There were at least two such groups with close ties to the Electro String company in the 1930s. Mark Allen and his Orchestra's string section were first to use Beauchamp's electric violins. The company pictured them in the 1935-36 Rick catalog. This group was popular in Southern California and at hotels across the country.

San Francisco's Bert Lynn All Electric Orchestra took the prize as the best equipped of the electric groups. Besides a complete set of standard Electro instruments, the group had instruments made by Bert Lynn himself. One of his creations included an odd shaped aluminum body guitar with a horseshoe pickup. In 1940 Lynn planned to build a glass guitar and a glass violin using original Rickenbacker hardware. Photos show that he conducted his orchestra with one hand while adjusting volume controls on a mixer and amplifier board with the other.

Sol Hoopii, master of the steel guitar, was one of George and Adolph's friends. This picture of Sol with one of the first Bakelite steels appeared in the late 1935 catalog.

This flyer appeared in the mid 1930s.

LOS ANGELES, CAL., March 8, 1935

ELECTRO STRING INSTRUMENT COMPANY

6071 South Western Avenue, Los Angeles, California

DEBTOR

WILLIAM H. MAXWELL
PATENT ATTORNEY
1032 VAN NUYS BUILDING

PHONE TUCKER 7779

Mar. 1, 1935	Prep. & File Appn. re T.M. "Electro"	$50.00
	Search re T.M. "Electro"	15.00
	Search re Bakelite Musical Instrument	15.00
	Title Search on Bakelite Instrument Patent	15.00
	Wire re Searchs	1.71
	Interviewing Examiner & Demonstrating Instrument at Washington	50.00
		$146.71

Paid AR.

Bert Lynn and his All Electric Orchestra in 1939 or 1940. Notice Lynn's odd shaped aluminum guitar balanced on the amplifier in front.

Electro String distinguished its new instruments with a total disregard for traditional styling. George and Adolph proved that electric instruments did not have to look like their acoustic counterparts. They proved traditional materials were not necessary for fine instruments. Their ideas helped to liberate the thinking of instrument makers and helped to modernize the industry.

The expansion of the instrument line helped to make 1935 Electro String's most profitable year in the 1930s. Steel guitars were the biggest reason--total sales more than quadrupled 1934's. The company picked up distributors in Europe, in Australia, and in New Zealand. (The 1930s British export instruments had the Premiervox label.) To a large extent, this increase was made possible by the sound of the new Bakelite steels and by the popularity of Hawaiian music. Yet, there was little more than curiosity in the new Bakelite violin and Spanish guitar. Rickenbacker made only one dozen electric violins in 1935. The Spanish guitar production was probably higher, but not by much.

In 1936 Electro String became the sole manufacturers of the manually operated Vibrola tailpiece invented by C.O. "Doc" Kauffman. Doc had met Beauchamp through the Southern California Music Company, the first distributor for the Vibrola, when George was National's general manager. Soon Adolph Rickenbacker, George Beauchamp, Paul Barth, and Doc Kauffman all became friends, sharing many ideas about guitars and manufacturing techniques. The hand Vibrola became standard on the Spanish guitars, tenor guitars, and mandolins in May of 1936.[14]

Ironically, business fell off in 1936 as fast as it had improved the year before. The company was on an economic roller coaster ride that would last until World War II. Adolph felt that steel guitars had saturated the market. Of course, the failure of the standard guitars, electric violins, and bass viol did not help. Rick told George more than once that he wanted to get out of the music business or at least, keep things stable. Beauchamp wanted to expand the company. Apparently, George's ideas prevailed because the company continued to grow.

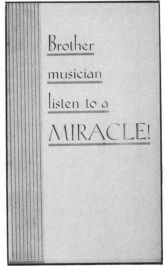

Ro-Pat-In published one of the first Electro brochures, left, in 1933. The brochure on the right was from 1934.

Bert Lynn and group in a publicity photo.

15

The Frying Pan patent drawing from 1934.

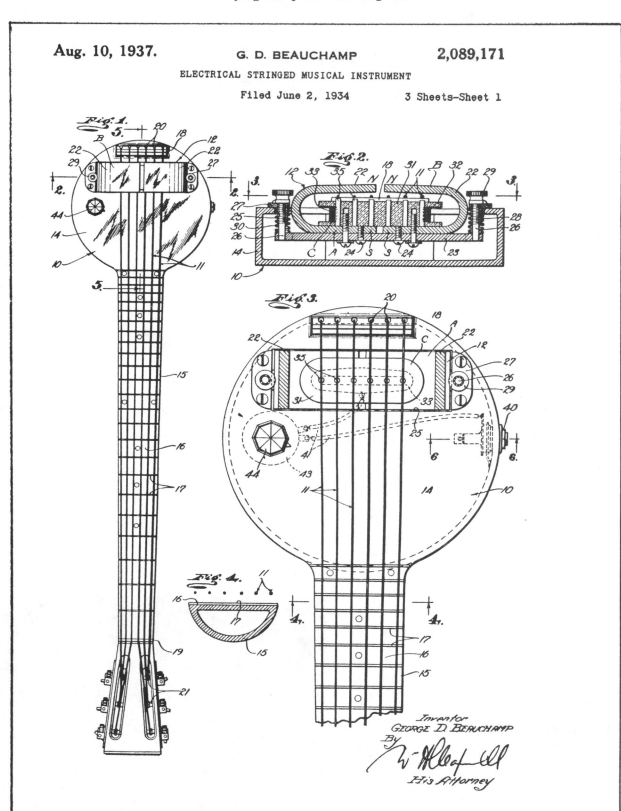

Aug. 10, 1937.   G. D. BEAUCHAMP   2,089,171

ELECTRICAL STRINGED MUSICAL INSTRUMENT

Filed June 2, 1934   3 Sheets—Sheet 1

Inventor
GEORGE D. BEAUCHAMP
By
His Attorney

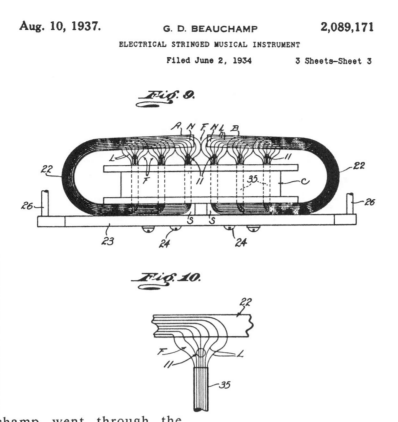

Aug. 10, 1937.   G. D. BEAUCHAMP   2,089,171
                        ELECTRICAL STRINGED MUSICAL INSTRUMENT
                            Filed June 2, 1934   3 Sheets—Sheet 3

Fig. 9.

Fig. 10.

Inventor
GEORGE D. BEAUCHAMP
By
[signature]
His Attorney

George Beauchamp went through the patent ritual several times in his prolific fifteen years designing and manufacturing musical instruments. At National he patented two versions of the single resonator guitar and the perforated National finger pick.[15] George patented two different styles of electric violins and the "roller vibrola" tailpiece for Electro String. Receiving the patent for the Frying Pan electric guitar pickup was a hard-fought accomplishment that took over five years.

It was clear Beauchamp did not create a new art with the Frying Pan. Many patents, going back to 1876, already related to electrical sound reproduction and musical instruments. The idea behind an electric guitar pickup was remarkably close to the idea behind a telephone pickup. Using the logic of the patent process, these devices were the same if you substituted a string for the telephone's mouthpiece diaphragm.

The Electro String attorney's job was to demonstrate the novelty of the new electric guitar or at least, the novelty of its individual features. For example, he had to show how the electric guitar pickup was not just a modified piece of telephone hardware or some other older electrical invention. In addition, the attorney had to show that George had advanced the art of electric instruments substantially with his pickup and electric guitar. That is, he had to prove to the examiner that the new device was not the result of mere mechanical skill.

George filed the first patent application (serial #615,995) for the Frying Pan on June 8, 1932, shortly before the Ro-Pat-In Corporation started commercial production. The patent application went through many small revisions as George improved his invention and clarified his claims. Other changes in the application were in response to actions by the examiner. By the middle of 1934 the revised document probably bore little resemblance to the original, although the basic design concepts of the pickup were the same. George completely rewrote and resubmitted the application on June 2, 1934.

There was a long delay in the examination of George's second application. Part of the patent process was comparing a new application

This 1934 patent diagram showed the horseshoe pickup installed in a wooden Spanish guitar body.

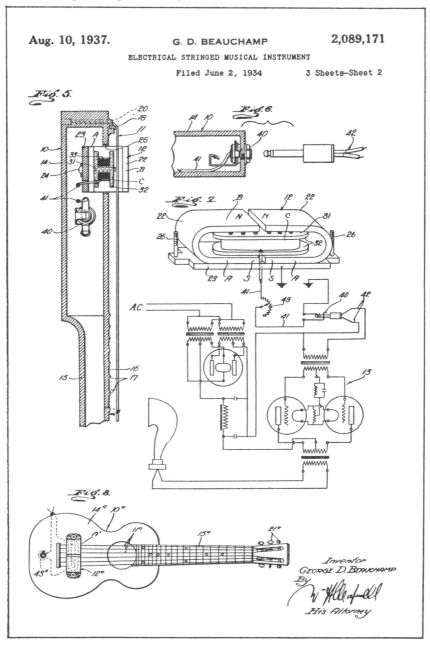

Aug. 10, 1937.   G. D. BEAUCHAMP   2,089,171

ELECTRICAL STRINGED MUSICAL INSTRUMENT

Filed June 2, 1934   3 Sheets—Sheet 2

Inventor
GEORGE D. BEAUCHAMP
By
His Attorney

to older inventions. An examiner's work determined if earlier patents disclosed an applicant's claims or if the claims were truly new and original. Just the size of George's application guaranteed a long, arduous process: it contained sixty claims, each requiring careful scrutiny.

To confuse things even further, the Patent Office could not decide if the new guitar was an electrical device or a musical instrument. There were separate divisions for each category. After two years in one division, the Patent Office shifted George's application to the other. Essentially, the second examiner started the process again from the beginning. He considered a whole new group of patents pertinent to George's claims.

Another cause for delay in the Californian's application was the issue of "inoperativeness." The first examiner did not believe the Frying Pan worked. A successful demonstration by the attorney convinced him. The second examiner in the bureaucratic maze came up with the same notion--after the guitar had been on the market for over four years. Adolph Rickenbacker told John Hall he sent Sol Hoopii with some other musicians back to Washington to perform at the Patent Office. Letters from Beauchamp's attorney indicate an electrical research firm conducted a detailed examination of the Frying Pan and submitted a report to the Patent Office. Fifteen minutes of Hawaiian music and the technical report proved to the examiner that the electric guitar worked.

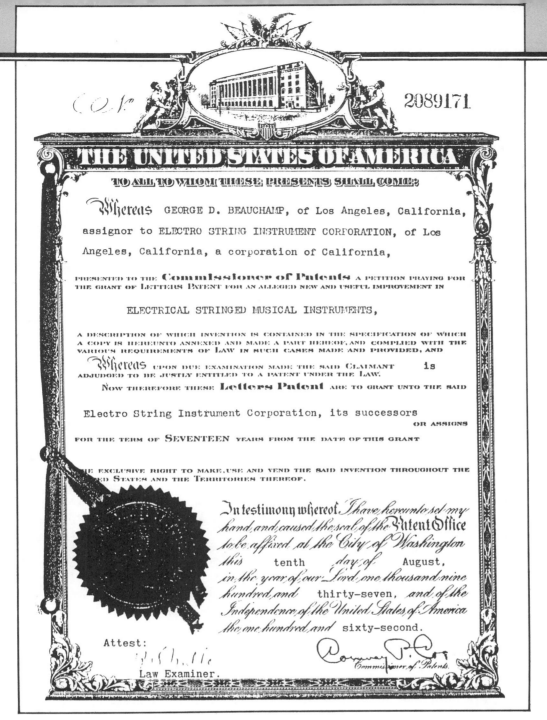

By August of 1936 Beauchamp and his lawyer complained about the delays in processing the patent. In a letter to the Patent Office attorney William Maxwell said in part:

"The careless piecemeal actions on the part of the Patent Office in connection with this application are causing the applicant great and irreparable damage. The applicant, through a licensee (Electro String), placed his invention upon the market several years ago and at that time, as far as he is aware, he was the first to introduce an electrical amplifying stringed musical instrument to the trade. From time to time since applicant's invention appeared on the market various competitors have introduced similar imitating devices until today there are in the neighborhood of twenty competing devices on the market, some six or eight of which are being manufactured and distributed by concerns doing nation wide business.

"It seems futile to continue prosecuting the application in the manner that it has been prosecuted heretofore. In light of the considerations just outlined, applicant requests that the Examiner give this application prompt consideration and that the next action be either a final allowance or a final rejection."

The Patent Office granted the patent, #2,089,171, a year later on August 10, 1937. It contained twenty-one of the original sixty claims, the bulk of these covering the pickup unit's design and adjustments. The rest of the claims covered the pickup as a hand rest for the player's right hand.

In Beauchamp's case the patent process demonstrated how the system actually hurt the inventor. After five years in consideration, getting the patent was almost anticlimactic.

The Early Electric Guitar Market

After the Rickenbacker guitars made their debut, many competing companies rushed to get their own electric guitar onto the market. But few of the companies did extensive original research.[16] Al Frost, who started at National in 1934, says: "At the time I came into the business, everyone was either stealing or buying the other's secrets. So, everyone was close to the vest on their experiments and inventions." He says that some companies dunked their pickup coils into tar or shellac. This made it difficult to check the number of turns, the wire sizes, and other design secrets. "It was a very competitive world and was filled with a lot shady operators when it came to (patent) claims made."

By late 1937 Electro String had many potential patent infringements cases. Adolph sent an attorney back to Chicago to confront a competitor and got a fat bill for legal fees. After that, he decided not to fight.

His lawyer thought Electro String could win some of the cases, but the others were doubtful. Rickenbacker did not think the electric guitar would ever be worth the cost of the legal battles.

By chance, the laissez faire attitude towards the competition started to pay off-- electric guitar fever was contagious. As Adolph said in 1972, "When everybody started to make them, everybody started to buy them." Rather than hurt business, the competition expanded the market for all the companies by creating more interest in electric instruments. The new business did not change the fact many of the competitors used elements of George's design in their instruments.

A problem for Electro String was Miessner Invention, Inc., a company that had done basic research and pioneering work in the field of sound reproduction. Miessner held many patents on electronic organs and pianos. Although they had not developed an electric guitar per se, Miessner argued that all electric pickups operated on the same principles--the ones covered by their patents. They threatened costly legal action against the guitar manufacturers producing electric instruments without a license from them. The Miessner group bluffed Kay, Epiphone, and Vega into these agreements. Miessner tried the same strategy with Rick's

company, even after the government patented the Frying Pan. Electro String resisted.

To protect themselves, several companies producing electric guitars circled their wagons against Miessner. Electro String, National-Dobro, and Gibson planned to challenge the invention company together, if necessary. Miessner backed off their claims in the 1930s after the guitar companies claimed estoppel for all of the phony threats.[17] Nevertheless, Miessner took some of the electric guitars makers to court years later. By that time it was too expensive and time consuming for the manufacturers to put up a good fight; they settled out of court.

The Late 1930s

The first hard years had already taken their toll on Beauchamp's health. Nolan Beauchamp says that his dad had a tireless routine: "Work, eat, drink, and fish--a lot of fishing. Almost every morning, before work, he would get up at 3 or 4 A.M. and surf-fish or fish the breakwaters, any place there were fish." He worked so hard that his doctor ordered him to slow down and take care of himself. George was not one for slowing down. In fact, he pushed himself even harder to expand the company.

In 1937 Electro String started to stamp Hawaiian guitar body parts out of sheet metal. They soldered these together like the metal body National guitars. The result was a wider range of models in the Rickenbacker line--from simple student guitars to advanced professional guitars. The new models made *step-up* sales of Electro guitars possible. In a *step-up* sale the customer started with a student model guitar. As his playing improved, he would buy a higher priced instrument. In this way the sale of student model guitars created a demand for professional models.

In December 1937 the company started to manufacture Doc Kauffman's Vibrola Spanish Guitar. The company had high expectations for the guitar's success and believed its versatile sound would overtake the steel guitar's in popularity. In its own wacky way this Bakelite guitar with a motorized vibrato tailpiece was a revolutionary instrument. The advertising literature read like a catalog for a modern day guitar synthesizer: "The Vibrola guitarist can simulate the organ's majestic

Hugh Pendergraft from the R.K.O. and the 20th Century Fox studios. He was one of the professionals including Les Paul who used a Vibrola Spanish guitar.

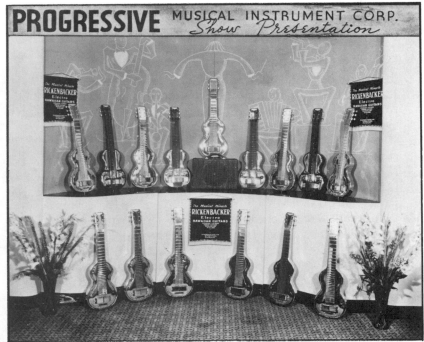

A 1937 display for Electro guitars. Pictured are Silver and Bakelite Hawaiian models.

Brochure for Doc's Vibrola Spanish guitar, 1938.

Model 59 flyer from 1938.

Doc Kauffman pictured in 1985 with a handle off one of his manual vibrato units.

diapason, the resonance of the vibraharp, and in slow moving melodies the accordion's reedy tone, or for beauty and elegance, amplify and swell a crystal harmonic in amazing crescendo."

By the late 1930s the steel guitar was reaching its peak of popularity. Not only was it used in Hawaiian music, but also increasingly, the steel became a Western swing music instrument. Many professional players embraced Rickenbackers because they sounded great. Thousands of the guitars were sold through instrument wholesalers to students and hobbyists. One reason this happened was the onslaught of World War II. The war inflamed Europe, and imported accordions used in many music instruction studios became scarce. This scarcity encouraged many studios to switch to steel guitar instruction.

After fifteen years in the fast lane of guitar development and manufacturing, Beauchamp became frustrated and disenchanted with the instrument business due partly to his deteriorating health. His second passion, fishing and designing fishing lures, had captured his full time attention. To raise the necessary capital to manufacture lures, he sold his shares in Electro String to Harold Kinney, Adolph's bookkeeper.

Beauchamp resigned his corporate position on October 11, 1940 with this message: "In resigning as Director of the Corporation, I want to express my appreciation of the friendly and cordial relationship that existed during the years we have been associated, and to wish you individually, as well as the corporation, prosperity and success in the years to come."

Shortly after leaving Electro String Beauchamp had a heart attack. He was on a deep sea fishing boat against his doctor's orders. A private yacht took George to Newport Harbor and a waiting ambulance drove him to St. Joseph Hospital in Santa Ana. He died that night.

George Beauchamp's funeral procession was over two miles long--he had a few friends. George was one of the true guitar industry pioneers. It is unfortunate that he did not live to see the electric guitar reach its full potential.

The War and Postwar Years

During the year 1941 Electro String continued to manufacture musical instruments and amplifiers, despite the World War in Europe;

Dick McIntire in the late 1930s playing a long scale Frying Pan.

Cover of the 1939 Electro catalog.

Trade show display in 1941.

Harold Kinney became the sales manager. It had already become difficult to obtain all the parts and materials necessary to complete instruments. The company ordered and bought heavily in anticipation of shortages, regardless of slow deliveries. Back orders for instruments increased as the other music manufacturers started to change over to war production. The company was able to continue guitar and amp production until the end of June 1942.

The Rickenbacker company started war related production in July of 1942. They used the tools for winding electric guitar pickups to wind armatures for electric gyroscopes. (The military employed these in navigation.) In the beginning they were able to wind only two hundred coils per month. Then they started a crash program to improve the machinery and increase productivity. By September of 1944 Electro String was winding two hundred and seventy coils a day. The payroll increased from six workers before the war to fifty workers at the peak of war production in 1944.

It is possible that the company scrapped some of the original dies and tooling during the war. In any event, the war effort postponed the company's development of electric instruments.

Paul Barth had worked with the company from the beginning, but assumed a new pivotal role after Beauchamp left. He perfected and patented a detachable version of the horseshoe pickup in 1941. During the war years he designed new tooling and trained new workers. After the war he continued as the factory manager and oversaw the transition back to peacetime production.

Electro String's job building gyroscope armatures ended in late 1944 after they had filled all their orders. The company was anxious to continue musical instrument production as they had all the parts necessary leftover from their heavy prewar stockpiling. (This fact makes the distinction between prewar and postwar instruments more difficult.)

Charlotte Rickenbacker, "Mrs. Rick," went on a trip to the Midwest and Washington D.C. in the winter of 1944. She tried to get new orders for amplifiers from the Oahu Publishing Co. She asked for permission from the War Production Board in Washington to resume guitar production. Mrs. Rickenbacker took a stack of letters from servicemen requesting guitars to prove that musical instruments were needed for the troops' morale.

The company returned to full-time musical instrument manufacturing in early 1946 with an expanded factory building. They had added 2500 sq. feet during the war. The steel guitar line remained relatively unchanged because they used prewar parts. The standard guitar line included the arch-top SP Model. They deleted the S-59 and the Bakelite Spanish models. Nolan Beauchamp, who had worked for Electro just before going into the service, returned to his job developing the amplifier line. Most of the amps in this period were student models. Nolan did make some custom ordered professional models.

The Electro String company made instruments and amplifiers for different music schools and jobbers. Bakelite guitars and small amplifiers were made for the Bronson company, a major Midwest distributor, under their brand name.

After the war, Rick felt the guitar's popularity had run its course and it was no longer a viable business proposition. His manufacturing company made increasing commitments to defense work. Since they had a limited capacity, sometimes there were delays supplying Electro String with parts for musical instruments.

As he approached retirement age, Rickenbacker started to shop around the idea of selling his instrument company. During the late 1940s the Electro String stagnated compared to the exciting period of the thirties. All of this changed in 1953 when Adolph found an enthusiastic buyer for his company. This man, F. C. Hall, would shape the company's history for the next thirty-one years.

Adolph did stay in touch with the instrument business. In fact, his manufacturing company continued to make many musical instrument parts for Electro String. He enjoyed the attention he got because of the growing awareness of his and George Beauchamp's accomplishments. He had many musician friends, especially steel guitarists. When he visited Hawaii, they treated him like a celebrity. However, he jokingly told John Hall that when they recognized him at a bar, he ended up paying for the drinks.

Adolph lived out his retirement in the hills of Fullerton, California. He built a large home equipped with an elaborate charcoal air filtering system. It was so efficient at cleaning

the air inside, he never had to dust the furniture. Rather than sit around idly, Adolph stayed active. He plowed up the fields around his house with his own tractor every Spring. He drove a car to his favorite restaurant--CoCo's on St. College Blvd.--even after he entered a rest home for his last months. Adolph finally passed away in 1976.

Adolph Rickenbacker in 1972 with the first Frying Pan.

Instruments From 1931 to 1953

When you own a Rickenbacker "Electro" you have the finest instrument it is possible to buy. Not one with an over-embellished exterior, but rather one beautiful in its simplicity and perfection of design quality materials and superb craftsmanship.

Behind each Rickenbacker "Electro" . as a bulwark for your protection, are years of experimentation and manufacturing. No other maker of electrical stringed instruments can substantiate a similar claim. Superlative performance with a Rickenbacker "Electro" is a maxim . a by-word among musicians and universally accepted in the musical world.

These essential qualities and many other excellent features you will cherish in all Rickenbacker "Electro" instruments . guitars . mandolins . violins . bass viols. . . . . Write for Complete Catalogue.

Electro String Instrument Corporation
Manufacturers
6071 South Western Ave., Los Angeles, California

From a 1937 brochure.

Hawaiian Steel Guitars

Pre-Production Steels--George Beauchamp reported to his lawyer in 1936 that he made unrecorded guitars sales before August 1932. He stated the first was in 1931. The instruments sold must have been Beauchamp's early experimental models.

No one knows exactly what all of Beauchamp's experimental guitars looked like, but a technical drawing of one remains in the Rickenbacker files. There were two coils and two horseshoe magnets in this design. One magnet was parallel to the strings and adjacent to the treble end of the pickup. The other magnet was parallel to the strings and adjacent to the bass end of the pickup. Each coil had a combination core and bobbin fashioned out of a flat piece of metal. Each coil assembly formed a link connecting the magnets with one coil over the strings and one under the strings.

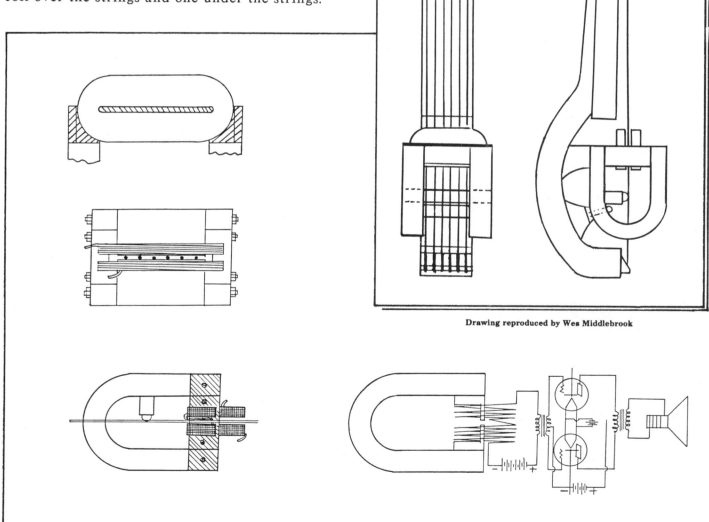

Drawing reproduced by Wes Middlebrook

These diagrams, dated January 30, 1932, illustrated George Beauchamp's earliest known experimental electric guitar.

The first Frying Pan.
Harry Watson crafted it from a single piece of wood.

The original Frying Pan guitar, the one on display at Rickenbacker's Santa Ana museum, appears to be maple.[18] The one piece neck and body had celluloid binding, and there were twenty-five frets hammered into the finger board. Instead of the conventional output jack used on most subsequent electric guitars, the first Frying Pan had two threaded terminals. The tungsten steel pickup magnets were 3/8 inch thick and 1 1/2 inches wide. The pickup was not adjustable for height; its mounting bolts went through the rear of the body. (There are unconfirmed rumors that Beauchamp and Watson made at least one other steel guitar out of wood.)

The first Frying Pan guitar apparently served as a guinea pig for Beauchamp's experiments; George probably modified it as he refined his designs. For instance, the first Frying Pan patent application described a core plate in the pickup coil rather than individual pole pieces. In fact, some of the first production model Electro guitars had the early version of the horseshoe pickup without pole pieces. Today the museum guitar has an old pickup, but a later one with pole pieces.

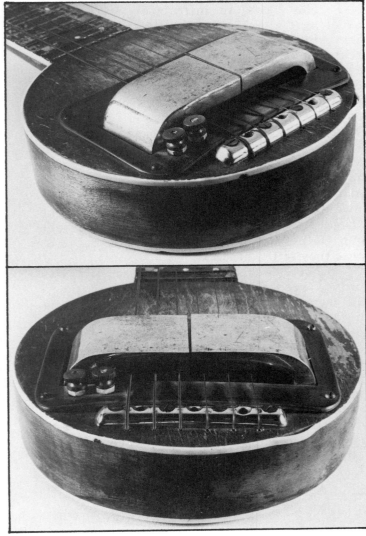

Close-up views of the first horseshoe magnet pickup.
The cord attached to the two threaded terminals, and the strings loaded through the rear of the body.

The first long scale Frying Pan and amplifier set pictured in a brochure cost $175.00 in 1933. The company reduced the price to $125.00 by 1935.

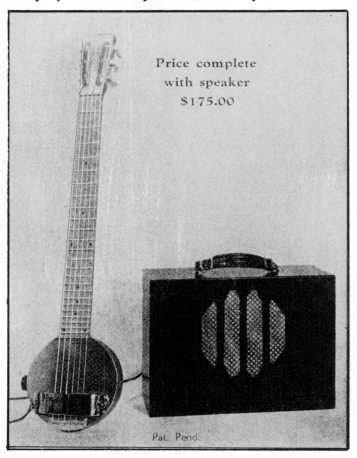

Price complete
with speaker
$175.00

Pat. Pend.

The Electro Hawaiian Guitar--This was the first official name for the production model Frying Pan. They added *Rickenbacker* in 1934.

The Hawaiian instruments were made out of cast aluminum. George theorized that there would be no acoustical interference from the body or the neck of a metal guitar. He thought that by using a metal body he could achieve the pure sound of the strings as translated by the pickup. In practice his theory worked, but with qualifications. There were two problems with the aluminum design. First, they made a few guitars with solid aluminum necks. To reduce their weight they started to core them out. George and Adolph learned that a hollow neck caused some unwanted resonances--the trade off for weight was tone.[19] In retrospect, Adolph once told John Hall, "The old ones are the best ones because they're the heaviest."

There was a second problem: it was hard to keep the aluminum guitars in tune. The metal expanded or contracted depending on the temperature. Performers experienced de-tuning with their guitars, especially under hot stage lights. There was no way to solve that problem short of redesigning the guitar.

The first Frying Pans had no volume or tone controls. A brochure photograph taken either in the last week of 1932 or in the first week of 1933 showed this. Jack Miller told <u>Down Beat</u> readers that the factory added a volume control to his first guitar.

The early Electro guitars had large pickup magnets like those used on the prototype. As mentioned above, the earliest production pickups had a single blade core rather than individual pole pieces. George specified this core in his 1932 patent application. Though undoubtedly used earlier, he first described pole pieces in a 1934 amendment to the early application.

The first brochure said they polished the top side of the steel guitar and finished the neck and body "in high polished silver duco." Sometimes, especially later in the 1930s, the factory used a baked crinkle paint on the Frying Pans. These steels were usually black.

When Ro-Pat-In started commercial production, they started precise record keeping. There were seventeen complete Hawaiian guitar and amplifier sets produced from August 1932 to December 31, 1932. The company sold thirteen sets that year, while they shipped two sample sets East to distributors. Two other sets were left in inventory to be sold in 1933.

Over the years there were two distinct

Frying Pan models: a 25 inch scale guitar (the A-25) and a 22 1/2 inch scale guitar (the A-22). The company introduced the long scale model first.

There were six and seven string versions of the short scale A-22. The most common ones had six strings.

The Frying Pans took a back seat to the other Rick steels after 1935. (The shortcomings of the aluminum Frying Pan led to the totally new Bakelite steel.) Electro String did not advertise them some years and ceased production entirely from 1950 to 1954. Nevertheless, many artists continued to play Frying Pans and customers kept on requesting the company to make them. The long scale guitars rarely appeared on price sheets after the war, but the factory manufactured some. The short scale versions were more common.

The company reintroduced and sold the last versions of the Frying Pan from 1954 to 1957. To provide easy access to the electronics, these had open backs covered with a Bakelite back plate. Unlike 1930s Frying Pans, the later ones had a Rickenbacker decal rather than a metal name plate.

One interesting point, the first Rickenbacker Hawaiian guitar's round neck made it possible to play as a standard guitar. This was intentional, as suggested by the patent forms prepared by Beauchamp.

Frying Pan pickup unit circa 1935.
(Courtesy of Micheal Lee Allen)

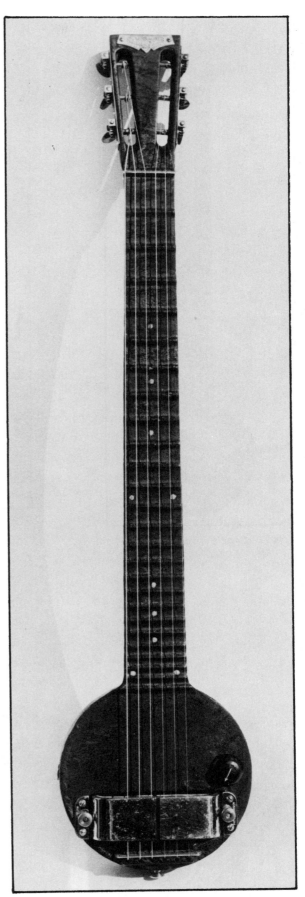

Late 1930s or early 1940s long scale A-25 with a black crinkle paint finish.

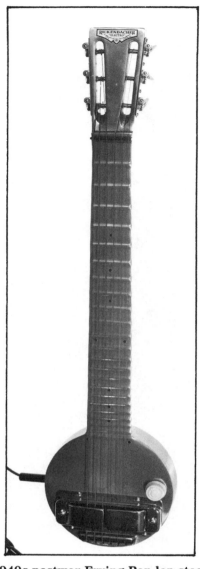

1940s postwar Frying Pan lap steel.

Early seven string Frying Pan from 1934.
The seven string price with an amplifier was $135.00 in 1935.

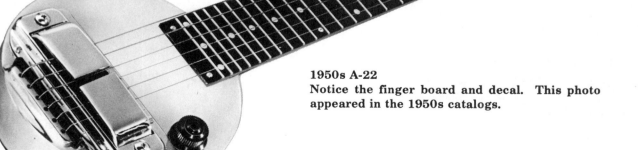

1950s A-22
Notice the finger board and decal. This photo
appeared in the 1950s catalogs.

The Bakelite Steels_____

Model B and Model BD Hawaiian Guitars-- These models were made out of Bakelite. This was the same easily molded, durable hard plastic Adolph used for making toothbrushes and other products. Electro String started commercial production of the Bakelite guitars in July of 1935; the earliest steel guitar like this was the Model B. The Model BD, first announced to the public in March of 1949, was a Deluxe version of the Bakelite steel guitar.

The structure and body design on these guitars remained basically unchanged before the war. The factory bolted the solid necks onto the near solid bodies. Beauchamp intended to solve two problems with this design. First, the heavy, rigid body minimized acoustic feedback and harsh overtones. Second, the Bakelite bodies were relatively insensitive to temperature changes; they were unlikely to detune like the aluminum steels did. In spite of this, the Bakelites still had a tuning problem. After the war, a metal insert was put into the neck to make it more rigid.

Jerry Byrd did more to promote the Rickenbacker steel guitars than any single artist of the 1940s and 1950s. He played Ricks on hundreds of records as a soloist and as a sideman for the top-name country singers. Influence by Hawaiian guitarists such as Dick McIntire, Jerry Byrd had flawless tone, technique, and intonation. His skill on the steel guitar made many listeners into loyal fans. This is Jerry Byrd pictured with a prewar seven string Bakelite with chrome plates, an instrument he had made into a collector's item by the mid 1950s. Today Jerry says that the Bakelite guitars had a great tone, but were hard to keep in tune. And it was the same problem that plagued the Frying Pans-- sensitivity to temperature changes. Byrd illustrates his experience: "When I started doing television shows in Cincinnati, Ohio in the late '40s and early "50s, the hot lights would really play hell with staying in tune." For that reason, all the Rickenbacker steels introduced after 1953 had hardwood bodies, including the Jerry Byrd CW Series.

JERRY BYRD

The detachable neck used on the Bakelite guitars was practical and advantageous in several ways. They were economical to make and easy to assemble onto bodies. All necks and bodies of the same models were interchangeable; the factory could service or repair a bad neck by replacing it. Likewise, dealers easily made repairs in the field without returning whole instruments. Interestingly, George first considered Bakelite necks for use on National guitars in 1930.

Several features on the Bakelite guitars changed before World War II. The earliest examples had a single volume control with an octagonal knob. There were five decorative chrome plates attached to the top. By 1938 these models usually had both tone and volume controls, with new shaped molded knobs. The molded fret markers probably had white outlines by 1938, and the metal plates had white enamel coatings by 1940.

There were features that distinguished the prewar Bakelite guitars (including those made shortly after the war with prewar parts) from the postwar examples.

For one thing, the pickups on prewar B Models had 1 1/2 inch wide magnets with 5500 turns of #38 wire on the coils. Postwar magnets were narrower. The strings on the prewar guitars loaded through the back of the body; later guitars usually had chrome tailpieces. The earlier guitars had knurled adjustment nuts on either side of the pickup magnet; later ones most often had Phillips head screws. (Since Bakelite guitars were not stuffed with newspapers, you cannot use this convenient dating method.)

Throughout the early years Electro String made special guitars and amps for customers, dealers, and jobbers. Nolan Beauchamp remembers one custom-ordered Bakelite guitar with the regular body, but with the edges rounded off. The metal parts were silver plated instead of chrome plated. This special guitar had fancy knobs too. It is quite possible other 1930s custom-built guitars had gold plated parts. After the war, the Bronson Melody King Bakelite guitar had gold plated tuners and metal plates bronze-flecked with gold to contrast with the burnished bronze tail assembly and mahogany colored body.

To some Hawaiian guitar players, Bakelite steels were the finest non-pedal steels

Japanese steel guitarist Noo Yuki Okami circa 1937.

This Bakelite steel had fret markers outlined in white, but no tone control.

32

Ernie Magann with a seven string Frying Pan and a seven string Bakelite circa 1937.

Over the years Bakelite guitars were available with six strings, seven strings, eight strings, and ten strings. The most common ones had six strings. Electro String intorduced the ten string model around 1940, though the exact date is unknown. They were structurally different from the others with metal necks instead of Bakelite necks.

After the late 1940s, the Model B and the Model BD appeared on price sheets, sometimes simultaneously. There was an eight to ten dollar variation in retail price. The literature was ambiguous about differences in the two models, but the Deluxe versions did have a plastic peghead cover in 1949 and in the 1950s. (Catalogs from the 1940s and early 1950s were notoriously deceptive; sometimes an illustrated guitar was a Model B and called a Model BD. Sometimes the jobber catalogs were totally out of date--they pictured guitars from years past.) Eventually, the company dropped the plainer Model B. Rickenbacker listed the BD6 on price sheets until 1974.

ever produced. Certainly, some of the most respected steel instrumentalists used them. Steel guitar fans consider Jerry Byrd one of the best non-pedal steel players. He played a prewar Model B6 and a prewar Model B7 for years. David Lindley, the famous sideman and solo artist, occasionally uses a Model B in the 1980s.

Bakelite steels from different years can sound different. Some purists believe that a mid 1930s change in the Bakelite formula affected the tone. They like the earlier ones. Some players also prefer the prewar style pickup with wider magnets. In the 1950s there was an intentional change in the Rickenbacker steel guitar pickup. The later steel pickups sacrificed rich tone for more treble. (This was a popular trend started by the Fender company during that period.)

The company pictured this Bakelite steel and Professional Model amplifier in 1941 ads.

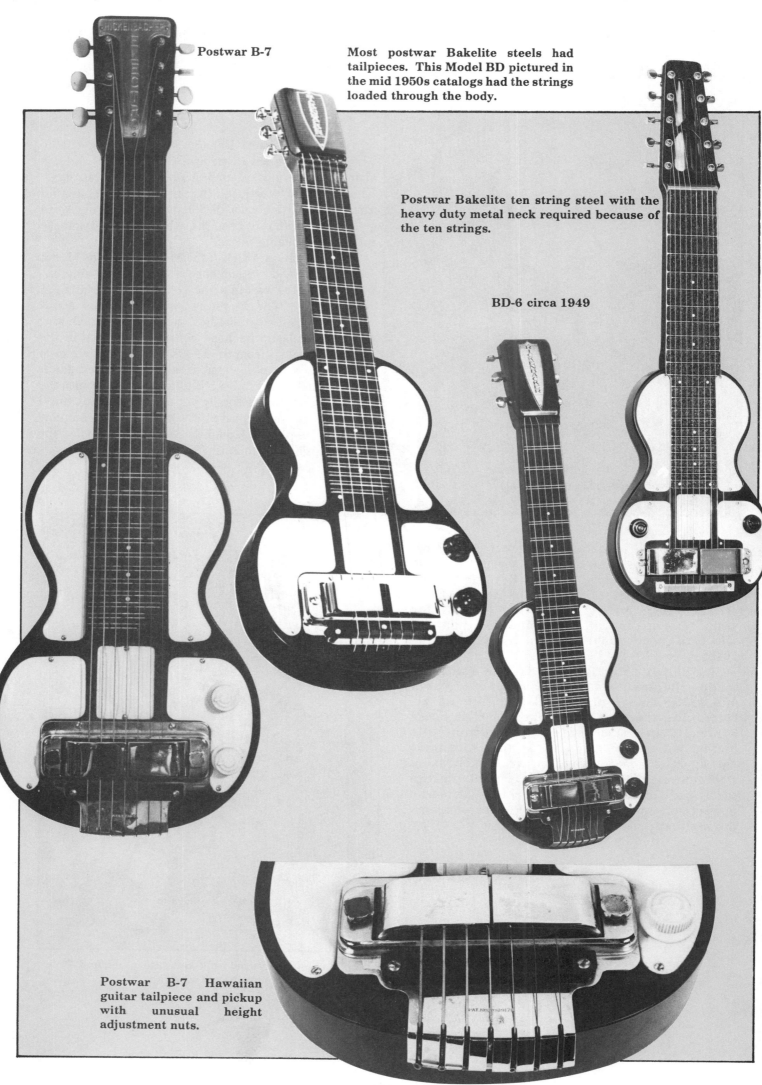

Postwar B-7

Most postwar Bakelite steels had tailpieces. This Model BD pictured in the mid 1950s catalogs had the strings loaded through the body.

Postwar Bakelite ten string steel with the heavy duty metal neck required because of the ten strings.

BD-6 circa 1949

Postwar B-7 Hawaiian guitar tailpiece and pickup with unusual height adjustment nuts.

34

Multi-instrument wizard David Lindley with his two Bakelite steels and custom-built road case.

Electro Hawaiian Guitar from the late 1935 catalog.

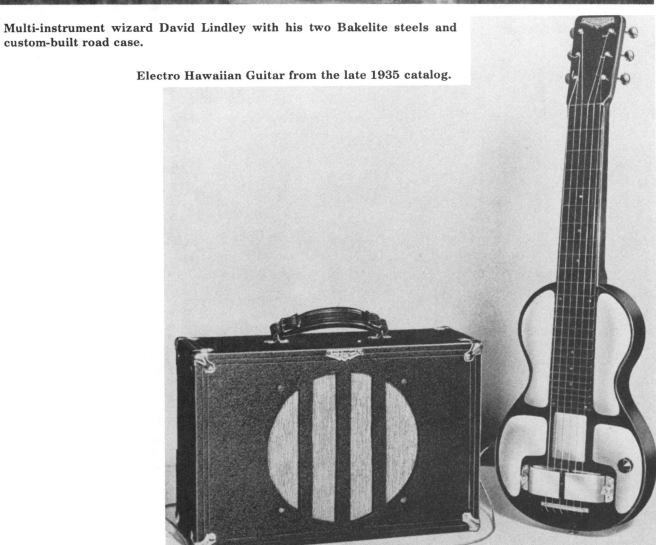

35

David Lindley and his beloved Bakelite steels.

We know that Rickenbacker made this
Bakelite after August 10, 1937 because it
bears patent #2,089,171 on the pickup.

1937 Bakelite Steel.

Rickenbacker "Electro" Guitars

No. 625-H—Six-String Hawaiian

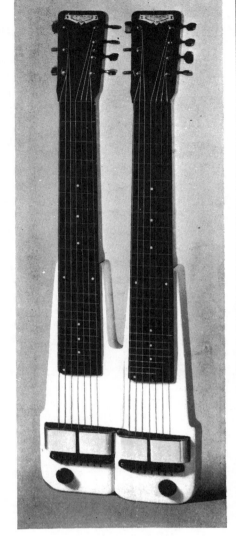

No. 125-H—Double Neck Hawaiian

Bakelite Model

The finest of all electric guitars for sweetness, purity, resonance, and depth of tone. Always the choice of professionals for outstanding performance. Equipped with both volume and tone controls.

The Spanish Guitar

Small in size and exceedingly easy to hold. The fingerboard has 14 frets to the body and the player may easily reach up to the twenty-fourth fret.
No. 625-S—Spanish Model Bakelite "Electro"
    Guitar..................................$62.50
    (Use amplifier No. 100-A or No. 200-A)

Hawaiian Guitars

All models made with arched back and neat square neck which makes the instrument easy to hold on the lap.
No. 625-H—Six-string model. Each..........$62.50
No. 725-H—Seven-string model. Each.... 72.50
No. 800-H—Eight-string model. Each........ 80.00
    (Use amplifier No. 100-A or No. 200-A)

Case for Above Guitars

No. 100-B—Three-ply veneer formed case with
    curly plush lining. State model of guitar
    when ordering. Each......................$15.00

Double Neck Hawaiian Guitar

Offers the advanced player greater freedom in musical expression, two tunings, fuller chord combinations, and smoother modulations. Designed to facilitate brilliancy of execution, the Double Neck Hawaiian has a cast alloy body with bakelite necks. The best materials and careful workmanship are combined in this instrument which permits the artist to escape the limitations of single tuning and fewer strings.
No. 125-H—Double Neck Hawaiian Guitar.
    Each..................................$125.00
    (Use No. 200-A amplifier)

Professional Model Amplifier No. 200-A

A new model (illustrated below with Vibrola guitar) designed to have a reserve power capacity and distinguished by its power sensitivity and efficiency with a minimum of harmonic distortion. These features are made possible through the application of the newest ideas in sound amplification and radio construction. Equipped with a 12" speaker and tone control for quality to suit individual expression. Output, approximately 15 watts. (Note: Does not include stand to hold guitar as illustrated.) No. 200-A—Professional Model Amplifier.
Each.......................$72.50

No. 198-S
$198.50

Electro's New Vibrola Spanish Guitar

An amplified Spanish guitar with a patented, electrically operated mechanism that moves the strings in a perfect vibrato—pulsating, rhythmic, throbbing tones that express emotions characterized in the past only by the human voice. The tonal quality surpasses anything you have ever heard before.

An important new feature of this model is the convenient stand which is part of the amplifier. It holds the guitar in playing position, and may be moved laterally or vertically as the player desires.

The amplifier is the Professional Model described to the left which incorporates the newest ideas in sound amplification and radio construction.

Hear for yourself what wonders can be done with the Electro Vibrola Spanish Guitar—Hawaiian effects with chord combinations (impossible for the Hawaiian guitar)—majestic organ crescendos—novel mimicry effects of reed and percussion . . . ALL are made with very little practice on this sensation new instrument!

No. 198-S—Electro Vibrola Spanish Guitar Outfit, complete with
    Professional Model Amplifier and stand.................. **$198.50**

114

Circa 1938

The Silver Hawaiian Model--Some old catalogs called this guitar the N.S. (New Style) Silver Hawaiian. It was a new style first produced in 1937. Rickenbacker made this model with body parts stamped out of sheet metal. They usually used brass, soldering the pieces together to form the guitar. The stamping process was economical and allowed the company to sell lower priced instruments. These instruments were often stuffed with crumpled newspaper or with crumpled tissue paper to eliminate unwanted resonances. (Some Hawaiian players filled them with sand.)

Though not a budget model, the Silver Hawaiian was the first stamped metal Rickenbacker. It had thirty-five frets and a chrome plated hollow body. The strings attached through holes stamped into the top. At first the Silver had a single volume control; by 1939 it featured a tone control too. The Silver Hawaiian Model had either six strings or eight strings.

The original flyer for the guitar described how to hook it up to a radio: "Any good radio service man will know how to make the attachment with these brief instructions."

The factory discontinued the Silver Hawaiian after World War II.

Silver Hawaiian steel from about 1939. Notice the positioning of the tone and volume controls.

Flyer for the first Silver Hawaiian Steel. 1937.

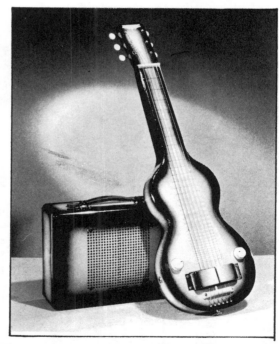

This Model 59 probably dates from early 1939.

38

Tin or aluminum nameplate and ivory colored crinkle paint finish on a prewar Model 59.

Model 59--This was the first Rickenbacker student model stamped from sheet metal. Electro String introduced it after the Silver Hawaiian guitar, in late 1937 or early 1938. The company discontinued the model after World War II.

During the prewar years it was available, the Model 59 came in different colors. The solid colors were textured crinkle paint. In 1938 the factory finished it with a solid ivory enamel. A 1939 catalog listed ivory and black finish options. According to the 1941 Grossman Music Company catalog, the Model 59 had a two-tone, high-lighted exterior. However that year they listed no color.

The first Model 59 had a volume control and thirty-five frets. The non-plated pickup had no height adjustments. By 1939 it had a tone control and an adjustable pickup. Distributors usually sold the Model 59 steel as a set with the Model 59 amplifier.

Model S or NS Model--Despite the NS title, this model was different from the prewar Silver Hawaiian. The postwar Model S was similar to a prewar shaded gray Model 59. However, the Model S always had a volume control, a tone control, and an adjustable pickup with narrow postwar magnets. It was available from 1946 until the early 1950s. (Although usually gray, the enamel color of this model probably varied.)

The Academy Model and the Ace Model--These two six string student guitars were usually

This was a 1941 Silver Hawaiian with tone and volume controls.

brown mahogany colored Bakelite. Electro String used colors such as maroon and white too.

The two models were nearly the same, although the Academy was the earlier version. The distinction between the two models was simple as the Ace had a plastic cover over the pickup. Both models had flocking material on the back to keep them from sliding off the player's lap. Both were equipped with tone and volume controls.

The company advertised the Academy after 1945. The Ace Model superseded the Academy in the late 1940s and lasted until 1953. Jobbers sold both models separately or sold them with an amplifier as a student set. At one time Adolph intended the Ace Model to replace the Model B.

Model SD--SD-6 (six strings) SD-7 (seven strings) SD-8 (eight strings). The Model SD was a Deluxe version of the NS Model. It had a two-tone tan mahogany colored enamel finish. Like other Deluxe metal body Rick steels, the SD had a peghead cover and a 24 fret lucite finger board. The Model SD had a tone and a volume control. The metal parts, except the body, were usually chrome plated. Electro String made these models from about 1949 until Adolph sold the company in late 1953.

Model G (or Deluxe Hawaiian Guitar)--G-6 (six strings), G-7 (seven strings), G-8 (eight strings). Introduced in the late 1940s, the Model G evolved from the Silver Hawaiian Model. It was the highest priced and most ornate of the stamped single neck guitars. Rickenbacker dropped the Model G steels from the guitar line in 1957.

The Deluxe Hawaiian Guitar features were simple yet striking. The body was chrome plated and highly polished. The guitar had a gold backed, clear lucite finger board. The pickup, tuners, tailpiece, and bridge were all gold plated. The peghead had a gold plated metal cover that concealed the string posts.

The Double Neck Hawaiian Guitar--There were at least two styles of double neck steel guitars produced by Rickenbacker before 1953. The first ones had metal bodies and detachable Bakelite necks; there were two versions like this before the war and another after the war. Prewar versions had 1 1/2 inch wide pickup

1938 Model 59 student steel with Model 59 amplifier.

Model 59 circa 1938.
This early version featured a non-adjustable pickup.

40

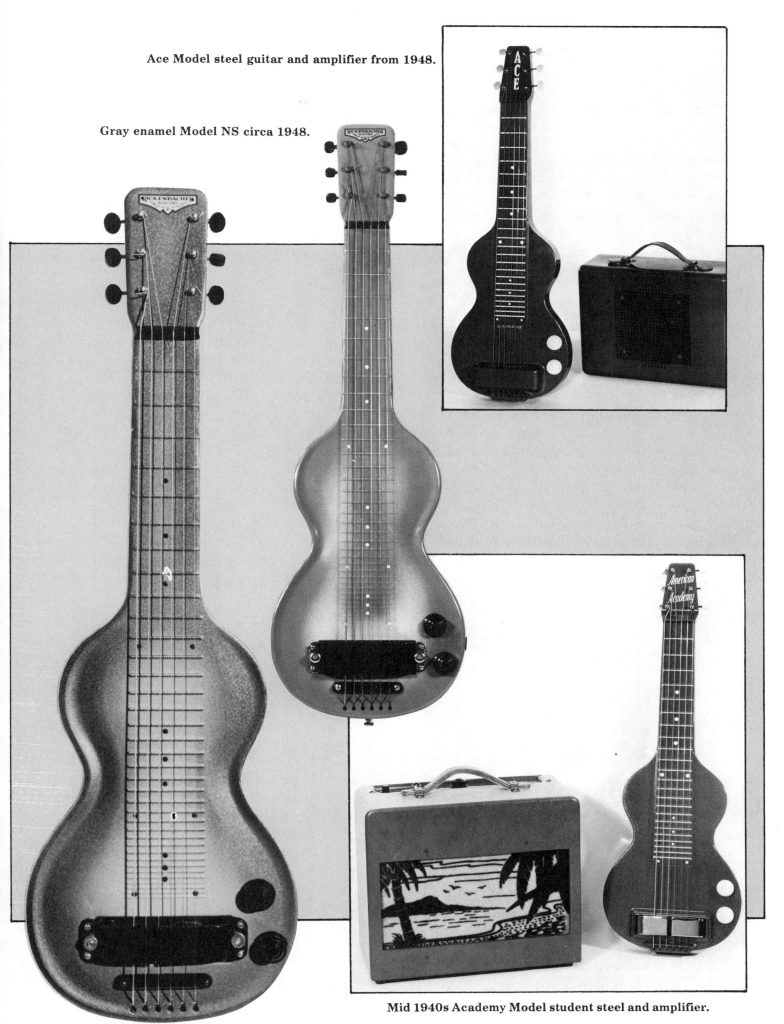

Ace Model steel guitar and amplifier from 1948.

Gray enamel Model NS circa 1948.

Mid 1940s Academy Model student steel and amplifier.

Mid 40s NS Model with a gray hammertone finish.
Notice that this model usually had a decal on the peghead rather than a metal nameplate.

41

Model G Deluxe Hawaiian guitar circa 1950.
This was the most ornate Rick lap steel ever.

Prewar D-12 double neck steel with detachable
Bakelite necks and a metal body.

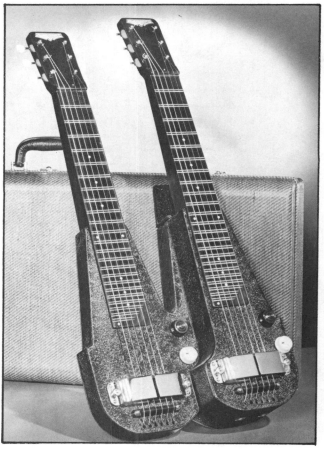

magnets.

The second style Rickenbacker double neck had a one piece metal body that included the necks. The Deluxe version of this style had lucite finger boards on each of its eight string necks. The finish on the metal body double neck was oven-baked enamel.

The double necks were available with six, seven, or eight string necks in any combination. The standard configurations were two six string necks (the D-12), two seven string necks (the D-14), and two eight string necks (the D-16). Rickenbacker probably discontinued the Model D-14 after the war.

Triple necks were available before 1950 on a special order basis. In 1950 Adolph wrote to one customer about triple necks saying that they were no longer available because pitch changing mechanisms made them obsolete. In fact, the company had trouble with the bulky metal bodies the triple necks used. Mr. Hall made completely redesigned triple necks available when he acquired the company.

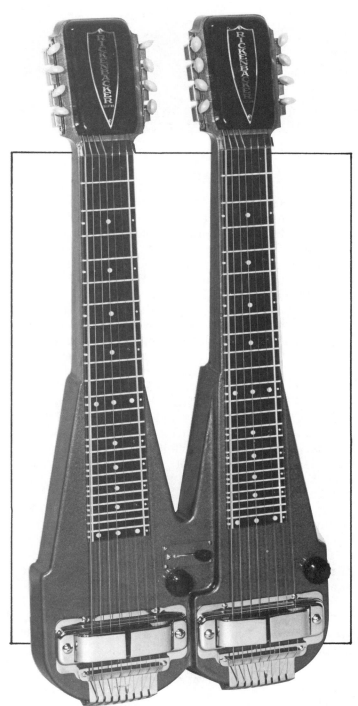

Deluxe model double neck steel with sixteen strings circa 1950. Note the peghead covers and lucite finger boards.

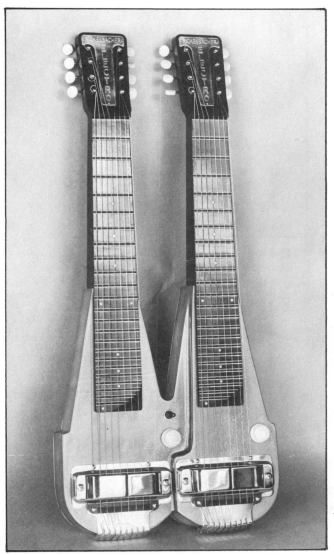

Postwar double neck with Bakelite necks and a metal body.

43

Spanish Guitars

The Electro Spanish Guitar--(six string standard and four string tenor) Rickenbacker sold acoustic/electric Spanish style guitars beginning in 1932. The earliest Electro Spanish guitars were similar to the wood body National Trojan models because the Harmony Co. in Chicago made both.[20]

The first Spanish guitar illustrated in the 1933 advertising literature had a flat-top hollow body and a slotted peghead. The tenor version, though not illustrated, had a solid peghead. The neck joined the body at the fourteenth fret; the finger board had nineteen frets. There were small F-holes on the upper top. This guitar had a single horseshoe pickup unit, but no volume control. The peghead had a plastic mother of pearl like veneer. On the earliest Spanish models, they simply silkscreened the Electro name in gold onto the headstock.

Brochures from the 1934 and 1935 period pictured a Spanish guitar with a slightly different tailpiece. It had a volume control with the same octagonal plastic knob seen on the steel guitars. The plywood body had a shaded mahogany finish with more of a sunburst effect than earlier. The neck was solid mahogany with a twenty-five inch scale. The Ken Roberts Model replaced the wood body Electro Spanish.

Price complete with speaker $175.00

The first style Electro Spanish Guitar pictured in early 1933.

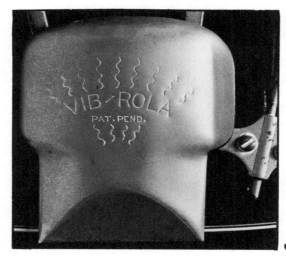

Early style adjustable horseshoe pickup from a 1934 Spanish electric.

Cover plate on the earliest style Kauffman Vibrola.

Octagonal volume control knob used on Rickenbacker Electro instruments from 1933 to 1937.

The Ken Roberts Model--The Ken Roberts Model was an acoustic/electric standard guitar manufactured by the Harmony Co. in Chicago. Ken Roberts was one of Beauchamp's friends and a top movie studio guitarist. This model appeared in catalogs and ads from late 1935 through 1939.

The Ken Roberts guitar had a bound neck that joined the body at the seventeenth fret. There were twenty-two frets total. The body was a concert sized flat-top with F holes, equipped with the Kauffman manual Vibrola tailpiece. The finish was a shaded two tone brown. It had one horseshoe pickup installed by Electro String.

Rickenbacker Electro Spanish guitar circa 1934. Someone added the Kauffman hand Vibrola.

Ken Roberts Model circa 1937.

Close-up of a circa 1937 Ken Roberts Model with the Electro made Kauffman Vibrola.

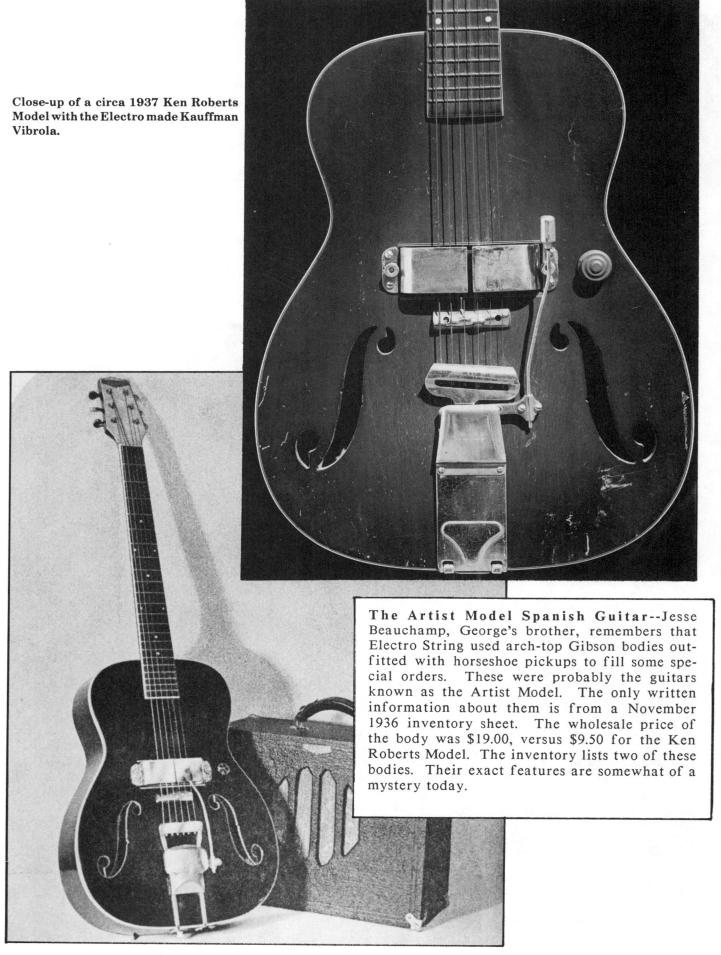

The Artist Model Spanish Guitar--Jesse Beauchamp, George's brother, remembers that Electro String used arch-top Gibson bodies outfitted with horseshoe pickups to fill some special orders. These were probably the guitars known as the Artist Model. The only written information about them is from a November 1936 inventory sheet. The wholesale price of the body was $19.00, versus $9.50 for the Ken Roberts Model. The inventory lists two of these bodies. Their exact features are somewhat of a mystery today.

The Ken Roberts Model with an old style hand Vibrola.
The company pictured this instrument in the late 1935 catalog.

The Electro String Model B--(six string standard and four string tenor). These were the Spanish versions of the molded Bakelite Model B Hawaiian Guitar. Electro String introduced them in the summer of 1935.

The features on the first Bakelite Spanish Guitar included a detachable neck with twenty-three frets. (The Hawaiian necks and bodies were incompatible with Spanish necks and bodies because the two different neck styles attached at different points on the length of their scales.) The Spanish body had five decorative chromed plates attached to the top. The guitar had one adjustable horseshoe pickup and one octagonal volume control knob. There was a brass name tag on the headstock.

Changes in the Spanish guitar features paralleled those of the Bakelite Hawaiian guitars. Nearly all these early instruments were black, but Rickenbacker did make Alvino Rey a white Bakelite Spanish guitar in the 1930s. The company discontinued the Spanish Model B during the war.

Beauchamp designed these guitars to be simple and economical to produce. One important feature that cut production costs was the detachable Bakelite neck. The frets were a molded part of the finger board and when they wore out the player replaced the whole neck. The choice of Bakelite, a relatively cheap and uniform material to work, showed Adolph's influence. (The factory supplied wooden replacement necks for the Bakelite Spanish and Tenor guitars after the war.)

Though the Bakelite standard guitar was semi-solid, many people believe that it qualifies as the first solid body electric Spanish guitar.[21] The design reflected Beauchamp's philosophy of the non-resonant guitar body which is also the conceptual basis for all modern solid body guitars. Since the hollow parts were there merely to eliminate excess weight, for all practical purposes the instrument was solid. At least, its design unveiled the future of fully electric guitars.

There were several reasons the Model B Spanish guitars did not become fashionable with players of the thirties. For one thing, steel guitar playing was more popular than Spanish guitar playing and that did not change until the 1950s. The Bakelite Electro standard was unpopular with professionals because its size and shape made it difficult to play sitting down. And most orchestra guitarists played sitting down. (A Bakelite guitar the size of other depression era ones would have been as heavy as a sack of bowling balls.)

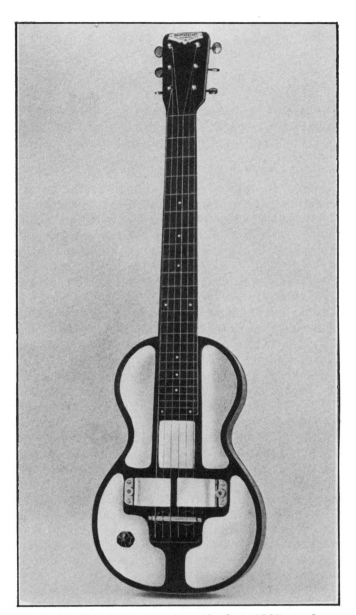

Bakelite Spanish guitar from the late 1935 catalog.

Harold Aloma with a Bakelite Spanish guitar on November 8, 1935.

47

The Vibrola Spanish Guitar--This guitar, a variation of the Bakelite guitars, was invented by C.O. "Doc" Kauffman. It had an extra thick body that housed a motor and pulleys. The pulleys attached to the motorized tailpiece which changed the pitch of the strings as the player strummed. It sounds like an underwater sound effect today, but it was marvelous in the 1930s.

Doc built five prototypes of the motorized Vibrola guitar at his home workshop in Fullerton, California. Three of these had handmade walnut bodies and Bakelite necks. The others were all Bakelite. George and Adolph came down from Los Angeles to hear a demonstration of the guitar on the night of July 7, 1936. Doc convinced them that the guitar had possibilities, and they negotiated an agreement for Electro String to manufacture the invention.

The first name for Doc's new instrument was the Vibratone Guitar. The name changed to the Vibrola Spanish Guitar when Rickenbacker took over production. Introduced in December 1937, they manufactured them on a regular basis until October 1941. Rickenbacker produced a total of ninety complete units before the war. Inventory sheets from 1942 listed two Vibrola Spanish bodies. These were probably the last ones made--if the factory finished them--as there were no advertisements for the instrument after the war.

The Vibrola guitar sold for $175.00, complete with a stand and amplifier. Rickenbacker gave Doc a one dollar royalty fee for every one manufactured. Doc and Electro String sold Vibrola guitars to some of the most predominate guitarists in 1930s show business: Pinky Tomlin (a popular Hollywood comedian), Georgie Smith (Paramount Studios), and Perry Botkin (of the Kraft Music Hall and Bing Crosby Show), Hugh Pendergraft, and Les Paul.

Besides being rather unconventional, Doc's Vibrola Spanish had a few serious shortcomings. First, it was so heavy a player needed a stand to hold it up. Second, the guitar had a switch to turn the vibrato motor/tailpiece off. But on the production models the strings, tailpiece, and gears were still engaged to the motor when this switch was off. And as a result, almost invariably the guitar was left out of tune when the Vibrola stopped. Essentially the guitar was only useful with the motor running.

Perry Botkin with his Vibrola Spanish guitar in 1938.

Perry Botkin, who played his Vibrola guitar without the vibrato on the Hoagy Carmichael record *Hong Kong Blues,* pointed out the Vibrola guitar's tuning problem to Doc in a letter dated November 3, 1938. Doc went into action and figured out a way to release the gears when he turned the motor off. With this simple modification, it was possible to play without the vibrato, always in tune. Kauffman installed this feature in his personal guitar and in Perry Botkin's too.

Model S-59 Spanish Guitar--Introduced in 1940 and deleted after the war. This guitar was an acoustic/electric with a detachable version of the horseshoe pickup created and patented by

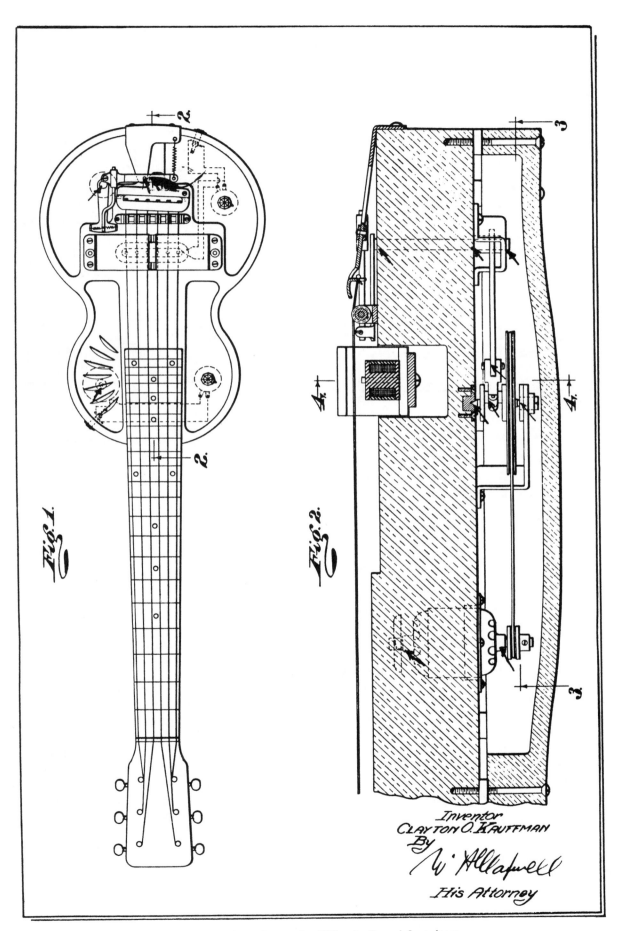

Drawing that shows the Vibrola Spanish guitar.

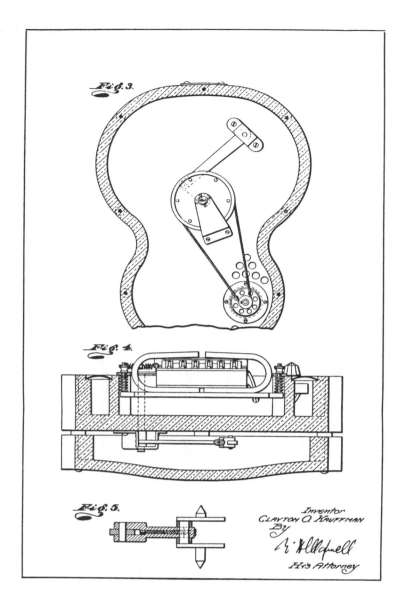

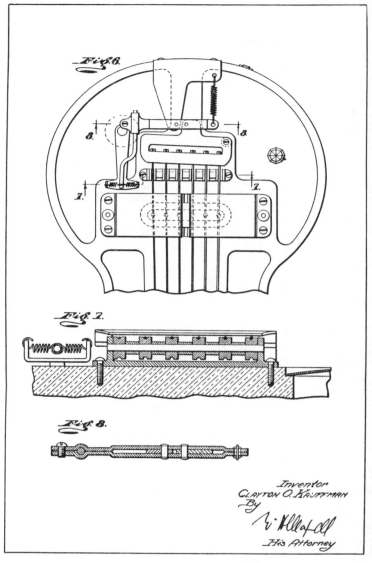

Inner workings of the Vibrola Spanish guitar.

Paul Barth. (Electro String sold the pickup separately as an accessory.)

The 1941 Grossman Music catalog had this description of the S-59: "A new Blonde, arch-top and back, Super Auditorium size, having shell bound edges, ovalled, rosewood finger board, with pearl inlay position markings, adjustable bridge, and celluloid guardplate. Has good quality, deep tone alone without amplification."

The catalog went on to describe the advantages of the new floating pickup unit: "The new Rickenbacker Electro pickup does not interfere with the instrument's use as a rhythm unit and by a turn of the control knob the magic of electric amplification makes possible those 'hot licks' and fancy effects that distin-

guish name players and point the spotlights of publicity on the guitarist. A turn of the knob and the guitar is again a rhythm 'box.' The possibilities of expression offered by this combination will prove a sensational advancement for the standard guitar."

The Kay Guitar Co. made the S-59 and Rickenbacker installed the pickup, but the records contain a mystery. Inventory sheets indicate that in 1941 the Kay Guitar Co. made an $8.50 (wholesale) guitar and a $16.50 (wholesale) guitar for Electro String. Electro String advertised only one model, but obviously there were two. The $16.50 guitar was probably another Artist Model type guitar comparable to the earlier ones made by Gibson.

Short-lived S-59 acoustic/electric with the detachable pickup.

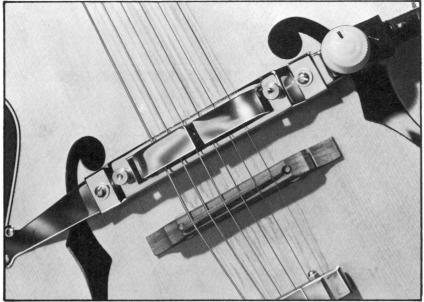

Close-up view of the S-59 pickup. Rickenbacker sold this unit as an accessory too.

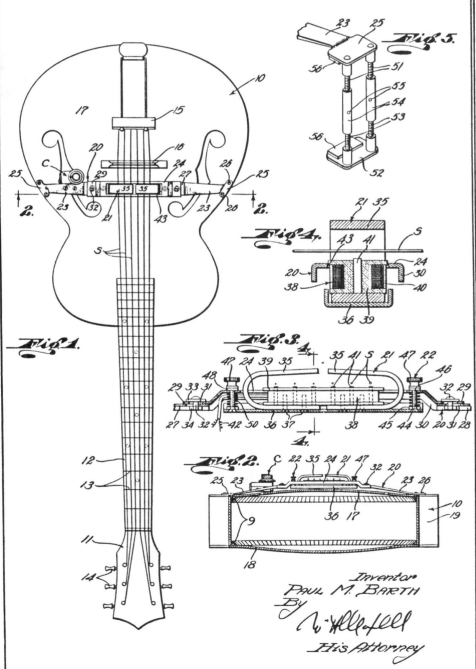

Paul Barth's detachable horseshoe pickup from the patent filed October 1941.

The Rickenbacker Spanish (SP)--Another company made the SP body and neck for Rickenbacker. Adolph's company offered the SP for sale in the mid 1940s and dropped the model in 1950 because the cost of the bodies became prohibitive.

The SP was an arch-top acoustic/electric guitar with a maple body and a spruce top. The body and neck were bound while the finger board had large block pearloid inlays. The guitar's bridge was adjustable for height. The electronics included an integrally mounted horseshoe pickup unit, a volume control, and a tone control.

Other Electro String Instruments

The Electro Mandolin--The early 1930s Rickenbacker electric mandolin was a hollow body flat-back acoustic/electric. It had a round sound hole. The body and neck were made out of mahogany by the Harmony Co. in Chicago. Electro String sold the first in 1933. The earliest mandolin looked quite similar to its contemporary Harmony Patrician model.

In literature from the late 1930s, Rickenbacker described the mandolin as an arch-top made out of curly maple. The neck had a rosewood fingerboard. The in-struments probably varied from those cataloged, and the company actually made few.

Price complete with speaker $175.00

Pat. Pend.

Top-The SP Model made after the war until 1950.
Bottom-The Harmony Co. in Chicage made Electro's 1930s mandolin.

The Electro Violin, Viola, and Cello-- Beauchamp started to experiment with the electric violin after he developed the Frying Pan steel. His goal was to develop a full line of violin family instruments. George designed two different electric violins.

Introduced in 1935, the first versions of the bowed instruments were more futuristic in appearance than the later examples. They did not have conventional headstocks; the tuning pegs were in between the chin-rest and the bridge. This headless look resembled the Steinberger electric bass popular in the 1980s. The first Electro violins had molded Bakelite bodies and necks. Neither the tuning peg setup nor the plastic finger board appealed to the string players who used them. In Nolan Beauchamp's words, "They were flops."

The second violin had a tubular aluminum body, a conventional peghead, and an ebony finger board. The chin-rest was Bakelite and the neck was maple. Electro String made a viola and cello like this too. They were available as early as 1939. Even with a less radical look and feel, the new Electro String violins were still too far out for the classical players. They were never popular, and Rick did not produced them after 1941.

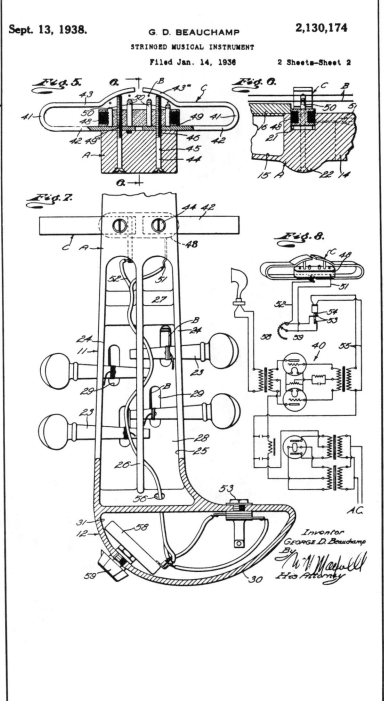

Patent drawing for Beauchamp's molded Bakelite electric violin.

The first Electro violin tuning keys, pickup, and chin rest.

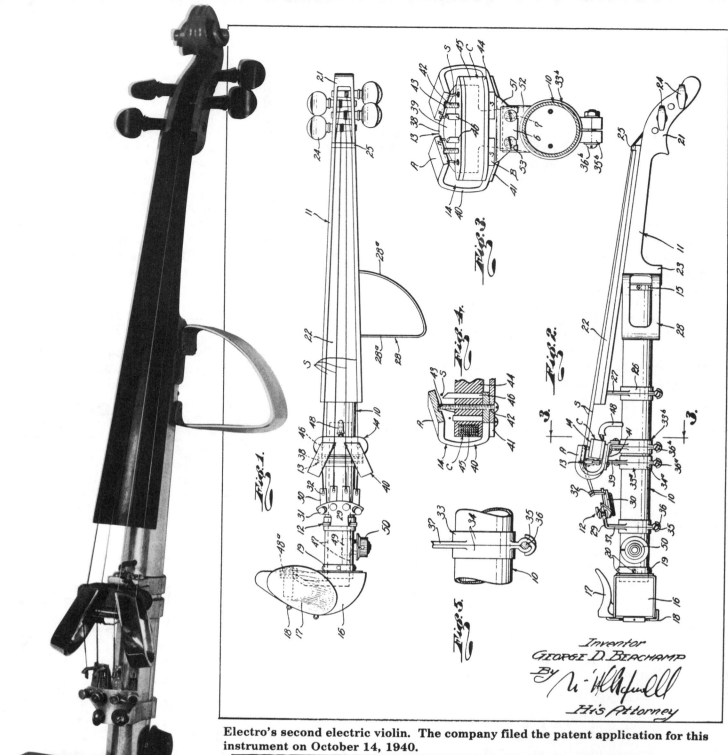

Electro's second electric violin. The company filed the patent application for this instrument on October 14, 1940.

An Electro violin with a tubular aluminum body circa 1939.

This was a violin pickup, a Bakelite knob, and a Bakelite chin rest on a 1939 Electro violin.

The Electro Bass Viol--Rickenbacker produced the first fully electric basses with string driven pickups.

The Electro Bass Viol--Rickenbacker produced the first fully electric basses with string driven pickups. Introduced in the 1930s, they were not bass guitars, but rather, stand-up fretless bass viols. Like the Electro violins, there were two versions of the bass viol. The first had a cast metal body which sometimes used a bass amplifier as a support stand, and the second had a tubular aluminum body which either stood free or had a separate stand.

George Beauchamp designed the first version of the bass viol in 1935. The instrument was fifty-eight inches in length and six inches at its widest point. It had an ebony finger board, an adjustable end pin, and a rheostatic volume control. There were two known photos of this style bass: in one photo the bass had a black crinkle paint finish, and in the other photo the bass had a polished metal and lacquer finish. The Electro bass viol used gut strings with about two inches wrapped with metal to excite the pickup.

The second version of the bass viol appeared in 1938. The tubular body supported a maple neck with a traditional style bass viol peghead and an ebony finger board. A catalog photo of one 1938 bass showed narrower pickup magnets than used on the earlier basses. However, the tubular bass used by Bert Lynn's orchestra had the wide magnets. The later Electro bass also had both volume and tone controls.

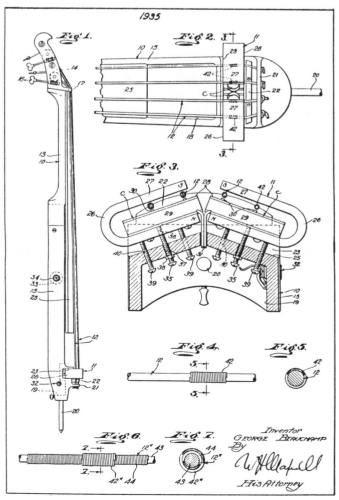

The first version of the Electro Bass Viol had a pickup with two coils side by side. One coil was under the low E and A strings, and one coil was under the D and G strings.

George Beauchamp's first electric bass viol.

Miscellaneous--Electro String produced several prototype instruments in the 1930s, each worthy of a short note. The most interesting of these was an electric harp made for Harpo Marx. Harpo paid two hundred dollars cash as a down payment on this instrument in January of 1933.

A prototype Electro piano sat in the front office at the factory on Western Avenue for years. One early brochure asked customers to "watch for announcements" about it. Considering the trouble the company had with the violin instruments, it is possible it chose simply to stay out of the crowded piano market. Today, no one knows much about Beauchamp's electric keyboard or where it is.

The Electro harp made for Harpo Marx in 1933.

Close-up of the electric harp strings and pickups.

Collectors have found several instruments recently that have Rickenbacker parts but no Rickenbacker or Electro String markings. It is possible the Electro String factory produced some unmarked instruments as test guitars, prototypes or samples. There is another explanation for these. During the thirties the factory sold parts, including pickups, to the public. There were some instrument makers known to Rickenbacker producing instruments legitimately on a small scale using these parts. Bert Lynn, the orchestra leader, was one. Usually, it is impossible to know the certain origin of unmarked instruments. Despite what they might be, their originality and true value will always be in doubt.

Part Two

The Modern Rickenbacker Company

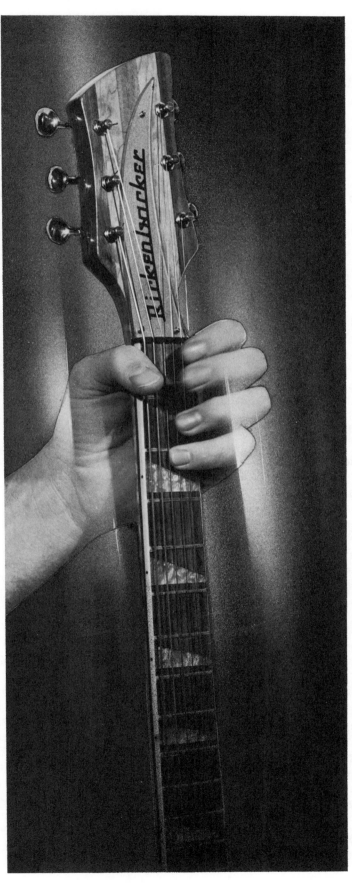

Rickenbacker in the 1950s____

F.C. Hall had a humble beginning for a man that would become one of the leading figures in the Southern California music business.   He was born in Iowa in 1909 and moved to Santa Ana, California in 1919 where his father opened a small store on Oak Street. As a boy, the younger Hall spent some summers working in the lima bean fields located near what is now Irvine, California. In high school he studied radio and electronics. F.C. made one of the first radios in the mostly rural 1920s Orange County. By then there was no question about his interests.

F.C.'s hobbies led him to start a part-time business recharging batteries for local residents, making home pickups and deliveries throughout Orange County. By 1927 he was manufacturing batteries at home and selling them through his dad's store. The battery business evolved into a radio repair shop called Hall's Radio Service, and that grew into one of So. California's most prosperous electronics parts distribution companies. By the late 1930s, F.C. called his business the Radio and Television Equipment Company (R.T.E.C. or Radio-Tel).

Mr. Hall's company did much more than distribute parts. It installed public address systems in many Southern California public buildings such as schools, halls, and churches. They had a speaker re-cone service that repaired all major brands of hi-fi speakers. In addition, Radio-Tel was the exclusive distributor for Tele-King television sets. Hall's willingness to enter all fields of electronic merchandise and service made his transition into the blossoming amplified music industry a natural step.

F.C. Hall with an early two tone sunburst Model 325 in February 1958.

In 1946 Radio-Tel started distributing Hawaiian guitars and amplifiers made by Leo Fender of Fullerton, California. Soon, Hall became Fender's exclusive distributor and set out to build a national distribution network for Fender products. Several people say that F.C. Hall played a key role in the early success of Fender instruments. He provided Leo with financial backing at a time when electric guitar manufacturing seemed like a high risk venture to most businessmen. Clearly, F.C. Hall was one of the people to recognize the bright business possibilities of electric guitars.

In December 1953 Adolph Rickenbacker sold Electro String to Mr. Hall.[22] Since a new company, Fender Sales, Inc., had already taken over the distribution of the Fender instruments, Mr. Hall devoted his full time to Rickenbacker. Eventually, he sold his interest in the new Fender distribution company setting in motion the modernization of the Rickenbacker company and guitar line.

58

The New Rickenbackers

In the early 1950s the guitar business was going through major changes. The popularity and sales of steel guitars dropped off as the Hawaiian music craze had run its course. At the same time, popularity and sales of standard guitars increased. Gradually the standard guitar completely overshadowed the steel.

The electric standard guitar became more and more popular for several reasons. For one thing, the electric guitar had become highly visible in popular music with the recordings of the King Cole Trio, Les Paul & Mary Ford, and others who often featured it. Another reason the electric guitar became more popular was a trend towards smaller sized bands after the war. For instance, two electric guitars playing ensemble arrangements took the place of whole horn sections in some postwar Western swing bands.

Since the electric standard guitar was effective as a rhythm instrument and as a solo instrument, it proved to be a versatile tool for musicians adapting to the changing styles. The standard guitar already had a central role in folk, blues, and country music. As these styles became more popular after the war, increasing interest in the standard guitar followed. Of course, rock'n'roll did as much for electric guitar popularity as electric guitars did for rock. While the tone and volume of the electric standard guitar propelled the music, interest in the music propelled electric guitar sales. By the time Hall had purchased Electro String, the trend in the guitar business was away from the company's best known products: its fine electric steel guitars. In response to the change, Hall introduced the Rickenbacker Solid Body Combo Series of electric Spanish guitars. By the late 1950s the company had one of most diversified standard guitar lines in the business. Despite the new emphasis on standard guitars, the steels remained important to the company throughout the 1950s and into the 1960s. The company

The 1954 Rickenbacker catalog.

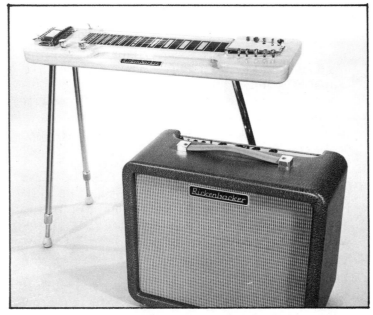

Steel guitars remained important to Rickenbacker until the mid 1960s. Here was a ten string Model TW with an M-15 amplifier from about 1956.

The Bob Kennedy Bandwagon played Combo guitars and a Console 508 steel in March 1955.

The 1955 Rickenbacker catalog.

Rickenbacker

ELECTRIC GUITARS
AMPLIFIERS ● CASES
STRINGS AND ACCESSORIES

ELECTRO

maintained many of the original steel models and added several new ones.

Mr. Hall changed the way Rickenbacker sold guitars wholesale to dealers. Before he bought Rickenbacker, the company used the traditional channels of the music industry: wholesale distributors.[23] These companies carried many different lines of musical merchandise and had their own salesmen. F.C.'s idea was to sell Rickenbacker guitars exclusively through the Radio and Television Equipment Co. as he had sold Fender guitars.

Radio-Tel was one of the first in-house distributors in the guitar business. (The Hall family owned the instrument's manufacturing company and the instrument's sales distribution company.) In-house distribution benefitted the customers, dealers, and the manufacturer; today it is almost universal in the business. However, in the beginning, the best way to sell guitars was not the easiest. Mr. Hall started from square one creating a new out-of-state sales network for Rickenbacker. He hired a new crew of on-the-road salesmen and opened accounts with many new Rickenbacker dealers.

By early 1954 the forces were set into motion that would make Rickenbackers the choice for thousands of modern guitarists. The company was a family owned business and responsive to its customers' needs. It had a small manufacturing facility and experienced employees. Because the factory was responsive to the distributor, they could provide better service to the dealers. Furthermore, the increasing popularity of the standard guitar encouraged the company to experiment and introduce new ideas.

On April 20, 1956 Mr. Hall moved the sales office for Rickenbacker to a larger facility at 2118 S. Main Street in Santa Ana. There he set up a showroom in the front and established a warehouse in back. Besides Rickenbacker guitars, steels, and amps, the company sold Nova, Starmaker, and Concerto band instruments. The band instrument business actually overshadowed the guitar business at times during the mid fifties. The company also sold a full line of instrument accessories and a record set called "The Talking Bible."

Although several people influenced the development of the 1950s Rickenbacker guitars, the most influential--and the last to seek any recognition--was Mr. Hall. He directed the overall thrust of the company, deciding

The Miller Bros. Western dance band and many other Western groups used Rickenbacker equipment in the 1950s and early 1960s.

(L toR) James Burton, Rick Nelson, and James Kirkland promoted Rickenbacker guitars in the late 1950s. Rick played a Model 390 in this picture.

This guitar was a late 1957 Combo 850.

Salesman Joe Talbot, with the Rickenbacker guitar, had many musician friends in the Southeast.

whether to introduce new models or to improve old ones. Specifically, he contributed to the circuitry designs in guitars and amps. Several employees helped to shape the modern look of the new guitars and helped to design their features. However, as owner, Mr. Hall always guided the workers to the finished product.

One important employee was Paul Barth, who stayed with Electro String until May 1957. He left to design instruments for other companies: Magnatone and Barth Guitars. Roger Rossmeisl, a new factory employee in the 1950s, developed the enduring Capri and solid body designs of 1957 and 1958. He ran guitar making at Rickenbacker--a virtual custom shop and factory rolled into one--until 1962. When Rossmeisl left Rickenbacker, he went to work for Fender where he designed their original line of acoustic guitars.

The new Rickenbacker guitar shapes were some of the most interesting and artistic in the industry. It is no coincidence that people perceived a European flavor to the new Rickenbackers. Rossmeisl came from a family line of German instrument makers; he was a trained craftsman from the old European school. Rossmeisl personally handcrafted Rickenbacker prototypes and custom-built instruments during his tenure at the company.

There were many Rickenbacker traveling salesmen over the years: Joe Talbot, Al Razor, and Harold Buckner, to mention a few. They made many indirect contributions to the evolution of the guitar line. The salesman's daily reports were barometers that measured new trends and styles in the industry. They sent Mr. Hall reports and suggestions from dealers and musicians. Many of the ideas picked up in the sales territories materialized as Rickenbacker innovations.

Mr. Hall hired Harold "Buck" Buckner in 1956 for the Midwest sales territory. He was an excellent guitarist and an energetic salesman who stationed himself in Indiana. Buckner won a gold watch in 1960 for his efforts as the most successful Rickenbacker salesman. The wide popularity of Rickenbacker instruments in his sales area was largely the result of his efforts and dedication to the company.

In the late fifties, singer Rick Nelson and his band promoted Rickenbacker guitars on television and at personal appearances. Rick played several different models including a Model 390 and a custom made flat top acoustic.

This model greeted visitors to the 1956 N.A.M.M. show booth with a single pickup Combo 400.

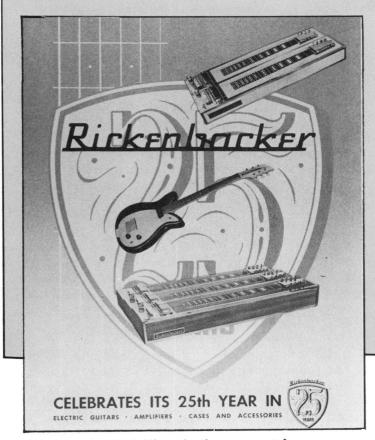

The 1956 Silver Anniversary catalog.

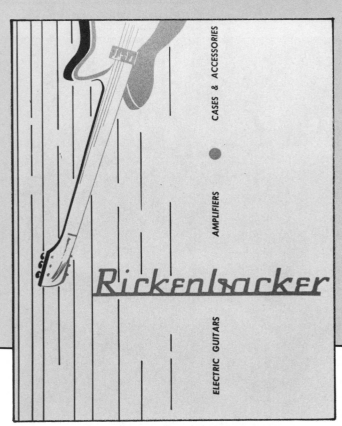

The 1957 Rickenbacker catalog.
The company used this catalog supplemented with single page inserts for several years.

Rock and Roll Hall of Fame singer Sam Cooke outside the Rickenbacker sales office in 1958.

Jerry Byrd at the 1959 N.A.M.M. show. The second guitar from the right was a rare walnut body Combo 850 with two chrome bar pickups.

Rick Nelson's band included one of rock's best guitarists, James Burton. He field tested a Model 381 and provided feedback that shaped the electronics and designs of the original electric Capri series. James Kirkland, Nelson's bass player during this period, used a Rickenbacker Model 4000 bass.

Another important Rickenbacker artist in the late 1950s was the great non-pedal steel player, Jerry Byrd. Jerry bought his first Rickenbacker in 1937 at Ron Dearth's Guitar Studio in Lima, Ohio, and he made many of his early recordings with a prewar seven string Bakelite. Byrd's use of the old Rickenbacker Bakelite and his great tone made a strong impression on many of his fans. By the 1950s, Byrd had turned the old Rickenbackers into some of the first collectible electric guitars.

Rickenbacker introduced the Jerry Byrd series of console steel guitars in the late 1950s. The factory made these to Byrd's specifications, and he promoted them with personal appearances for the company at the trade shows and festivals. The company's association with Byrd did much to reinforce its prestige among steel guitar players.

Longtime factory manager Ward Deaton retired in the early 1980s.

Legendary steel great Joaquin Murphy played a Rickenbacker steel with Spade Cooley's band in the late 1950s.

Rickenbacker in the 1960s

As Rickenbacker entered the sixties, it already carried the tradition of nearly thirty years in the music business. Some of the most important artists of the time played the steel and standard guitars. Music studios that taught guitar, especially in the Southwest and Midwest, equipped their students with Rickenbackers. The instrument line had a number of innovative models. In retrospect, this calm period really was the lull before the storm the Beatles would soon create around Rickenbacker.

In 1962 Mr. Hall moved the Electro String factory from the original location in Los Angeles to the present location on Kilson Dr. in Santa Ana. It took at least six months to move because the moving schedule minimized the disruption of the manufacturing schedules. It was a particularly difficult time for Mr. Hall who had to make additional trips to Los Angeles from his home in Laguna Beach. The situation eased when the factory in Los Angeles finally closed. In Santa Ana there were originally two buildings with a much larger one added in 1964.

The 1960 Spanish guitar color brochure.

Harold Buckner with a 4001 bass standing beside Mr. Hall at a 1963 trade show.

Radio & Television Equipment Co.
2118 S. MAIN ST.
SANTA ANA, CALIFORNIA
KIMBERLY 5-5574

F. C. HALL
PRESIDENT   WHOLESALE MUSIC DIVISION

One of Mr. Hall's early business cards. He changed the name of his distribution company to Rickenbacker, Inc. in 1965.

At times there was some confusion over the Radio and Television Equipment Co. name and its connection with Rickenbacker. As Harold Buckner once said, "We don't sell radios. We don't sell televisions. And we don't sell equipment." It was true that by the sixties Mr. Hall was dealing almost totally in musical instruments and accessories. To Buckner and others, it made sense to update the sales company's name by including the word Rickenbacker in it.

For good reason, Mr. Hall was reluctant to change the distribution company's name because of its long standing reputation. Although many people knew the company informally as Rickenbacker, a change might have confused many longtime customers. Eventually Mr. Hall's thinking changed. In 1965 he decided to call his sales company Rickenbacker, Inc.

This pre-British Invasion teenage band used two Fireglo 460 solid bodies and a Model 365 hollow body in 1962.

The Beatles in late 1963. John Lennon was holding his first Model 325 after Jim Burns refinished it black.

The Beatles————————

In the early 1960s the history of Rickenbacker guitars became wedded to one of the biggest music phenomenons of the Twentieth Century: the Beatles from Liverpool, England. At one time or another, John Lennon, George Harrison, and Paul McCartney each played Rickenbacker instruments. John was the first, during the Beatles' early days in Hamburg, Germany. Like everything Beatle, from the haircuts to the boots, Rickenbacker's unique styling was a new experience for the British.

When European Beatlemania first started, several British music instruments distributors contacted Rickenbacker. The three most prominent were Selmer, Jennings Musical Instruments, and Rose, Morris Ltd. Naturally, they wished to capitalize on the Beatle-created interest in Rickenbacker since the Beatles were the fastest rising stars in Europe. In spite of this popularity, F.C. Hall and most Americans were unaware of the group. Gradually, stories of their success spilled into American press reports, and Hall received clippings that showed both John Lennon and George Harrison using Rickenbackers.

By November 1963 the people at Rickenbacker realized a business opportunity was unfolding in Europe, but there was no way to gauge its dimensions. Only hints existed of what a Beatles/Rickenbacker connection would do for the company's business in the United

George Harrison had a Model 425 by late 1963, before the Beatles became widely known in the United States.

States. Still, the Beatles remained an unknown quantity. By 1963 Rickenbacker standards, they could have turned out to be insignificant compared to the fortuitous free promotion for the company by other artists. After all, Chet Atkins--probably the early 1960s most influential guitarist--pictured a Rickenbacker amp on the cover of his 1963 album *Teen Scene*.

However, by January 1964 F.C. Hall knew that the company he had carefully managed and cautiously expanded was on the brink of a major turning point with the Beatles the cause. He wrote a letter to salesmen Harold Buckner in Indiana on January 2, 1964: "Buck, this is the hottest group in the world today as they have the two top records by popular poll in Europe; and, in addition, they have the two top LP albums for the same territory."

Hall went on to tell his salesman that the Beatles were coming to America and that a short Beatles' film would be on the Jack Paar TV show. The group would appear in person on the Ed Sullivan show three times in February. He added: "If the boys are as popular in the United States as they are now in Britain, it will be impossible for us to begin to make enough guitars to supply the demands. You may think I am boasting, but this a fact."

Buckner's response illustrated the competitive forces at work in the 1960s guitar market: "To keep them on Rick would prove a promotion so big that it could not be measured in dollars and cents." Then he added: "But, watch out for those Fender promoters, or they will have them all using Jaguars and Piggybacks (and don't say I didn't warn you.)" Although they would occasionally use Fender amps in the studio, the Beatles never played Fender Jaguars.

Rickenbacker was a big part of the Beatlemania phenomenon. Many of the teenagers who were excited about the Beatles were just as excited about Rickenbackers. The frenzy caught the company by surprise. They received fan mail--from simple inquiries to hand sketched drawings of the Beatles and their Rickenbackers. Some of the letters were addressed erroneously, "Rickenbacker, Liverpool, England." Somehow, they made their way to the company's office in Santa Ana. One teenager wrote Mr. Hall: "All the guys in my band have things in common with the Beatles and someday we're all going to have Rickenbackers too."

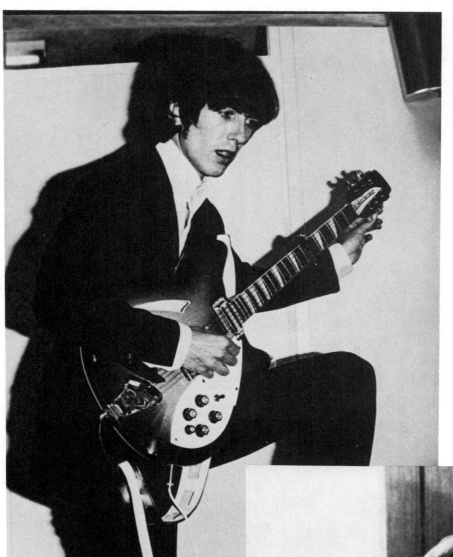

George Harrison got this twelve string
on the 1965 American tour.

John Lennon with his second Model
325.   This guitar has the Accent
vibrato.

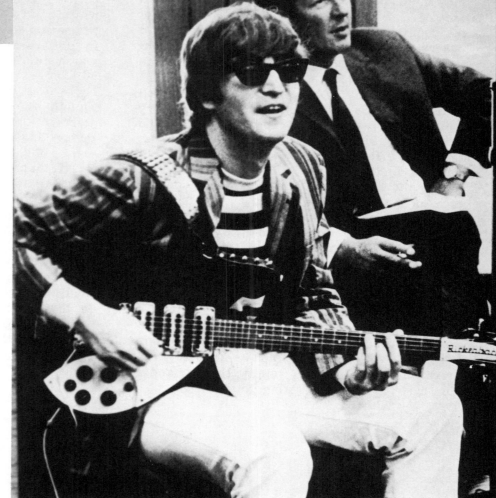

George Harrison with his Model 425.

George Harrison with his first Rickenbacker twelve string Model 360/12.

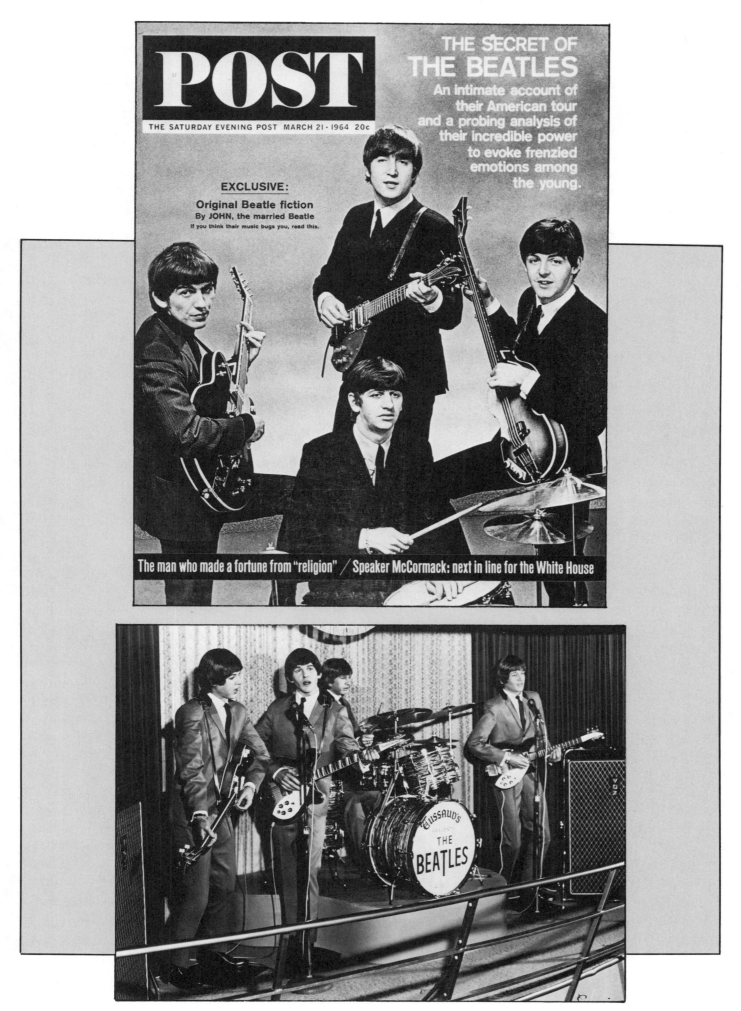

Wax Beatles played Rickenbacker too.

John Lennon with his first Model 325 when it still had a Kauffman Vibrola.

Today people connect the sound and shape of Rickenbacker guitars to the image of the Beatles and other 1960s British invasion groups; old Rickenbackers are a symbol for the mid 1960s period. Naturally, the Beatles made the Rickenbacker models they played famous. As for the Model 325, in big demand during the mid 1960s, some people nicknamed it the John Lennon Model. The Rick electric twelve strings used by George were among the company's most important instruments. The Rickenbacker bass gained the respect of many players after McCartney popularized it.

Although Mr. Hall later gave "the boys" several guitars, he never paid the Beatles to endorse Rickenbackers. In fact, George and John bought their first Rickenbackers. The Beatles turned down money to endorse guitars from other manufacturers presumably because they did not want to lose their freedom of choice. (The group had learned the endorsement game the hard way. Because of an agreement with Vox, they could not use Rickenbacker amps on stage during their first visit to the United States.)

The Beatles' Rickenbackers

John Lennon's affair with Rickenbacker guitars started in 1960 as a result of Jean "Toots" Thielemans, a Belgian born American. Thielemans had endorsed Rickenbacker guitars for several years, both while he was the guitarist in George Shearing's jazz group and while he pursued a solo career. Lennon heard guitarist Thielemans perform in West Germany where he had done a series of recorded broadcasts over German public radio in 1959 and 1960. Lennon was clearly enthusiastic about the Rickenbacker sound in the hands of the jazz great and went to local music stores in Hamburg looking for one.

The Rickenbacker Lennon bought was a natural finish Model 325, a three-quarter size guitar with four control knobs and three pickups. Mr. Hall remembers selling this guitar to West German dealer Walter Hofner at a Chicago trade show in 1959. John's guitar was exceedingly rare: it was one of eight such guitars made in 1958. (In October 1958 Rickenbacker shipped three of these maple finish 325 guitars to Framus Werke in West Germany. If the guitar Mr. Hall remembers selling to Hofner was not Lennon's, then certainly John's

guitar was one of the three sent to Framus Werke.)

Pictures of the Beatles in Hamburg cataloged the evolution of John's first 325. Lennon was no stickler for original parts on this guitar, which he was quick to modify, removing the stock Kauffman vibrato tailpiece to add a Bigsby replacement. (At the time the Bigsby vibrato was an atypical Rickenbacker feature.)

The next parts to go were the original T.V. style control knobs; there were at least two different types of replacements. For a while, according to Beatle guitar enthusiast Bob Mytkowicz, the knobs on John's guitar were like Hofner violin bass knobs.

John had his first 325 refinished black by British guitar maker Jim Burns (Burns, London) in 1963. A 1964 Beatle fan magazine said the original finish got "rubbed and scratched from many encounters with walls and stages." Even with the new paint job the guitar was easy to identify. It had a single gold backed lucite pickguard. All of John's other Ricks had double white pickguards. Beatle fan magazines indicate that someone stole John's first Rickenbacker in 1964.

The company shipped an updated 1964 Model 325 to John in Miami the week of their second performance on the Ed Sullivan show in February 1964. John's second Model 325 had a black factory finish, an Ac'cent vibrato unit, the fifth knob mixer control, and white double pickguards. Like John's first Rickenbacker, his second one had a solid top with no F hole. Unlike John's early "short arm," his new guitar had a slim body with a slightly smaller headstock, both characteristics of the mid 1960s 325 guitars.

Lennon had at least two more Rickenbackers between 1964 and 1966. One of these was the first Model 325/12 electric twelve string which had a stock black finish and a solid top. Rickenbacker shipped the 325/12 Rickenbacker guitar to the Beatles' London office in March of 1964. The shippers either temporarily lost it in transit or customs agents delayed its delivery. There was concern on both sides of the Atlantic because it did not arrive on time.

Eventually, the little electric twelve string made its way to Lennon. John played it in a promotional film for the 1965 single *Ticket to Ride,* suggesting that he used the guitar on

Jeffery Foskett guitarist with the Beach Boys and dedicated Rickenbacker advocate with his rare Model 381/12.

Susanna Hoffs lead singer of the Bangles with her 1980s Model 620/12.

Jean "Toots" Thielemans with his 1956 Combo 400.

the record too. In fact, the twelve string tone on this cut is quite different from other Beatle recordings that feature a twelve string guitar.

John's fourth Rickenbacker was like a Rose, Morris Model 1996. The standard finish on the Model 1996 was Fireglo. John used this F hole Model 325 as a backup guitar and in the studio. The Beatles' reputation as Rickenbacker players was so strong, sometimes British ads called the Rose, Morris instruments "the Beatlebackers."

The second Beatle to have a Rickenbacker was lead guitarist George Harrison. George bought his first Rick in 1963 while visiting his sister who lived in St. Louis, Missouri. It was a stock black Model 425 with one pickup. He used this guitar on the 1963 New Year's Eve broadcast of the British television show *Ready, Steady, Go.* However, the Model 425 was not the Rickenbacker guitar most people remember George playing. Soon fans identified George Harrison with the Rickenbacker 360/12 Deluxe electric twelve string. During the Beatle years, he played two different versions of this model. Harrison might not have known it, but the twelve string was

still an experiment when first presented to him.

Mr. Hall made arrangements to meet the Beatles in New York City during the week of their first February appearance on the Ed Sullivan Show. He and a sales representative took several guitars, including a twelve string and a left-handed bass. They set up what amounted to a complete Rickenbacker display in a suite at the Savoy Hotel. Toots Thielemans was there to entertain the group when three of the Beatles--all but George--dropped by on February 8. The first Beatle to try the new twelve string was John Lennon. Of course, Paul tried the Rickenbacker bass.

George was sick with the flu, isolated from the rest of the group in his suite at the Plaza Hotel. Anxious to show George guitars, the Rickenbacker entourage packed up the essentials and went to his room at the other hotel. Harrison played the Rickenbacker twelve string sitting in bed while talking to a Minneapolis radio audience on the phone. The interviewing disc jockey asked George if he liked the guitar. The Beatle replied in his dry, deadpan Liverpudlian accent, "Yes, it's a Rickenbacker." According to Rickenbacker

George Shearing and Jean "Toots" Thielemans in 1958 with his Model 330F.

The Brook Twins in the early 1960s with Model 365 and Rickenbacker pedal steel.

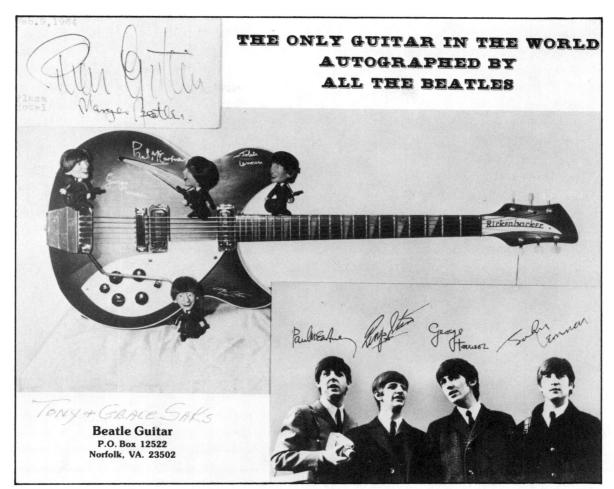

THE ONLY GUITAR IN THE WORLD AUTOGRAPHED BY ALL THE BEATLES

Beatle Guitar
P.O. Box 12522
Norfolk, VA. 23502

A December 1963 Model 365 shown to the Beatles in New York on February 8, 1964. Music studio operator Tony Saks bought the instrument and later had the Beatles autograph it.

legend, later that day a radio station person bought the guitar from Mr. Hall and gave it to Harrison. It was a present for the interview.

George's first electric twelve string was made in December 1963. It was the first of the new Rickenbacker twelve strings to have the reversed style stringing. (George's was actually the second known Rickenbacker twelve string made.) Like most Ricks of the day, it had a Fireglo finish with binding on the top and back of the body. There were Deluxe triangle finger board inlays. The guitar had double white pickguards and small black knobs. By late 1964 the company changed the body shape of the 360. George's second twelve string was the newer style with a Fireglo finish.

Paul McCartney was the third Beatle to use a Rickenbacker. His first Rick bass was a double pickup, left handed Model 4001S with a Fireglo finish. The factory made it in January 1964 in time for Mr. Hall to take it to New York in February. Paul said in a 1980 interview that he was quite comfortable doing T.V. shows with his light weight Hofner bass.[24] The Rickenbacker was heavier than the Hofner; this fact explains why Paul passed on the Rickenbacker the first time he saw it. However,

Mr. Hall showed it to him again in the summer of 1964, during the week of the Beatles' Hollywood Bowl concerts. John Hall was there and remembers McCartney taking delivery of the solid body bass then.

When the Beatles quit live performances and moved into the studio, Paul turned to the Rickenbacker bass. McCartney used its punchy sound and string mutes to define his new melodic bass style. The Rickenbacker sound was especially clear on the Sgt. Pepper album and on other late Beatle recordings.

Paul's 4001S was the same as models being exported to England. Unlike most American 4001 basses, these basses had dot finger board inlays. There were no bindings on the neck or body and no Rick-O-Sound stereo output. Paul refinished his first Rick with a psychedelic paint job during the Beatles' Magical Mystery Tour phase. Later he stripped the bass to a natural maple. In the 1970s he removed the horseshoe pickup and installed a new under-string unit in its place.

The British Invasion Groups and Rickenbacker

The Beatles opened many doors for

The Beatles in 1964. George Harrison playing his double-bound Model 360/12, and John Lennon playing his 1964 Model 325.

other new English rock groups. The British music invasion of 1964 through 1966 followed-- the American record and music business was never the same. It would be an exaggeration to claim the British invasion groups used Rickenbackers exclusively. In fact, they used a variety of different European and American guitars. However, Rickenbacker guitars were as visible as any other single manufacturer's instruments. The list of British groups and guitarists who used Rickenbacker guitars read like a who's who.

An early English Rickenbacker artist following the Beatles lead, Jerry Marsden, was a client of Beatle manager Brian Epstein. With his own group from Liverpool, Jerry and the Pacemakers, Marsden helped to expand the so-called Mersybeat sound. His success in England and the United States--although shorter lived-- followed on the heels of the Beatles. Marsden's 1964 doublebound Rick Model 360/12 was nearly the same as George Harrison's. Rickenbacker shipped Jerry's guitar with John Lennon's 325/12 in March of 1964 as a favor to Epstein.

Television shows introduced many British groups using Rickenbacker guitars to

an American audience. (The company exported instruments to the U.K. in quantity by mid 1964.) The 1965 television special, *Shindig Goes to London,* featured several British bands playing live at the Richmond Jazz Festival. The Animals knocked out their hit *We Gotta Get Out of This Place.* Animal guitarist Hilton Valentine played a Rose, Morris Model 1997. A young Denny Laine of the Moody Blues played a similar two pickup Rickenbacker export model. On a later *Shindig* show, produced in Los Angeles, Laine played a three pickup Rose, Morris Model 1998. Another British group seen with Rickenbackers on *Shindig* was Lulu's band, the Luvvers.

There were many other important English acts using Rickenbackers. The Kinks' bass player, Peter Quaife, had a Rickenbacker. The Rolling Stones, although not usually remembered as Rick players, used two on a 1965 BBC *Ready Steady Go* television show. The Who's bassist, John Entwistle, had many Rickenbacker basses. These included a Rose, Morris 1999 and a light show 4005L. One guitarist that stood out as a sixties Rickenbacker artist was Peter Townshend of The Who. He played a two pickup export Model

Pete Townshend on Rickenbacker

March, 1987

What influenced you to buy your first Rickenbacker?

The fact that they were used by The Beatles. Prior to seeing Harrison and Lennon with them I'd never seen them before. I thought they were beautiful, unique and classic in design on a level equalled only to Fender.

How long did you use the Rickenbackers on stage and in the studio?

I used Ricks on stage until 1967. In the studio I still use them today; I have a couple of 12 strings and 6 strings 360 types, not special models. They sound clear, bright and play very well. I use tape wound Rickenbacker strings on the 12 strings; it's important.

The Rose, Morris Model 1993.
(Jeffrey Foskett collection)

Pete Townshend (r) used an assortment of Rickenbackers in the mid 1960s. Here he played a three pickup Rose, Morris 1998 while an American Model 360/12 rested against his amplifier. (Courtesy of Guitar Player).

What were the good points and the weak points of the instruments?

The Rickenbackers are eccentric and unique as I said above. The strings are closely spaced on a narrow neck. The fingerboard is highly varnished and the woodwork is lightweight but superbly balanced. This suited my chordal style and I invented several new shapes utilizing the neck shape that have become standard Rock shapes. What falls under the fingers on a Rick might dislocate your hand on an old acoustic Martin. The lightweight neck allowed me to produce vibrato techniques by moving the neck backwards and forwards. This became another characteristic of my style. The weak points of the guitars were that the necks would literally break off in my hand if I went too far. I think some modern players might find the neck shape quite restrictive too, but the delicate body shape, the

lightness of the woodwork, the carefully constructed craftmanlike neck all contribute to a guitar that is utterly different in every way from all other makes. I often feel that Rickenbacker are like violins rather than guitars, modern and delicate.

How many Rickenbackers did you break on stage?

I broke about 8. This was in the days these guitars cost around L250 a piece; i.e. well over L1,000 today. I had many reasons for these theatrical outbursts, but I was perversely proud of the fact that I was smashing up the most expensive guitar in London shops during the early '60s, when I still didn't own a car or an apartment. The guitars on the wall in the famous picture by Colin Jones of the Observer newspaper were all taken by a roadie to be repaired by his father. I never saw them again.

The Who's guitarist Pete Townshend (r) with a Rose, Morris Model 1993 twelve string in 1965.

(Courtesy of Guitar Player).

82

Pete Townshend with his new Pete Townshend limited edition Rickenbacker guitar introduced in early 1987.

Roger McGuinn with a 1960s Model 370/12 with custom wiring.

1997, a three pickup export Model 1998, and an export Model 1993 twelve string. He also had American versions. The Rickenbacker on the well known Marquee Maximum R&B poster was a Rose, Morris 1998 with an added switch and a replacement Gibson tailpiece.

Besides his brilliant songs and performances, Townshend's habit of destroying guitars on stage gained him notoriety. The first was a Rickenbacker banged through a ceiling and broken by accident at the Railway Hotel in England. Showing a total disregard for a quality product, Pete perfected his craft. He soon learned that the Rickenbacker necks had a certain weakness when he flung the guitars over his head at full speed against a Marshall stack.[25]

Rickenbacker
and the
New American Rock Groups

While George Harrison brought attention to the Rickenbacker twelve string, James Roger McGuinn put it on the map. The electric twelve was the foundation for the Byrds' first albums. The intros to *Mr. Tambourine Man, I'll Feel a Whole Lot Better*, and *Turn! Turn! Turn!* were quintessential electric twelve string licks and the embodiment of electric folk rock. Ironically, McGuinn bought his Rickenbacker after he went to see *A Hard Day's Night* a second time to learn what guitar George was playing.[26]

Roger McGuinn and Jeffrey Foskett.

SPANISH GUITARS Combo Series (Solid Bodies)	List Price	Shipping Weight
420—Jet Black, Natural or Fireglow Finish	$179.50	7
425—Jet Black, Natural, or Fireglow Finish, Vibrato Unit	189.50	7
450—Two Pickups, Jet Black, Natural or Fireglow Finish	224.50	7
450-12—Two Pickups, Twelve Strings, Jet Black, Natural or Fireglow Finish	294.50	7
456-12—Two pickups, Twelve Strings, String converter, Jet Black, Natural or Fireglow Finish	339.50	7
460—Deluxe with White Binding, Two Pickups, Jet Black, Natural or Fireglow Finish	284.50	7
600—Blond or Fireglow Finish	169.50	12
615—Two Pickups, Vibrato Unit—Jet Black, Natural or Fireglow Finish	334.50	7
625—Deluxe with White Binding, Two Pickups, Vibrato Unit, Rick-O-Sound Jack, Jet Black, Natural or Fireglow	394.50	7
800—Two Pickups, Turquoise Blue Finish	199.50	12
900—¾ Neck, 21-fret, Natural or Fireglow Finish	184.50	7
950—¾ Neck, 21-fret, Two Pickups, Jet Black, Natural or Fireglow Finish	199.50	7
1000—¾ Neck 18 fret, Natural or Fireglow	179.50	7
310-375 Series, Thin Body (Hollow Bodies)—Available in Fireglow or Natural Grain Finish—Deluxe models have white binding, inlaid finger boards, and Rick-O-Sound Jacks.		
310—¾ Neck, Two Pickups	329.50	8
315—¾ Neck, Two Pickups, Vibrato Unit	389.50	8
320—¾ Neck, Three Pickups	339.50	8
325—¾ Neck, Three Pickups, Vibrato Unit	405.00	8
330—Full-Size Neck, Two Pickups	339.50	9
330-12—Full-Size Neck, Two Pickups, Twelve Strings	474.50	9
335—Full-Size Neck, Two Pickups, Vibrato Unit	405.00	9
336-12—Full Size Neck, Two Pickups, Twelve Strings, String Converter	529.50	9
340—Full-Size Neck, Three Pickups	359.50	9
345—Full-Size Neck, Three Pickups, Vibrato Unit	419.50	9
360—Deluxe, Two Pickups	414.50	9
360-12—Deluxe, Two Pickups, Twelve Strings	524.50	9
365—Deluxe, Two Pickups, Vibrato Unit	479.50	9
366-12—Deluxe, Two Pickups, Twelve Strings, String converter	579.50	9
370—Deluxe, Three Pickups	429.50	9
375—Deluxe, Three Pickups, Vibrato Unit	494.50	9

From a 1966 price sheet.

1968 Catalog

Billy Hinsche with his mid 1960s Model 360/12.

Before the Byrds disbanded in the 1970s, McGuinn had an assortment of Rickenbacker guitars. The factory modified his first 1964 Model 360/12 in February 1966 adding a middle pickup, custom wiring, and a new nut. At the same time the factory modified his original guitar, McGuinn bought a new walnut finished 370 and a black Model 325. Later he owned a light show 341/12, a Bantar, and a current style twelve string.

Roger told Guitar Player Magazine in 1967 that he installed a Vox treble booster in his original guitar. A 370/12 guitar from the factory wired like McGuinn's, except for the treble boost, was a Model 370/12Byrd which was available on a special order basis.

During the British invasion many other American rock groups besides the Byrds dis-

(Continued on page 119)

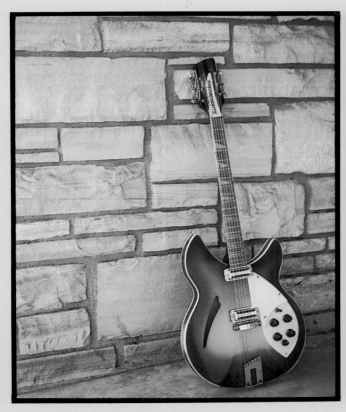

Mr. Hall photographed George Harrison's December 1963 Fireglo 360/12 before taking it to New York for his first meeting with the Beatles.

In early 1964 Rickenbacker made John Lennon the first Model 325/12.

The first Rickenbacker electric twelve string had gold backed pickguards and TV style knobs. The factory made it in mid 1963.

(L to R) Fireglo 360/12, Mapleglo 360/12, and Fireglo 450/12. When Mr. Hall took this photo in 1965, the Rickenbacker twelve string was already the industry's standard.

Mid 1960s Model 366/12 convertible.

Late 1960s Model 456/12 convertible guitar.

Custom-built 1970 Model 381/12 with three pickups, checkerboard binding front and rear. (Jeffrey Foskett collection)

Fireglo 1966 Model 330/12 (John Peden/Guitar World)

An early 1980s Model 360/12 with a Walnut finish.

Slanted frets Model 481 with chrome cover humbucking pickups.

This all girl band lit up Las Vegas in the early 1970s with an assortment of light show guitars and a rare 4005L light show bass.

This 1971 Model 331 with the original circuit and filtered lamps gave its owner "the thrill of a light show." (John Peden/ <u>Guitar</u> <u>World</u>)

The company pictured this non-vibrato Model 320 in the 1975 catalog although the guitar probably dated from the late 1960s.

Two early 1958 Model 325 guitars, one natural maple and one dark brown sunburst.

By the time Mr. Hall took this snapshot in January 1964, fans already referred to the 325 as the John Lennon Model.

One of the Kim Sisters played this 1960 Model 310.

December 1961 Model 460 (left) and prototype Model 615 (right) with split white pickguards.

An extremely rare black 1963 Model 460 with custom-ordered gold plastic parts.
(John Peden/Guitar World)

1962 Model 625.

This was a November 1961 protoype of the Model 615. Its invoice called it a Model 450 w/vibrato. Notice how the factory carved the guitar's top to accommodate the Ac'cent vibrato. (John Peden/<u>Guitar</u> <u>World</u>)

The Model 450 pictured in the 1975 catalog.

This was the wave cresting style Model 450 as produced in 1958 and 1959. Notice that it had two control knobs and two tone selector switches.

A 1960 Model 450. By 1960 these models had separate tone and volume controls for each pickup.

A mid 1957 Model 450 with chrome bar pickups and a three position selector switch.

One of the first Model 450 tulip shaped guitars came with the pre-chrome bar pickups and a rotary selector switch.

A rare pink Combo 400 from 1956. Notice there was only one switch. The Combo 800 had two switches.

A white 1956 Combo 400 guitar with vibrato.

One of the first of several custom show guitars made by Roger Rossmeisl, called the Custom Built. 1956

A Cloverfield Green Combo 400 (left) and a Montezuma Brown Combo 400 on display at a 1956 show.

1957 Model 1000.

The Model 425 was a full sized student model with one pickup.

Two 3/4 size Model 1000 guitars from 1960.

Roger Rossmeisl working on a Combo at the Electro String factory in 1957.

This was the 3/4 size Model 950 with the wave cresting style body pictured in the 1975 catalog.

Tom Petty and the Heartbreakers. Michael Campbell on right with Tom's 360/12.

Tom Petty with his reissue Model 1997 in early 1987.

Tom Petty with Michael Campbell's modified Model 615.

One of the first Model 4000 basses. 1957.

A Fireglo Model 4000 pictured in March 1960.

(L to R) Fireglo Model 4000, Mapleglo Model 4001, and a Fireglo Model 4005/6 six string bass pictured in October 1965.

This bass (left) was an extremely rare Model 4000 with Deluxe features made in 1960.

This 1957 Capri prototype had Model 330-like standard features, but on a longer body unlike the production models.

Although no one dated this picture, undoubtedly Rickenbacker made this guitar in 1957 or in early 1958. It is possibly the first Model 335.

This was the Model 365 Deluxe prototype from 1957.

Another Capri prototype from 1957, this thick body guitar was closest to the Model 381. However, most of the Model 381 guitars had carved tops.

This picture of a Fireglo Model 335--with a missing Vibrola handle--dates from January 1960.

A 1959 Model 375 with a highly figured natural maple top.

This thick body Capri Model 384 illustrated the inconsistent features found on the 1958 hollow bodies. Although it was a Deluxe model, it had Standard dot inlays. The factory rarely used the traditional F sound hole on the full sized Capris made for domestic sales.

Another one of the few long body Capris, this one had Model 345 features, but with an unusual solid top.

A 1958 Model 335 vibrato guitar with another variety of the brown sunburst.

The Electro factory delivered this Model 365 on December 14, 1959. The invoiced described the finish as "Brown," which usually meant Autumnglo. Clearly, this guitar was actually one of the early Fireglo guitars; Fireglo became a standard finish a few months later. (John Peden/Guitar World)

This Model 365 had an Autumnglo finish, and this picture appeared on a Rickenbacker promotional postcard.

A 1959 Model 360 with the flat tailpiece used before the 1963 introduction of the R tailpiece.

A 1958 Model 345 vibrato guitar with a two tone brown sunbrust.

This 1958 Model 325 in the foreground had a traditional F sound hole. Model 345 is in the background.

This was the one of a kind El Toro model solid body guitar shown at the 1958 trade shows.

Trade Show 1957.

Trade Show 1958.

1963. The first twelve string, pictured third from the left, appeared at this show.

Trade Show 1962.

Toots Thielemans in July 1958 with an early
Model 330F guitar.

Trade Show 1966. Notice the eight string bass on the left.

Jim Reeves and the Blue Boys displayed their custom-built powder
blue 1961 Rickenbacker guitars and amps in this promotional
photo. The instruments from left to right were a Model 360F, a
custom acoustic, and a Model 4000 electric bass.

The late singer Rick Nelson in 1958 with a 385.

A 1959 Model 360F
with a natural maple finish.

A 1968 Model 360F   A 1968 Model 370F

Early 1980s Model 360 W.B.

This 1975 Model 330 had twenty-one frets. Compare the position of the rhythm pickup to Model 330s with twenty-four frets.

111

Early 1980s Model 330 with a twenty-four fret finger board.

1975 Model 360 with a twenty-four fret finger board.

1975 Model 460.

Early 1980s Model 620.
Non vibrato 600 Series guitars had adjustable bridges
like the non vibrato 300 Series guitars.

113

1975 Model 4001 bass.

Paul McCartney in the 1970s with his modified and updated 1964 4001S.

Close-up of the Vintage Series Model 4001V63 in Mapleglo.

A double-bound 4005 W.B. from the early 1980s catalogs.

An early 1980s Model 4002 in Mapleglo.

Early 1980s Model 4001S.

1987 reissue Model 381.

covered Rickenbacker guitars. The Beach Boys'
Carl Wilson used at least three different Rick
Twelve strings: a 1964 double bound 330S/12, a
rounded top 1965 style 360/12, and a mid 1960s
360/12WB.

Dino, Desi, and Billy used the Rickenbacker twelve string. The Turtles' guitarist, Al
Nichol, had a Rick 360/12. The Jefferson
Airplane's rhythm guitarist Paul Kantner
played a 360/12.

Another influential group, probably one
of the biggest hit makers of the late sixties and
early seventies was Creedance Clearwater
Revival. John Fogerty, Tom Fogerty, and Stu
Cook all used Rickenbackers on their first
albums. John is best known for his three-
quarter size Model 325. However, he had a
whole assortment of Rickenbackers, including a
Jetglo Model 360 and a Fireglo Model 450/12.

One American group that was an official Rickenbacker endorser and part of a major
promotion effort in the late 1960s was
Steppenwolf. John Kay, the leader and chief
songwriter of the group, used a 381 six string
and a 370/12. In a 1969 company news release
he said that he liked the Rickenbackers because
of the neck action. One picture shows their
other guitarist with a rare 1950s Combo 800. In
addition to guitars, Steppenwolf toured with
the large Rickenbacker Transonic amplifiers.

The Transonic Amplifiers

The Rickenbacker Transonic amplifiers
were the work of electronics designer Bob
Rissi, who headed up the Electro String
amplifier division from 1967 to 1970.[27] The
company advertised two basic series: the 200
watt (peak power), Series 100, and the 350 watt
(peak power) Series 200. The optional 350
Series Rick-O-Gain unit with amplifier and
speakers attached to a 350 Series amp created
700 watts of peak power. One bass amplifier
offered either four 15 inch heavy duty speakers
or one 30 inch speaker. Another option with
the bass amp was a set of three cabinets, each
with one 30 inch speaker. The Transonics were
for serious rock players.

The guitar amps had a variety of features, including built in fuzz tone. However,
players could achieve the best sounding distortion by running the second channel into the
first channel. Although unintended, the Transonic was one of the first amps to make this ef-

Late 1960s Series 200 Transonic amp.

119

Top-Jeff Beck with a Rickenbacker Transonic amp in the late1960s.
Bottom-Led Zeppelin on a late 1960s visit to the Rickenbacker sales office.

120

Ron Wood playing a Fender bass through a Rickenbacker Transonic amp in the late 1960s.

Steppenwolf in the late 1960s. John Kay (center) had a Model 381.

Carl Wilson, second from left, with his new style Model 360/12.

fect possible without modification. While manufacturers were ready for transistor amps in the late 1960s, the guitar buying public was not.[28] John Hall says that one reason the public soured on the genre was the dramatic failure of CBS Fender's first transistor amp design.

The Transonic's relatively short life was not for lack of support by some of the late sixties biggest rock bands. Besides Steppenwolf, bands that toured with Rickenbacker amps included Led Zeppelin and the Jeff Beck Group. Beck's group included bassist Ron Wood and vocalist Rod Stewart.

The Eko Guitars

Mr. Hall traveled to Europe extensively promoting Rickenbacker and investigating the possibility of distributing imported European guitars in America. Radio-Tel and Rickenbacker distributed the Ekos on the West Coast for several years in the middle 1960s. The Eko di Oliviero Pigini & Co. made the guitars in Italy. These instruments rated high among the most off-the-wall guitars ever sold. An Eko guitar was liable to have as many as four double polarity pickups with push button automatic tone selectors. Eko used exotic materials such as Jong-Kong wood from Thailand to make their necks.

Rickenbacker in the 1970s

In the early 1970s the company solidified its prestigious position in the quickly changing music industry. All the other great American electric guitar makers had either sold their companies to major corporations or closed shop. Many of the ones still in business had expanded so fast that they lost sight of their original purpose. Rickenbacker grew rapidly, but maintained consistency--the enduring trait of a family owned business. It is no coincidence that Rickenbacker and the most prestigious American acoustic guitar maker, Martin, are both family owned businesses.

In the 1970s Rickenbacker added many new models to the guitar line as they had plenty of new ideas. There are descriptions of the light show guitars, slanted frets, and the new solid body guitars in later sections of the book. Despite these new products, it was an old Rickenbacker idea that caught fire.

If the mid 1960s was the right time for the Rickenbacker electric twelve strings, the

Eko Model 500/4 with vibrato. 1962

Eko Model 700/4 with vibrato. 1962.

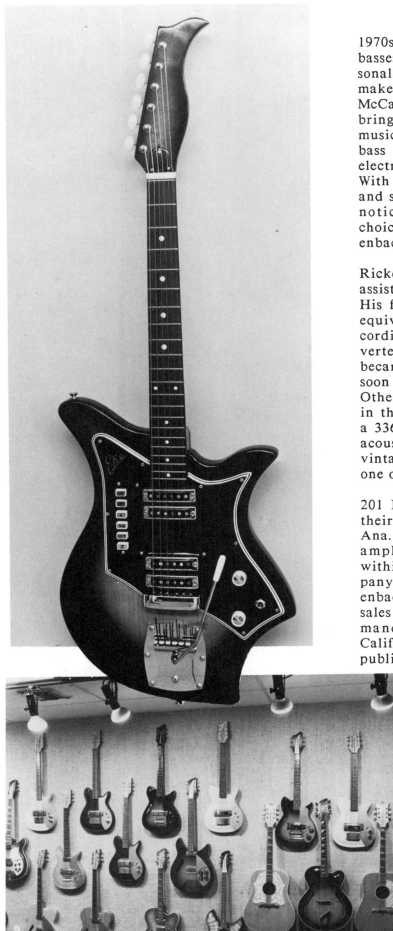

1970s was the right time for the Rickenbacker basses. It was another case where timing, personalities, and a good product came together to make an impact on our musical culture. Paul McCartney with his solo career did much to bring the Rickenbacker bass into the minds of musicians. However, a new force in the 1970s, bass virtuoso Chris Squire, was taking the electric bass into a different musical realm. With the group Yes, he explored the melodic and solo applications of the bass. Other players noticed that like McCartney, Squire's first choice for most live performances was a Rickenbacker.

Englishman Squire bought his first Rickenbacker bass when he worked as a shop assistant and salesman at a London music store. His first was a Rose, Morris Model 1999, the equivalent of the American Model 4001S. According to Guitar Player Magazine, Chris converted this bass from mono to stereo. When he became a star, and endorsed Rickenbacker, he soon added a six string bass to the Yes act. Other Rickenbacker instruments Squire bought in the 1970s included a white eight string bass, a 336/12 convertible, and a 1973 custom-made acoustic. Today he has a collection of original vintage Rick basses and according to John Hall, one of the first Model 4000 basses ever made.

In 1975 Rickenbacker Inc. moved from 201 E. Stevens, home since the mid 1960s, to their current address at 3895 S. Main St., Santa Ana. The new facility was adjacent to the amplifier factory; the guitar factory was within five minutes driving time. The company displayed many rare and collectible Rickenbackers in the museum located at the new sales office. For guitar enthusiasts, it was a mandatory stop on any visit to Southern California. (The museum is still open to the public.)

Some of the guitars displayed at Rickenbacker's Santa Ana, California museum.

124

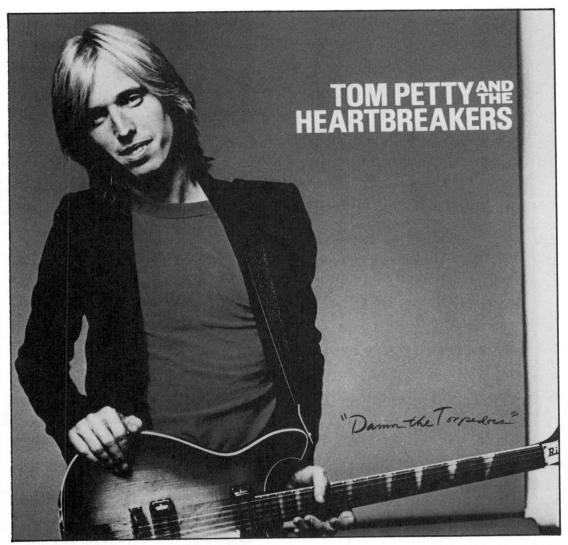

Tom Petty's 1979 album renewed interest in solid body twelve string guitars. Here Petty held Mike Campbell's 1963 Model 625/12.

Rickenbacker and the New Music of the 1980s

Nostalgia became a driving force of the late seventies new wave music movement. This trend continued into the 1980s. Although they did not consider themselves new wave artists, the sound and look of sixties groups influenced Tom Petty and the Heartbreakers. Petty almost single-handedly brought back the Rickenbacker twelve string sound with his hits. The *Damn The Torpedoes* album cover caused quite a stir among guitar collectors: People were trying to figure out what model Rick twelve string Petty had.

Tom Petty and his guitarist, Michael Campbell, have a number of original vintage Rickenbackers. Petty owns a 1960s natural 360/12, a Fireglo 365WB six string, and a black 362/12 doubleneck. The twelve string on Damn the Torpedoes is actually lead guitarist Michael Campbell's 1963 Model 625/12. Campbell also owns a modified Model 615 that Petty usually plays. According to guitar technician Alan Weidel, Tom prefers his 1960s 360/12 and his newer style doubleneck 362/12 for recording.

Not a company to rest on its laurels, in the 1980s Rickenbacker began a concentrated program of product improvement. This program included reorganization of factory assembly teams and installation of new machinery. The factory put a new emphasis on quality control. When veteran factory manager Ward Deaton retired, the company hired Forrest White to spearhead the factory effort.

Forrest was the plant manager and vice president of the Fender Electric Instrument Co. from 1954 to 1966. He is proud to say that he was Fender's only plant manager in the pre-CBS days. Forrest White was the key to the modernization of Fender manufacturing in the fifties, leading the company through its phenomenal expansion. In the 1970s White was co-founder and vice president of Music Man. His skill as an industrial engineer and his contributions to musical instrument manufacturing were well known inside the industry. (He worked for Goodyear Aircraft before he entered the music business.) Forrest worked at Rickenbacker for a short period in 1970 before starting Music Man. Then he helped to develop several prototype instruments that were never actually put into production. Some of these, including a unique bass guitar, were stolen in a burglary at the factory.

In the 1980s White helped to improve productivity, product design, and quality control at the Rickenbacker factory. He helped to revise the Rickenbacker adjustable bridge by adding springs and hex screws. White combined his experience with single truss rod necks used at Fender and Music Man with the old Rick double truss rod. With the help of Dick Burke and John Quarterman, Forrest redesigned the double rod neck into what many call the best neck in the industry.

Today, Brian Carman heads the Rickenbacker guitar factory. Besides being a long time Rickenbacker employee, Brian has credentials in the song writing world. He co-wrote the instrumental classic *Pipeline* while he was a guitarist for the Chantays surf-rock band.

Several other factory employees, like Dick Burke, are Rickenbacker veterans. Dick started with the company in the 1950s. Employees such as John Quarterman have much experience with other companies in the Southern California guitar industry. He worked with the Dopyera brothers at Dobro (O.M.I.) and Leo Fender at C.L.F. Research before coming to Rickenbacker.

Brian Carman holding his gold record for the hit Pipeline in March 1984.

Forrest White (left) and Alvino Rey (holding his early Electro Frying Pan.)

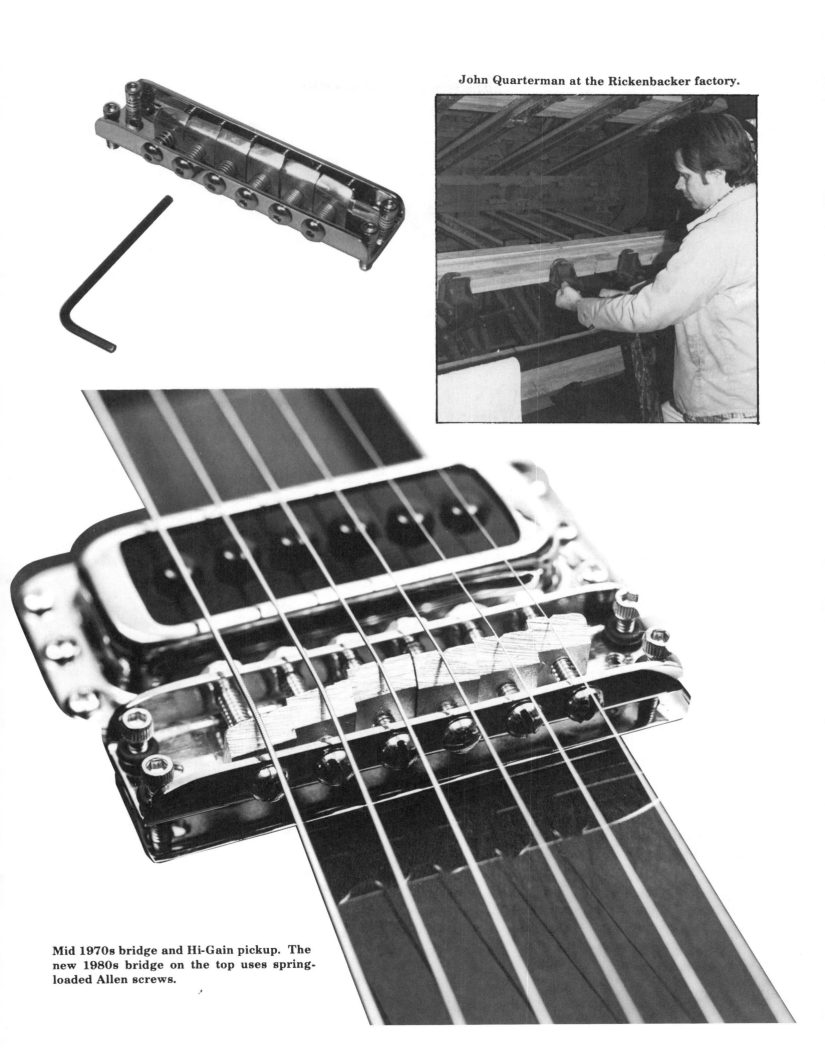

John Quarterman at the Rickenbacker factory.

Mid 1970s bridge and Hi-Gain pickup. The new 1980s bridge on the top uses spring-loaded Allen screws.

John Hall at Rickenbacker's Santa Ana museum.

The Vintage Series

There was a growing awareness at Rickenbacker of the interest in the vintage instruments. The models played by the Beatles and other rock stars of the 1960s and 1970s were in great demand. Up-to-date versions of these models have always been available, but purists demands were exacting: They wanted instruments that were cosmetically original.

Rickenbacker did not go through disabling management changes or lapses in consumer confidence like most other American guitar makers. There are no bench mark cut off points such as "Pre-CBS" for interest in post-1953 vintage Rick guitars. Most Rickenbacker collectors like certain models because of the artists associated with them. With this in mind, the company introduced the Vintage Series in 1984.

Rickenbacker International Corporation

In September 1984 F.C. Hall turned over control of the company to his son, John C. Hall, whose first move combined the manufacturing and distribution of Rickenbacker guitars and Road amplifiers into one company named Rickenbacker International Corporation (RIC). John then opened foreign offices in Japan and England for direct distribution there.

John Hall was born in 1950 and has known the guitar business his entire life. He vividly remembers visiting the sales office and the factory as a boy, playing the now vintage guitars and mandolins. And who could forget meeting the Beatles at age fourteen? Rickenbacker's previous owners were forward-looking men and so is John Hall. In 1972 he was the first to graduate from the University of California, Irvine with a degree in computer graphics.

John was an executive with Rickenbacker in the 1970s. In fact, he effectively managed many aspects of the company then as F.C. started to pursue other interests. John took one sidetrack from the guitar business with his own computer firm that was in business between 1979 and 1983. For John, returning to the guitar industry--where high technology is increasingly important, but largely untapped--was the vehicle for pursuing a wider variety of interests. These interests included designing for Rickenbacker. Undoubtedly, his hands-on skill with computers will give Rickenbacker an extra edge as this technology becomes more important to guitars and amplifiers.

John obviously believes that the future of the music business is as much in the international arena as it is in America. The 1984 opening of Rickenbacker's foreign offices in England and the founding of a sister company in Japan reflected this attitude.

The Japanese office represents the company Rick's Corporation of Japan. The headquarters is in the seaport town of Kobe headed by former Sony executive Toshio Sogabe. Toshio is a musician and an avid collector of vintage Rickenbacker guitars.

Managing Director Trevor Smith and Director Linda Garson are in charge of the British office. Trevor is a former television film director with both the BBC and the independent British networks. His film experience included work on *Brideshead Revisited*. Before taking up the promotion and distribution of guitars, Linda worked as a graphics designer.

Rickenbacker is integrating the best of its past with modern music manufacturing and marketing. The company's present and future include some diverse endeavors. The company is proud to manufacture a complete line of guitars and basses here in the United States. These instruments are among the best ever. Rickenbacker also makes the RIC Amplifiers in Santa Ana. In addition, they distribute to the world high quality power amplifiers with the RIC trademark, produced by the Sony Corporation in Japan.

No doubt, the future will write another chapter for the Rickenbacker company as it continues to change with the times.

Instruments from 1954 to the present.

Deluxe crushed-pearl inlay on a late 1960s hollow body.

General Notes on Modern Rickenbackers

Collectors want to know guitar features--when they appeared and when they changed. Although the features on Rickenbackers did not always make clear cut transitions, it is possible to point out many facts about them.

Deluxe and Standard Models

There were Deluxe and Standard versions for most of the different Rickenbacker body styles. Deluxe models had triangle shaped finger board inlays, bound necks, and bound bodies. Standard models had dot inlays and no bindings. Rickenbacker guitars usually had a rosewood finger board and a maple body. Descriptions of the different models note specific exceptions to this.

A Rick-O-Sound stereo jack was usually another Deluxe feature after mid 1960. Guitars equipped with it could use an accessory called the Rick-O-Sound kit that divided the signal from the guitar's different pickups. The kit produced a quasi-stereo effect when attached to two amplifiers. Mr. Hall explained in a 1971 letter that using Rick-O-Sound boosted the audio output while reducing hum and distortion.

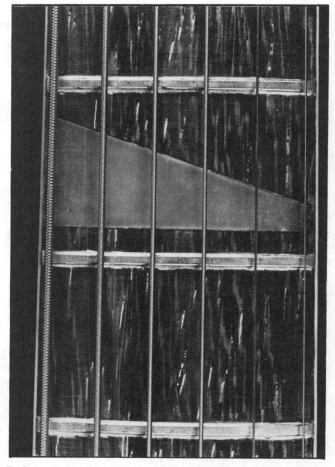

Deluxe finger board inlay on a early 1960s hollow body.

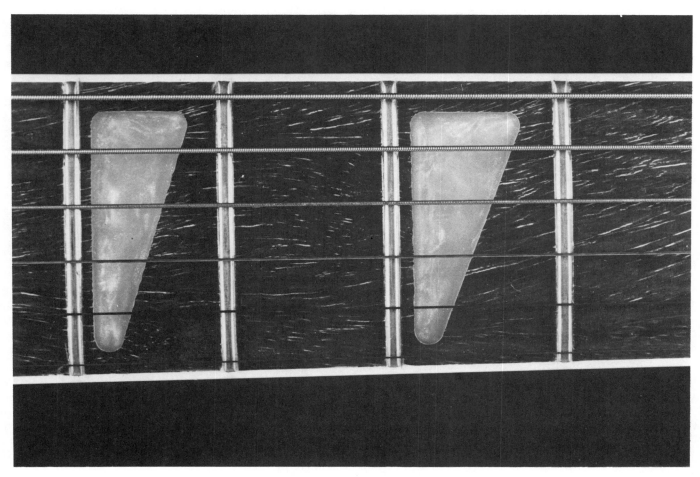

Deluxe inlay from the 1970s and 1980s.

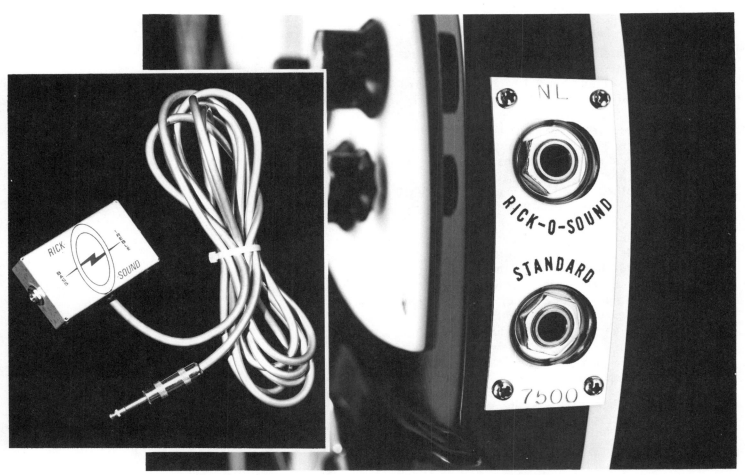

The Rick-O-Sound box could send the guitar's signal to
two amps for a stereo effect.

The Rick-O-Sound jack became a Deluxe feature in 1960.

131

The Rickenbacker Color Guide

The factory had some problems with finishes in the late 1950s. On one batch of guitars in 1959, a silicon wax used by mistake caused the finishes to check. This incident and others caused Mr. Hall to search for the perfect guitar finish. The factory developed what they called a new "no checking treatment." This Rickenbacker trade secret is among the most highly protected in the guitar industry.

Mr. Hall also wanted to find colors unique to Rickenbacker. The search paid off: since the 1950s Rickenbacker finishes have been some of the most attractive in the guitar business.

The late 1950s sunburst varied considerably. It was originally two-tone brown. In late 1958 and in 1959 the painters added increasing amounts of red to the sunburst. Eventually, they arrived at two distinct colors: Fireglo and Autumnglo. Autumnglo had both red and brown; Fireglo was a shaded red with no brown, but with a tinge of yellow. While many 1959 guitars in fact had a Fireglo finish, the factory still called them either dark or brown guitars on the invoices to the sales office; Fireglo became an official Rickenbacker finish in 1960. Factory invoices described a new "lighter shade of Fireglo" in late 1964.

Custom ordered colors were always available, but at an extra cost. Satin finishes were available too, after the early 1970s. Different models often had different standard colors, especially in the 1950s. (The descriptions of each model in later sections of the book list particular colors.) In the early 1960s black was a standard color on the solid body guitars; at the same time it was a custom ordered color on the hollow body guitars.

The colors listed as standard for all Rickenbacker guitars in 1968 were Fireglo, Mapleglo, Azureglo, Jetglo, and Burgandyglo. The Thick Body Series hollow bodies came standard in Mapleglo and Autumnglo, but the factory painted them all the other colors too. Although not listed, other colors from this period are orange, shaded blue, shaded green, walnut, and cherry red.

The January 1, 1977 price sheet listed these as custom colors: white, walnut brown, Mapleglo, and Autumnglo. Standard colors were Fireglo, Burgundy, Azureglo, and Jetglo.

The 1981 catalog listed the standard colors as Fireglo, Burgundy, Jetglo, and Azureglo. The custom glossy finishes were Ruby, Walnut, Mapleglo, and White. The custom matte finishes were Natural, Black, and Brown. This catalog pointed out a fact universally true with Rickenbackers over the years: "Instrument color may vary due to the hand finishing process."

In a move towards simplicity, later in the 1980s, Rickenbacker listed eight standardized Colorglo finishes: Midnight Blue (a radiant metallic blue), Metallic Silver, Ruby (a metallic red), White, Red, Mapleglo, Fireglo, and Jetglo. In addition, each color had corresponding hardware, pickguard, nameplate, and binding; some finishes got chrome hardware with white binding and some finishes got black hardware with black binding. Today a customer can also order these combinations reversed by specifying the Black Trim (black hardware) and White Trim (chrome hardware) options.

Rickenbacker Vibratos

Doc Kauffman patented the first hand vibrato tailpiece for stringed instruments in 1932. He called it the Vibrola and had it manufactured in Los Angeles. Doc sold the Vibrola through various jobbers as an accessory. Unlike the popular vibratos of today, Doc's worked sideways in the same direction as the movement of the player's strumming hand.

In 1936 Electro String signed a five year licensing agreement with Kauffman. They improved the Vibrola's design and manufactured it at the Electro String factory on Western Ave. After the War, Electro String no longer had the rights to make the tailpiece. Kauffman did not manufacture the Vibrola, even while working at the Fender Manufacturing Co.

Doc's patent ran out in the 1950s and all manufacturers were free to pursue Vibrola style vibratos. According to explanations given to Electro String customers in the early 1950s, Rickenbacker Mfg. (Adolph's metal shop) could not make the Vibrola. They had too many commitments to the government and there was a shortage of the necessary metals.

Rickenbacker reintroduced an improved Kauffman style Vibrola in 1957. This version had roller bridges. (The company used roller bridges on some non-vibrato instruments too.) Electro String utilized the Vibrola on all vibrato models until late 1960. The Vibrola's biggest problem was--even with the modern improvements--that players used it in ways Doc Kauffman's delicate 1920s design never imagined.

Inexplicably, Rickenbacker avoided equipping their guitars with the heavy-duty Bigsby vibrato until recently. In the early days some salesman believed it worked better than the Vibrola, urging that the factory make it standard. A factory invoice and correspondence indicates that Rickenbacker would supply Bigsby tailpieces on a special order basis, but rarely did. The most famous Rickenbacker with a Bigsby, John Lennon's first 325, originally had a Kauffman Vibrola.

Rickenbacker first installed the Ac'cent vibratos on their guitars in early 1961. The first versions said "Ac'cent" on the top cover plate. Later ones had no labels. The bridge had rollers and was adjustable for each string. Eventually, Gibson bought the company that produced Rickenbacker's Ac'cent; although Gibson continued producing the unit, the supply was undependable forcing Rickenbacker to discontinue its use by 1975.

Although it was superior to the Vibrola, the original Ac'cent design had problems. For one thing, both the flat mounting plate that bent over the end of the guitar and the handle easily broke. The roller bridges could cause rattling and loss of sustain if not precisely seated. Sixties guitarists such as Pete Townshend often removed or modified their Ac'cent units.

Rickenbacker first introduced the Boyd vibratos in late 1962. The company used them simultaneously with the Ac'cent on different models. Boyd made two different versions for solid body guitars and two different versions for hollow body guitars. Two of the Boyd tailpiece models had "pedal steel" levers for the second or third string. This was one of the first known tunable pitch changing devices for the standard guitar that imitated the pedal steel guitar. Rickenbacker also sold the Boyd Vibes as separate guitar accessories.

Rickenbacker developed a transposing vibrato in the mid 60s that kept the relative pitch of the strings in tune when the player used it. While the factory never commercially produced it, a prototype Model 335 equipped with this unit is on display in the Rickenbacker museum.

The vibrato unit used on the new guitars is an Ac'cent look-a-like called the Rickenbacker Torsion Vibrato. Its design remedies some of the original Ac'cent's problems. Most important, it is stronger than the breakable Ac'cent. It employs no rollers, coil springs, or cams in what the literature calls a "frictionless system." It is also available as an accessory.

Next Page
1. T.V. style control knobs, Kauffman vibrola, and split gold pickguards on a 1960 375F.
2. The modern Rickenbacker "Ac'cent" vibrato. Most vintage style Rickenbacker parts are available again.
3. Ac'cent vibrato on a 1967 Model 615.
4. Model 365 circa 1959 with a Kauffman Vibrola.
5. A Bigsby vibrato unit on a Vintage Series Model 325V59.

(Notice all guitars here are equipped with chrome bar pickups.)

1.

2.

3.

4.

5.

134

Rickenbacker Pickups

Rickenbacker has used several different style pickups since 1954. The horseshoe pickup, derived from Beauchamp's original design, showed up on the Combo solid body guitars and on the early basses. Various "under-string" pickup styles appeared in the mid 1950s until the factory decided on a final design. Mr. Hall once called this the True Tone pickup; today people commonly call it the chrome bar pickup. (The factory began chrome plating these pickups in October 1957. Earlier ones had no plating.) Although it looked like an old DeArmond pickup, the chrome bar was Rickenbacker from start to finish.

A new design Rickenbacker pickup, the so-called Hi-Gain pickup, appeared in 1969. This version (first developed for the Model 381) had a similar tone content, but with higher gain. The hotter design proved more suitable for the period's music. There was a transitional version that had exposed metal pole pieces which was used for about a year. The version that followed had six black dots covering the pole pieces.

Today there are four styles of Rickenbacker pickups for the standard guitars. One, available by special order, is a reissue of the original chrome bar. There is a humbucking design, the Hi-Gain 1970s model, and the Hybrid style.

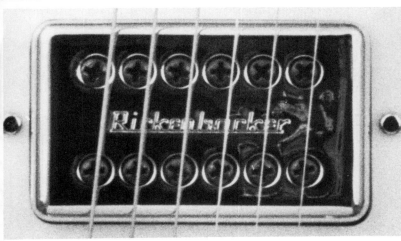

Top-The original Hi-Gain pickup on a slanted frets Model 360 circa 1970.
Left Top-Hi-Gain style pickup with the black dot type pole pieces.
Left-One old style Rickenbacker humbucking pickup from the 1970s.

Causes for Inconsistencies

Some Rickenbacker features were inconsistent, especially in the early years. As John Hall says, "It was not like an automobile company with clear cut transitions between model years." When features in one particular model changed, many times older versions were still in stock. A great example of this happened in the late summer of 1959. Radio-Tel shipped black Model 450s with newer, narrower necks. (Necks on all the bass and standard guitars became thinner in 1959.) At the same time they shipped two-tone brown ones out of inventory with older, wider necks.

The factory's production methods accounted for many variations in features. This is still true. Since handwork has always been a large component in making Rickenbackers, many slight variations in instruments occurred due to differences in workers. Body thicknesses, especially in the old days, varied considerably as a result of sanding procedures. Finish nuances, like the shading on the sunbursts, were inevitable because the workers hand sprayed all instruments.

Many features were dependent on parts manufactured outside the Rickenbacker plant. For instance, Rickenbacker used Kluson, Grover, and imported German tuning machines. Sometimes parts suppliers proved to be unreliable or the factory ordered insufficient quantities. Sometimes when a certain part was not available or there was a late delivery, they substituted another part for it. Often this was how older parts out of the inventory--like 1940s lap steel control knobs--ended up back in circulation.

Sometimes, especially before 1964, the factory used different style Rickenbacker name plates, knobs, and pickguards simultaneously for no discernible reason. The safest generalizations about these follow the development of specific models rather than any trend for all Rickenbackers. As the early 1960s unfolded, these features became more predictable. For instance, by 1962 white plexiglas pickguards became standard on the solid bodies; they became standard on the hollow bodies in late 1963.

Some pre-1970 Rickenbackers had integral bodies and necks. If the neck had problems beyond what the truss rod adjustment could fix and they could not remove the neck, there was a simple solution. The factory removed the parts on the bad guitar and installed them on a completely new body and neck. This practice explains some instruments with totally inconsistent bodies, features, and finishes. It also points out that virtually anything was possible from the Rickenbacker factory.

Another fact about some of the early Rickenbacker models is their rarity. Many were literally one of a kind, custom-made instruments. Even for some models considered regular production items, the factory made so few it never established consistent features.

Still another factor was Rickenbacker's willingness to accept orders for special features. Long time factory employee Dick Burke says that the first twenty-four fret necks on the 300 Series guitars were special orders. Soon they became standard, but there were still requests for twenty-one fret necks. In other words, the factory made the guitars both ways almost simultaneously.

John Hall says there are probably other examples of overlapping production of different features. No one knows for sure when the factory changed the bass horseshoe pickup to an understring pickup or if they did it all at once. Likewise, neck construction--solid maple or maple with walnut lamination--did not make a clear cut transition from one style to another.

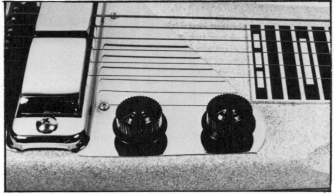

Top-Black plastic knobs and an anodized pickguard on a 1957 combo 450.
Bottom-Flying saucer knobs on a 1950s lap steel.

Odd, But Original

The neck on a few 1960s Rickenbackers had a highly unusual shape. This unmistakable feature was the patented Sceusa neck, invented by Peter P. Sceusa. On conventional oval or V-shape necks, cross sections of the neck were symmetrical. The Sceusa neck's profile was asymmetrical. The thickest section of the neck was behind the bass strings. The back of the neck tapered from the bass side to the treble side. Thus the neck was thinnest behind the first string.

The idea was to fit the neck to the arch between the thumb and forefinger on the player's left hand. It worked well when the player grasped the neck with his thumb over the finger board. Its advantages stopped when playing barre chords with the thumb behind the neck. The Sceusa neck was a special order item.

The factory first produced slanted frets in late 1969. They were a standard feature on some instruments and an option on others. On these instruments the nut, bridge, and frets were all set at an angle to the edge of the finger board. As with the Sceusa neck, the intent was to match the neck better to the player's hand. The original brochure said: "This slight slant of the frets across the finger board eliminates the long chord reaches, reduces stretch length, and matches precisely the natural angle of the fretting fingers."

A slanted frets Model 360 from 1970.

The sections that follow detail the solid body Rickenbacker standard guitars and the hollow body Rickenbacker standard guitars. There are additional sections for the Rickenbacker basses, twelve strings, doublenecks, custom guitars, and exports.

Solid Body Standard Guitars

Electro String was the first to design, produce, and sell anything like a solid body guitar. It is ironic that they got left in the dust as the idea started to take hold in the early 1950s. Nevertheless, the last several years Adolph Rickenbacker owned the company he added few new products to the line; there was no replacement for the Bakelite Spanish guitar after the War. Meanwhile, Fender and the Eastern establishment companies introduced their own solid body standard guitars. Of course, Mr. Hall had experience selling the Fender Spanish guitars and knew Rickenbacker needed comparable instruments.

The new solid body guitars showed Rickenbacker's energy and enthusiasm. They integrated exciting visual designs with the requirements of practical musical instruments. And the designs were original, not copies of Gibson, Gretsch or Fender. The first Combos were just a taste of the new direction the company headed, trailblazing philosophies of guitar technology and construction.

Rick solid bodies combined several significant innovations. The extreme cutaway, first used on the Combo solid bodies, combined a flare for style with a concern for utility. Neck-through-body construction, used on most models between 1957 and 1970, was the ultimate manifestation of the solid guitar. With these Rickenbackers, there were no bolts or glue joints on the plane between the end pin and peghead. The design enhanced the instrument's tone and sustain.

In the 1950s there were five body shapes for the production model solid bodies. The first was the shape of the Combo 600 and 800. The second was the so-called tulip shape (butterfly shape). The third had a slight variation of the tulip shape. The fourth had the extreme cutaway with pointed horns. The fifth had the extreme cutaway with the cresting wave shaped top horn.

In the mid 1960s solid body guitars took a back seat in sales to hollow bodies. At Rickenbacker this was true because of the overwhelming popularity of the Thin Hollow Body Series. In fact, the 1960s industry-wide trend towards hollow body guitars can be attributed in part to the success of Rickenbacker.

Solid body guitars regained their lost stature in the early seventies. Rickenbacker responded by introducing a variety of new body styles, pickups, and options. By the mid 1970s, Rickenbacker produced new solid body models with both detachable necks and glued-in necks. The company styled the new Models 480-483 after Rick's highly popular solid body basses. The company used humbucking pickups and modular electronics with varying degrees of success. Still, some of the stalwart models from the late fifties retained their appeal, thus proving the inherent soundness of their designs.

For Rickenbacker, the pendulum-like cycle of solid bodies versus hollow bodies returned to favor hollow bodies in the 1980s. There are only two groups of solid bodies on the current lists: the Hamburg/El Dorado group and the 610/620 group.

Mid 1950s Combo 800 headstock with a black backed lucite logo plate.

Combo 600 (Single pickup) and Combo 800 (Double pickup)--Rickenbacker introduced these two models in 1954 and officially dropped them in 1969. They were advertised as solid body guitars. However, on the early versions the factory cut out from the back sizeable portions of their double cutaway bodies. This reduced their overall weight.

Before late 1957, the Combo 800's pickup was the "Rickenbacker Multiple Unit." It was a horseshoe pickup with two coils: one wired to accentuate treble and one wired to accentuate bass. This pickup was humbucking when the player activated both coils. After late 1957, the second pickup on the 800 was a chrome bar type. The 800 guitar had a coil selector switch and a preset tone selector switch. The 600 had a single coil horseshoe pickup and the tone selector switch.

In 1954 the standard finish on these Combos was blonde. The volume and tone controls had chrome knobs. Two examples in the Rickenbacker museum have hollowed out bodies with sheet metal back plates. The necks on two of these museum guitars are the bolted-on variety.

The factory redesigned the headstocks before the end of 1954; the company pictured the new design in the 1955 catalog. The logo plates were black backed lucite. Also, black plastic knobs soon replaced the chrome ones for the volume and tone controls.

The dark finished Combo 800 pictured in the 1956 catalog appears to have had a contrasting gold backed lucite logo plate on the headstock and chrome knobs. It also had a larger pickguard made of gold backed lucite that extended back past the controls. The color of the lucite parts, either gold or black, possibly varied according to the body's finish.

By 1957 the standard finishes were blonde and Turquoise Blue. The double adjustable truss rod system appeared on some Rickenbackers in 1957. A museum example of the Model 600 has a solid body with a bolt-on neck. Another museum Model 600 with an undetermined date of manufacture has a solid body with a glued-in neck.

In 1957 factory manager Ward Deaton talked with Mr. Hall about making the Combo bodies thinner and more adaptable to the Vibrola, a project Roger Rossmeisl began. In fact, the factory made only a few solid bodies with vibrato tailpieces in the fifties.

1954 Combo 800. The two switches allowed nine tone settings.

Lou Walker with a rare Vibrola equipped Combo 800 circa 1957.

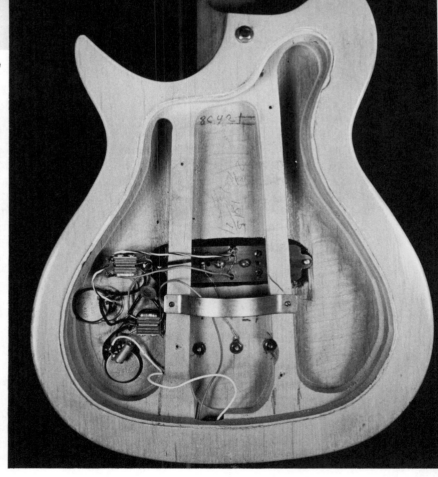

The back side of a 1954 Combo 800 with the metal cover plate removed. Notice the serial number written in pencil and the wire leads coming off the double coil horseshoe pickup.

This Combo 800 from 1955 or early 1956 had a small pickguard and flying saucer knobs.

Combo 800 from late 1957 or 1958. Earlier versions had just a double coil horseshoe pickup. Compare the pickguard on this guitar with pickguards from 1954 through 1956.

The 1957 Combo 400 had a new pickguard shape.

The first Rickenbacker with neck-through-body construction was the 1956 Combo 400.

Combo 400--Rickenbacker introduced the Combo 400 in 1956 and dropped it in 1958. The Model 425 replaced it. This was the first of the tulip shaped guitars and the first Rickenbacker with neck-through-body construction. The single pickup was in the neck position, recessed into the body. Standard colors for the Combo 400 were Cloverfield Green (blue-green), Montezuma Brown (golden), and Jet Black. The first press release for the Combo 400 said it had a an aluminum pickguard with "gold color impregnated into the metal so that it will be difficult to scratch." In other words, it was gold anodized.

142

Combo 450 pictured in the 1957 catalog.

Combo 450--The first Combo 450, introduced in 1957, was a two pickup version of the Combo 400. It was available in the same colors as the 400. The company maintained several variations of the 450 over the years before it was deleted from the guitar line in 1984.

The 1957 Combo 450 had the tulip body with neck-through-body construction. Two long bolts and glue connected the outside sections of the body to the center neck/body section. The controls included a rotary selector switch with a plastic pointer knob and black plastic knobs for the volume and tone. Mr. Hall revised the original wiring of the two pickup solid bodies in late 1957. The new control setup allowed the player to switch from rhythm to lead, and vice versa, with a minimum change in volume. Early 1957 photos show the 450 with the pre-chrome bar pickups used on the 1956 Combo 400.

All guitar manufacturers made an effort in the 1950s to produce a neck that was warp resistant and still highly playable. Rickenbacker's solution for more strength was a double truss rod system. In 1957, to make the necks more playable they rounded one edge of the fret board on some guitars. The Combo 450 was the first Rickenbacker to have rounded fret board edges.

1958 was a transition year for the Rick solid body guitars. In the early part of the year the 450 still had the tulip shape body, but with redesigned pickups. It had a gold colored logo plate on the headstock and a metal pickguard. There were two black plastic control knobs and a metal style selector switch on the lower horn of the body.

Electro String delivered a two color sunburst 450 with the new cresting wave cutaway body on March 28, 1958. It appeared at the summer trade shows. The metal pickguard was a new shape to conform with the new body. The Model 450 came out with the strings close to the body. As a result, vibrato units used by Rickenbacker did not fit well. (In a few cases the factory modified either the guitar body or the vibrato unit to install vibrato on the 450.)

There were two black plastic control knobs and two selector switches on an example photographed by Mr. Hall in April 1959. This guitar had a gold backed lucite logo plate.

By 1960 the Model 450 had separate volume and tone controls for each pickup and a single selector switch below the treble pickup. Fireglo, black, and natural maple were the standard colors. The guitars had embossed metal logo plates and metal pickguards.

A press release to The Music Trades magazine stated that the Model 450 had a new look in 1961. The width of the guitar was now "super-slim." This made it lighter, easier to play, and easier to handle. The first factory invoice to indicate a new 450 body thickness was on May 11, 1961.

Model 450 guitars photographed in 1962 had white plastic pickguards and gold backed plastic logo plates. By 1963 the plastic hardware was consistently white. The Boyd vibrato was adaptable to the 450 and sometimes installed on the guitar starting in late 1962. Model 450 guitars had the new Hi-Gain pickups sometime shortly after 1969, but had no other significant changes in features from 1962 through 1984.

Model 450 circa 1967.

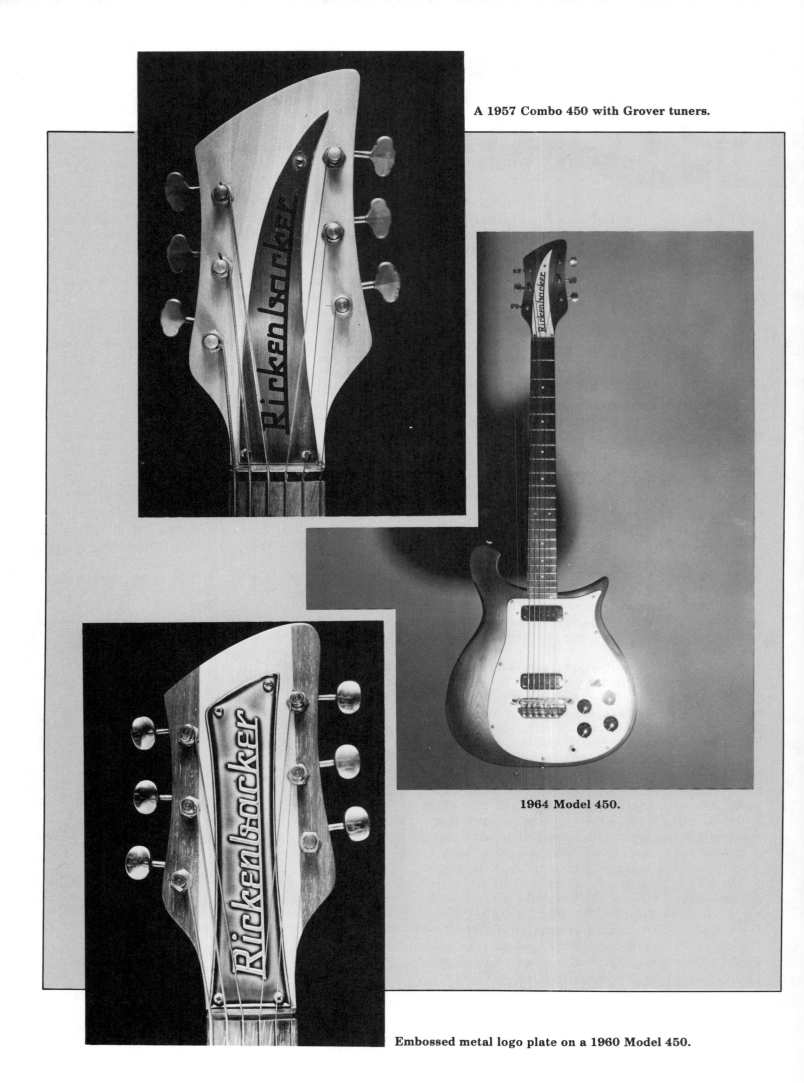

A 1957 Combo 450 with Grover tuners.

1964 Model 450.

Embossed metal logo plate on a 1960 Model 450.

144

Models 900, 950, and 1000--These short scale student guitars came out in 1957. The 900 had a single pickup and a twenty-one fret neck. The 950 was the same as the 900, but with two pickups. The 1000 had one pickup and an eighteen fret neck. These guitars had neck-through-body construction. (The original factory designation was C150-18 fret, C150-21 fret, and C150-21 frets-2-pickups.)

One prototype had what the factory called a standard body--presumably shaped like the Combo 600. The production models were three-quarter size tulip shaped guitars. They amended the shape slightly in the last part of the year to include a "new cutaway feature." The new shape had less than perfect symmetry which allowed easier access to the upper frets. Original colors included brown, black, gray, and natural. At least one prototype was light blue. In the 1960s, the added Fireglo finish became popular.

After 1968 and before 1975, the body shape on the 900 and 950 changed from the tulip style to the cresting wave style.

The 1000 disappeared from the price sheets in 1962 and reemerged in 1966. In fact, the factory still produced them. Rickenbacker dropped the 1000 in 1971 while they dropped the Model 900 and Model 950 in 1980.

The Model 1000 was the eighteen fret student model. This was a late 1950s version with the modified lower cutaway played by seven year old Tommy Mustain.

The S-1000 set in 1957: a Combo 1000 student guitar with amp.

1957 Catalog picture of the Combo 950.   1957 Combo 900.

Combo 650 (Single pickup) and Combo 850
(Double pickup)--Mr. Hall ran several ads in
1957 music magazines introducing these new
Combos. They dropped the 650 in 1961 and the
850 in 1966. The two guitars were identical except for the number of pickups and their
electronics.

The Combo 650 and 850 were the first
Rickenbackers to feature the "extreme cutaway"
body style. The factory glued the neck into the
body on the Rickenbacker museum
850, probably the standard construction on
production models; yet, some photos show neck-
through-body 850s too. The cutaway reached to
the twenty-first fret on both sides of the neck.
The body horns of these Combos were pointed
like on the first Thin Hollow Body Capris--the
design of Roger Rossmeisl. The standard colors
were natural maple and Turquoise Blue. Like
some other Rick solid body guitars, sometimes
these models had saxophone strap attachments.

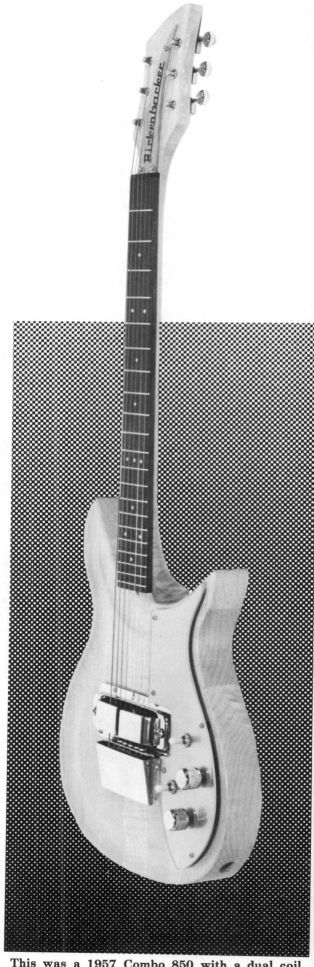

This was a 1957 Combo 850 with a dual coil
horseshoe pickup.

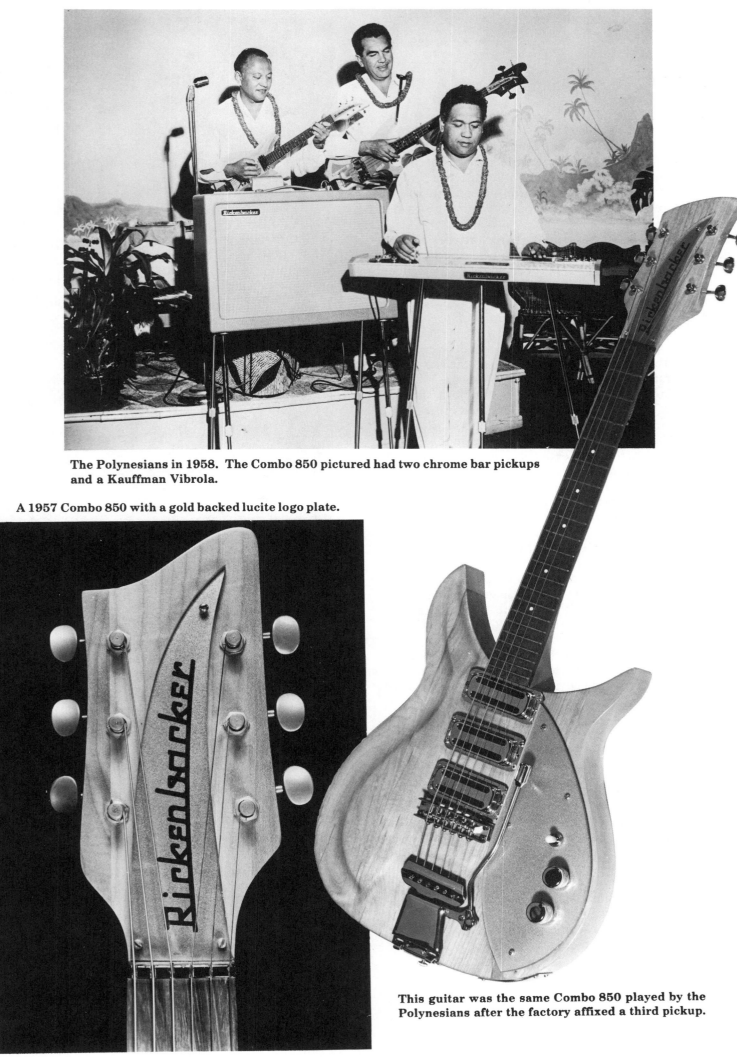

The Polynesians in 1958. The Combo 850 pictured had two chrome bar pickups and a Kauffman Vibrola.

A 1957 Combo 850 with a gold backed lucite logo plate.

This guitar was the same Combo 850 played by the Polynesians after the factory affixed a third pickup.

147

Both of these solid body guitars had the horse-shoe pickup. Some of the very first Combo 850 guitars had double coil horseshoe pickups. As on the Combo 800, the double coil counted for two whole pickups in 1957. Before the end of the year, the 850's additional pickup was a separate chrome bar unit positioned close to the finger board.

Other standard features advertised in 1957 included the Rickenbacker double truss rod and a rosewood fingerboard. The finger board helped to reinforce what the company called a thin neck. Mr. Hall told the Miller Bros. Band in a letter that the factory rounded the frets on one side to ease playing.

One of the rarest and most interesting Rickenbacker solid body guitars was a special sunburst Model 850 made in November 1958. The factory invoice said it had an inlaid, bound fret board and complete body binding. Photographs of the Rickenbacker exhibit at the 1959 N.A.M.M. (National Association of Music Merchants) show revealed one of the company's most appealing prototype instruments. It had a natural walnut 850 style body, a laminated neck, and a flat Capri style tailpiece. This beauty had two chrome bar pickups, with one in the place of the horseshoe.

There was another 850 without the familiar horseshoe unit that the company photographed several times in 1958. It had a maple body. In one photo, a guitarist for the Polynesians played it; here the guitar had two pickups and a Kauffman Vibrola. Other photographs shows the same guitar, but with three pickups. A close examination indicates that the company set the middle pickup in position for the photo without securing it with all the necessary mounting screws.

The factory made no 650-850 guitars after 1960, although the 850 remained on the price sheets until 1966.

Model 420 and Model 425--The Model 425 from 1958 through 1964 was a one pickup version of the Model 450 introduced in late 1958. It had a cresting wave cutaway body. Rickenbacker slimmed the 425 and the 450 down at the same time in 1961.

Unlike the 450, the Model 425, usually had a white plastic pickguard. (Early 450s usually had metal pickguards.) It had two control knobs and a tone selector switch. The pickup was in the treble position.

In 1965 the Model 425 came with a Boyd vibrato tailpiece. At the same time, the non-vibrato guitar became known as the Model 420. The Model 425 with vibrato disappeared from the line in 1973. The company dropped the non-vibrato Model 420 in 1984.

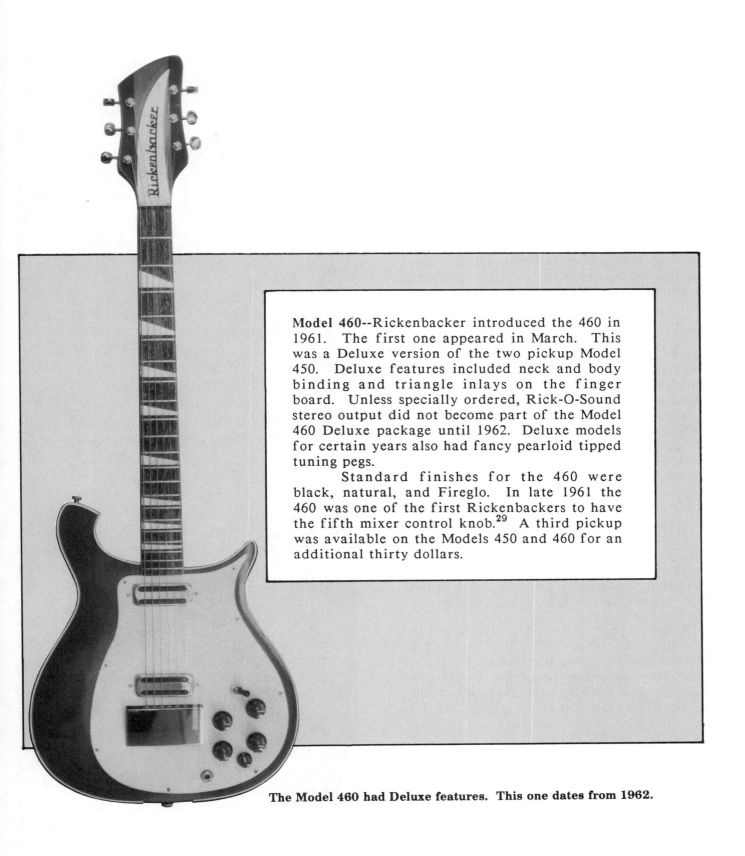

Model 460--Rickenbacker introduced the 460 in 1961. The first one appeared in March. This was a Deluxe version of the two pickup Model 450. Deluxe features included neck and body binding and triangle inlays on the finger board. Unless specially ordered, Rick-O-Sound stereo output did not become part of the Model 460 Deluxe package until 1962. Deluxe models for certain years also had fancy pearloid tipped tuning pegs.

Standard finishes for the 460 were black, natural, and Fireglo. In late 1961 the 460 was one of the first Rickenbackers to have the fifth mixer control knob.[29] A third pickup was available on the Models 450 and 460 for an additional thirty dollars.

The Model 460 had Deluxe features. This one dates from 1962.

Model 615 and Model 625--The company introduced these models in early 1962 after testing successful prototypes in 1961. They were Standard and Deluxe versions of the same double pickup solid body guitar. Both models had the familiar cresting wave shaped body; the 625 had Deluxe features and the 615 had Standard features.

The Models 615 and 625 differed only slightly from the non-vibrato 450/460 models. In fact, the 1961 invoice for the prototype 615 simply called it a "450 w/Ac'cent." However, the bodies of the Models 450 and 460 did not easily accommodate the Ac'cent vibrato tailpieces; on the prototype 615 they carved the instrument's top to seat the Ac'cent properly. The factory designed the 615/625s with the strings higher off the body, thus allowing the craftsman to mount the vibrato on a flat top.

Some of the earliest examples of the 600 series photographed had gold backed logo plates on the headstocks and four control knobs. Most of the production models had double adjustable pickguards, and most had the master mixer control knob. By 1962 the factory used white logo plates on the 615/625 guitars to match their white pickguards.

The original standard finishes were Fireglo, natural maple, and Black Diamond. A third pickup was available on these guitars for an additional thirty dollars or as a substitution for the vibrato unit. One three pickup 625 went to Canada in 1964.

Rickenbacker deleted the 615 and 625 from the price sheets in 1977. The Model 620, a non-vibrato version of the 625 Deluxe, replaced them. 1985 price sheets listed the Model 610 and 610VB. The 610VB is the modern version of the old 615. The 610 is the same with no vibrato. The 620VB listed in 1985 is a modern version of the old 625.

The Model 625 had Deluxe features, split pickguards, and vibrato. This 1962 example was one of the first production models

1980 Model 620.

1967 Model 615.

1980s Model 610 V.B. In the old numbering system this guitar was a Model 615.

151

Model 430--Introduced in 1971, the 430 was dropped by the company in 1982. Rickenbacker advertised at least three different versions. Without a doubt, the guitars pictured in the first brochures were prototypes the company never produced. The earliest, one of Forrest White's projects, had a Fender style headstock with six tuners on one side. This one and the second one shown had single tone and volume controls.

The 430 guitar produced varied considerably from the earlier experiments. Although it had a similar body shape with a twenty-four fret detachable maple neck, almost everything else was different. There were two pickups, each with its own volume and tone control. The mahogany body had a natural finish and the finger board had dot inlays.

The Model 430 as it appeared in an early 1970s brochure. The factory never produced this version.

A 1975 production Model 430.

Model 470--This was a Deluxe rendition of the Model 430. It had body and neck binding. The finger board had dot inlays, and the brochure described the pickups as "hot wound." The guitar pictured had single tone and volume controls, but the ad copy described dual volume-tone controls. Rickenbacker listed the Model 470 on the 1971 price sheets only. Like the prototype 430 guitars, the factory never produced the 470 for sale.

The factory patterned the Model 480 after the Model 4000 bass with Standard features.

This prototype Model 470 was a one of a kind Deluxe version of the 430 never commercially produced.

Model 480--Introduced in 1973, this guitar lasted until the end of 1984. It used the body styling of the Rickenbacker 4000 electric bass, with two pickups and a detachable neck. The neck had dot inlays, a flat finger board, and binding. There were separate tone and volume controls for each pickup.

153

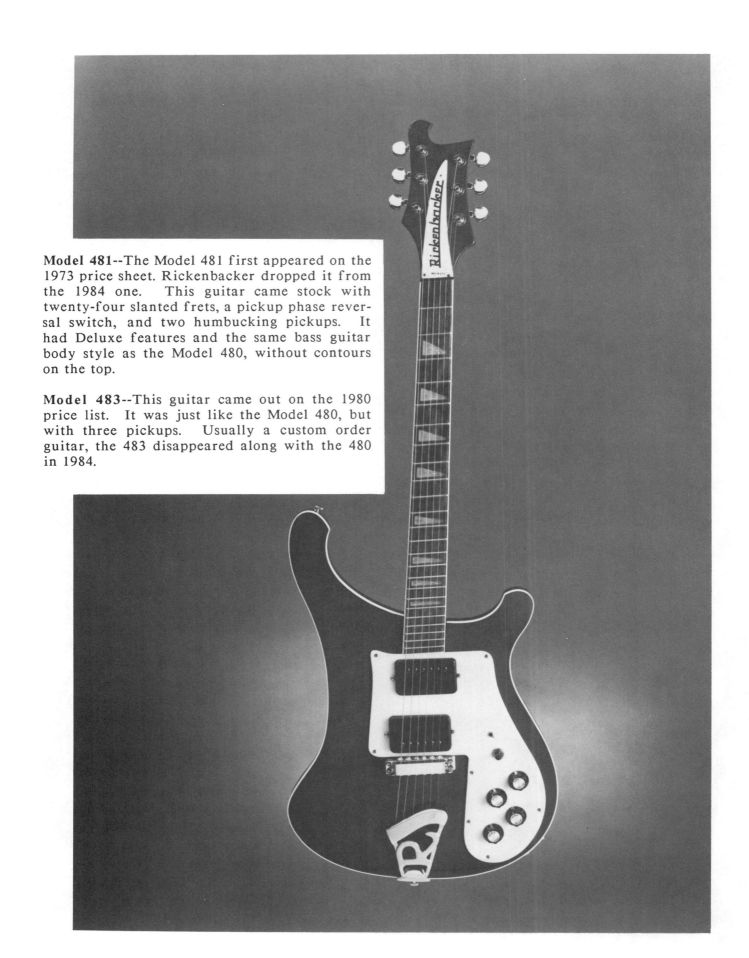

Model 481--The Model 481 first appeared on the 1973 price sheet. Rickenbacker dropped it from the 1984 one. This guitar came stock with twenty-four slanted frets, a pickup phase reversal switch, and two humbucking pickups. It had Deluxe features and the same bass guitar body style as the Model 480, without contours on the top.

Model 483--This guitar came out on the 1980 price list. It was just like the Model 480, but with three pickups. Usually a custom order guitar, the 483 disappeared along with the 480 in 1984.

The Model 481 had slanted frets and Deluxe features.

Rickenbacker

The Smithereens

Carla Olson of the Textones with her Model 620 special made in 1980. It has a blue body with checkerboard binding.

155

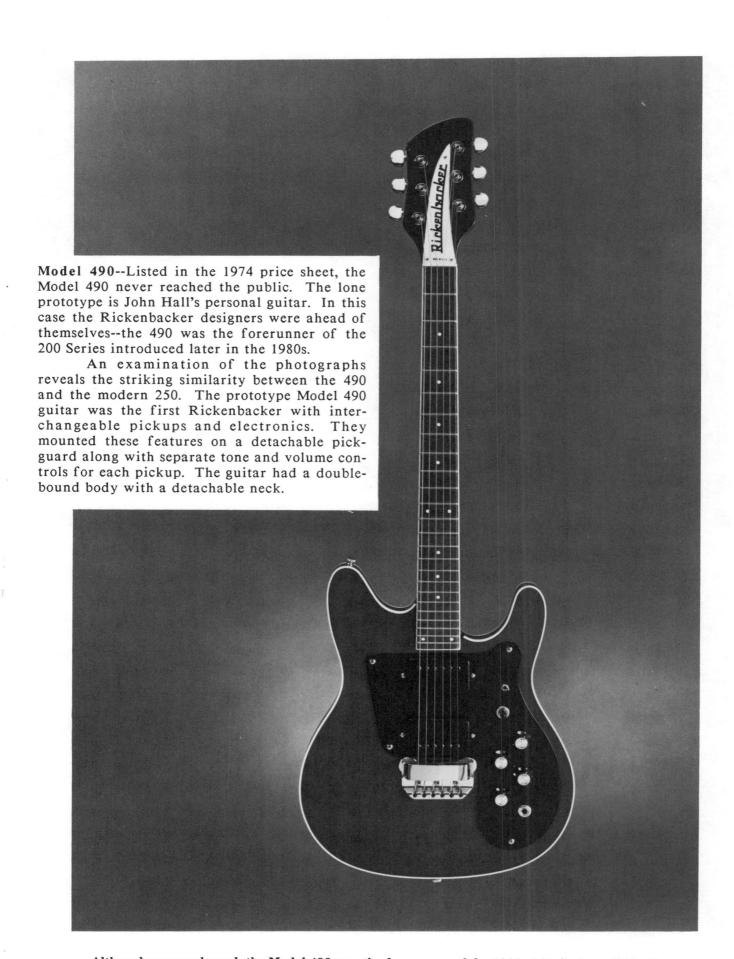

Model 490--Listed in the 1974 price sheet, the Model 490 never reached the public. The lone prototype is John Hall's personal guitar. In this case the Rickenbacker designers were ahead of themselves--the 490 was the forerunner of the 200 Series introduced later in the 1980s.

An examination of the photographs reveals the striking similarity between the 490 and the modern 250. The prototype Model 490 guitar was the first Rickenbacker with interchangeable pickups and electronics. They mounted these features on a detachable pickguard along with separate tone and volume controls for each pickup. The guitar had a double-bound body with a detachable neck.

Although never released, the Model 490 was the forerunner of the 1980s 200 Series soild bodies.

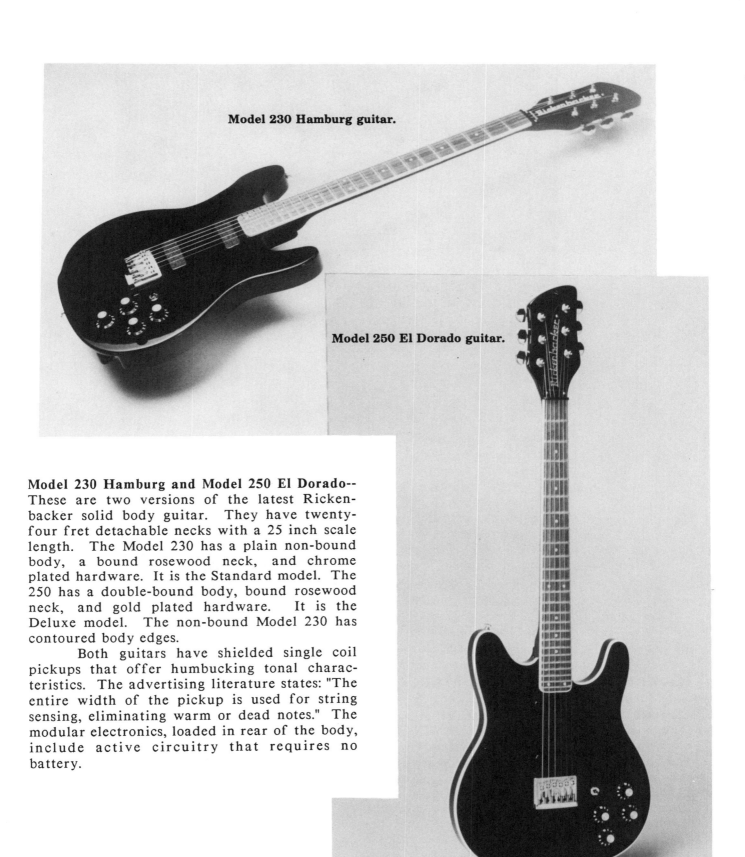

Model 230 Hamburg guitar.

Model 250 El Dorado guitar.

Model 230 Hamburg and Model 250 El Dorado-- These are two versions of the latest Rickenbacker solid body guitar. They have twenty-four fret detachable necks with a 25 inch scale length. The Model 230 has a plain non-bound body, a bound rosewood neck, and chrome plated hardware. It is the Standard model. The 250 has a double-bound body, bound rosewood neck, and gold plated hardware. It is the Deluxe model. The non-bound Model 230 has contoured body edges.

Both guitars have shielded single coil pickups that offer humbucking tonal characteristics. The advertising literature states: "The entire width of the pickup is used for string sensing, eliminating warm or dead notes." The modular electronics, loaded in rear of the body, include active circuitry that requires no battery.

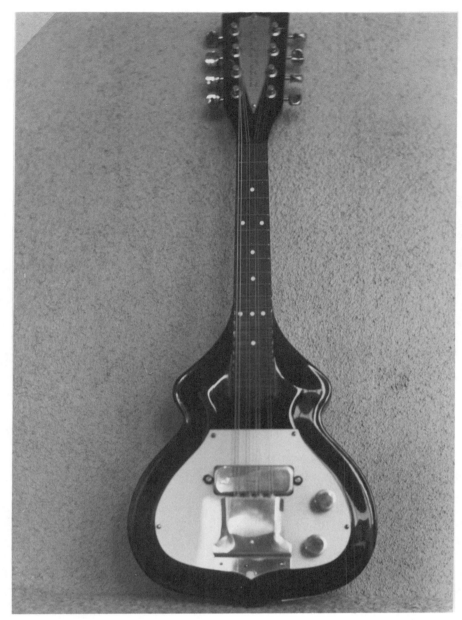

The 1957 Rickenbacker prototype electric mandolin.

Rickenbacker Electric Mandolins

Electric Mandolin--Rickenbacker created a sample solid body electric mandolin in 1957. Since there were no mandolin invoices for 1957 and there were no listings in the price sheets, this instrument was probably one of a kind. In 1958 they introduced a redesigned production model available in three different finishes: Natural Light, Natural Walnut, and Combination Light and Dark. Fireglo was available after 1959. Although the factory still made one for the Byrds in late 1965, the electric mandolins last appeared on 1961 price sheets.

There were factory invoices for nine individual Rickenbacker electric mandolins from 1958 through 1965. There were three models:

Model 5000 (four string).
Model 5001 (five strings).
Model 5002 (eight strings).

Mando Guitar--The Electro String factory made at least one Mando Guitar in early 1971 with a Fireglo finish and vibrato. Unfortunately no further information is available. The Mando Guitar probably had a body and a scale comparable to a mandolin. If it was like other manufacturers' Mando Guitars, the Rickenbacker had twelve strings tuned like a twelve string guitar, but one octave higher.

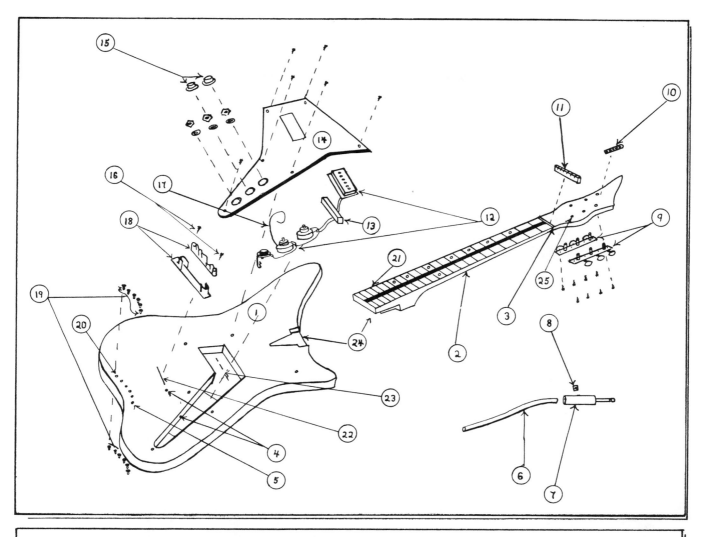

EXPLANATION OF NUMBERS ON PARTS DRAWING
Astro Guitar Kit, Model AS-51

1 – Body

2 – Neck

3 – First fret acting as nut

4 – Hole extending out to top of body for ground wire

5 – Hole – location where smallest string is threaded through body of guitar

6 – Cord

7 – Guitar plug

8 – Set screw for guitar plug

9 – Machine heads

10 – Name plate

11 – String spacer

12 – Controls (volume and tone), jack, and pickup wired

13 – Rubber pad

14 – Pickguard

15 – Knobs

16 – Set screws for bridge

17 – Ground wire

18 – Bridge

19 – String bushings

20 – Holes – locations for string bushings

21 – Fret – location for checking string height

22 – Mounting position for bridge

23 – Location for rubber pad

24 – Neck and body joint

25 – Hole – location of machine head for first string on head of guitar

The Astro Kit guitar from the mid 1960s.

Astro Kit--The Astro was a solid body kit guitar produced in the mid 1960s. It came unfinished. One sample shown at the trade shows was red and another was white.

Electro ES-16.

Electro ES-17 from 1969.

The Electro Guitars

The Electro line was a separate line of guitars produced by the Electro String Instrument Corporation and sold by Radio-Tel. They were not Rickenbacker guitars; they were separate items sold to studios and dealers not carrying the full line of Rickenbacker guitars. Radio and Television also sold some Model 425 guitars with the Ryder label and the Contello label.

There were two Electro solid body models: the three-quarter size ES-16 and the full scale ES-17. The ES-17 was similar to the 1960s Rickenbacker Model 425, and the ES-16 was similar to the Rickenbacker Model 1000. However, in contrast to the Rickenbacker models, the Electro guitars usually had glued-in necks rather than the neck-through-body construction.

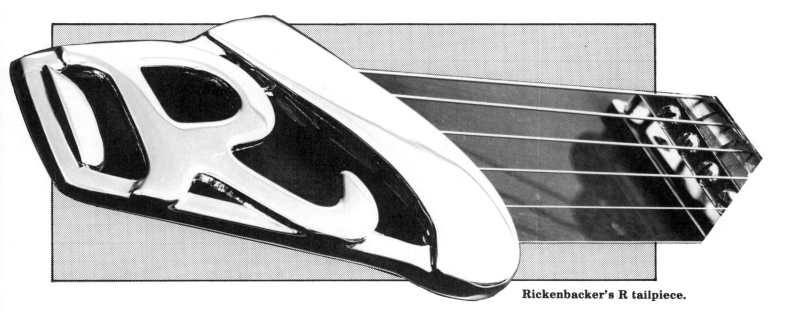

Rickenbacker's R tailpiece.

Hollow Body Standard Guitars-- The 300 Series

The first hollow body Rickenbacker guitars introduced after Mr. Hall acquired the company were called the Capris. At first the name referred to the three-quarter size hollow bodies. The Super Capri name--that never got past the sales office--referred to the full sized ones. On the 1958 and 1959 price sheets, the Capri name referred to the entire line of hollow body guitars. (John Hall remembers that his family named their cat Capri too.) A popular misconception is that Rick made one Capri style or model. The choice of the unfamiliar word to describe such a large category of instruments probably led to this confusion.

The name Capri did not catch on; so, the company dropped it from the price sheets in 1960. After this time, Rickenbacker usually called the hollow body guitars the 300 Series. Their development began in 1957 with their introduction to the public in 1958.

There were three different Capri model series: the Thin Body Series, the Thin Full-Body Series, and the Thick Body Series. By 1959 there were six different body styles and thirty-five different models within these three series. Some of these models existed only on price sheets as the factory never produced them. Certainly, many of the other 1958-59 Capris produced were virtually one of a kind.

The first numbering system for the different Capri models was inconsistent. Consequently, there is no easy, systematic way to explain it. The only hard and fast rule is that all the hollow body guitars had a number between *300* and *395*--hence, the title 300 Series. Usually, vibrato models had a 5 as the last digit. However, there were several exceptions, including vibrato Model 394 and non-vibrato Model 385. The best way to become fluent with the scheme was to memorize it.

The Rickenbacker company bases today's numbering system on the original scheme. However, now it relies on suffixes to designate vibrato and other options. For example, a 360VB has vibrato and a 360VP has vintage style pickups.

The Rickenbacker hollow bodies changed gradually. Sometimes, the changes were slightly different for each group. For example, the Model 360 had an R tailpiece before the Model 330. The company slimmed the body width on most of the electric hollow bodies in the 1961-62 period. A frontal view of the slimmer bodies on the full sized guitars reveals slightly wider horns with a different body waist position.

Some models in the original Capri line, especially ones out of the Thin Body Series, became well known Rickenbackers. Other models were evolutionary dead ends. All Rickenbacker hollow bodies from the sixties and seventies had roots in the 1950s Capri line. They were either updated versions of original models or second generation descendants of original models.

Current Rick hollow bodies continue the tradition of the original Capri guitars forward into the eighties. The 300 Series professional guitars represent the new generation of Rick hollow bodies with up-to-date improvements. The Vintage Series represents modern versions of the classic models, nearly the same as the original editions.

The Thin Hollow Body Guitars
Models 310-375

There were three divisions in the Thin Hollow Body category, but just two different body styles. The first division, Models 310-325, had extreme cutaway three-quarter size bodies. The second and third divisions, Models 330-345 and Models 360-375, had extreme cutaway full sized bodies. Originally, all guitars in this group had bodies roughly two inches thick. The necks had twenty-one fret finger boards.

Models 310-325--This set consisted of three-quarter size guitars with standard features:

    Model 310 (two pickups, no vibrato).
    Model 315 (two pickups, vibrato).
    Model 320 (three pickups, no vibrato).
    Model 325 (three pickups, vibrato).

On January 2, 1958 the factory delivered the first Model 325 to Radio-Tel. The 325 was the first Capri advertised to the public; the company pictured one with a brief description in The Music Trades April 1958 issue.

Mr. Hall intended the 325 to be a hollow body guitar with all the qualities of a solid body, obviously feeling a short twenty-one inch scale and a light body would make the model widely accepted. (The bodies measured 16x13x2 inches. The fully assembled guitars weighed only 5 1/4 pounds.) However, it took several years and the British invasion to make it happen. Because of their three-quarter size, most players probably thought the 325s were either student guitars or specialty instruments.

The first guitars from the 310-325 group had solid tops. Perhaps this is why many people thought they had solid bodies. (Nevertheless, at least one made in 1958 had the traditional F sound hole.) Other features included a single gold backed lucite pickguard and a rosewood fret board with dot inlays. The first finishes were a two tone brown sunburst and a natural maple. The company installed the Kauffman style vibrato on the 315 and 325 models.

The first 325 guitar had a single pickup

Mr. Hall in early 1958 with one of the first natural maple 325 guitars.

One of the first Model 325 two tone brown guitars in February 1958.

162

selector switch, a volume control, and a tone control. Factory invoices indicate that at least one 325 had the solid body Combo 850 circuit-- the same as above, but with an additional selector switch. Later in 1958, the factory refitted many of the 325 guitars in Rickenbacker's inventory with two tone controls and two volume controls.

In 1961 photos showed traditional F shape sound holes on some of these models. One example was a Model 310 seen in March. Another example was a Model 315 displayed at the summer trade shows. There is no consistent pattern in the production of F hole and solid top guitars. It was probably simultaneous throughout the history of the 325 style instruments.

A Model 315 guitar probably produced in 1961 and pictured at the N.A.M.M. show in the summer of 1962 had a traditional F hole. It also included a single gold backed pickguard, four knobs, and an Ac'cent vibrato tailpiece.

Thanks to the *Saturday Evening Post* and the *Ed Sullivan Show*, by mid 1964 nearly every young guitarist in America was familiar with Models 310-325. It was about this time that Beatle fans unofficially tagged the 325 "the John Lennon Model."

The standard finishes in 1964 were Fireglo and natural maple. Black was available for an additional twenty-five dollars over the retail cost. The traditional F shape sound holes became standard, but, as before, some solid top guitars were made too. Other regular features included white pickguards, Ac'cent vibrato, and the mixer control.

In 1969 a customer ordered a Jetglo 325 with white binding on both sides.

The 1970s brought changes to the three-quarter size hollow body group. In 1971 the factory deleted the Model 310 from the line. In 1975 the Models 315 and 325 disappeared leaving only the non-vibrato, three pickup Model 320. The 320 pictured in the 1975 catalog had the 1960s style chrome bar pickups, but actual production models had the newer style Hi-Gain pickups. In 1979 the Model 320 had a solid top as a standard feature. The F hole became optional.

In 1981 the company reintroduced the non-vibrato, two pickup solid top Model 310. The F hole was optional. The 1982 price sheets

A 1967 Model 325 with a missing Ac'cent handle.

listed the Model 320S.

Today the three pickup Model 325 is one of Rickenbacker's most collectible guitars--original pre-1964 examples are extremely rare. To satisfy the demand for these vintage style instruments, Rickenbacker introduced the 320B in late 1982. John Hall refers to this as "semi-vintage reissue." More precise re-issues soon followed.

The first reissue Rickenbackers--the B Series from 1982.

Modern Model 320.

Model 325V59--The Model 325V59 is a re-issue of the Model 325 John Lennon bought in Hamburg in 1960. Lennon changed his original constantly, thus making an exact copy impossible. Nevertheless, there are only slight differences in this version and the original. At first John's had a Kauffman Vibrola tailpiece with roller bridges and open-back Grover tuners. The 325V59 has a Bigsby B5 tailpiece like the one added to John's in Germany and Kluson style tuners. John's guitar used a Bigsby bridge while the reproduction has a new Rickenbacker bridge.

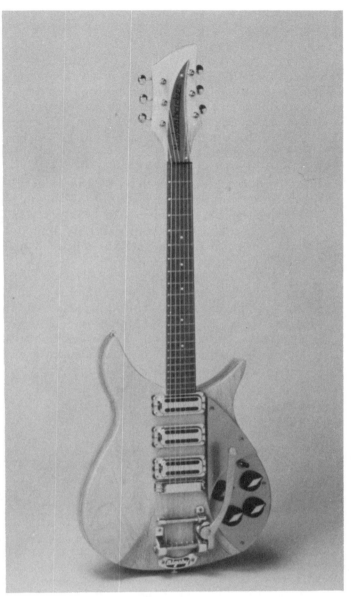

Vintage Series Model 325V59 in Mapleglo.

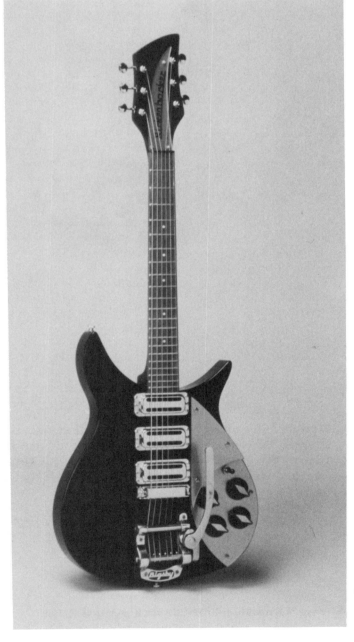

The knobs on the re-issue are the same as John's originals, rather than the replacements shown in most Beatle photos. Lennon's first guitar had a single pickguard rather than the double one used on the reissue. The 325V59 is available in either natural maple or Jetglo black. John's guitar was both colors in its Beatle days.

Vintage Series Model 325V59 with Jetglo finish.

Model 325V63--The 325V63 is a recreation of John's second Rickenbacker, the one sent to the Deauville Hotel in Miami Beach February 13, 1964. It is nearly the same as the original: it has a fifth control knob, a Jetglo finish, and white double pickguards. Like John's second Rickenbacker, the 325V63 has Kluson style tuners. (These are recreations of the originals-- the Kluson company is now out of business.) The company has improved the Vintage Series guitars structurally by employing an improved double truss rod system and an improved body bracing arrangement.

The Rickenbacker factory is quite similar in some respects to what it is was in the 1960s. The company found nearly all the original tools, dies, and patterns when preparing to make the re-issues. This is probably the only guitar company in the world making their re-issues with nearly original tooling.

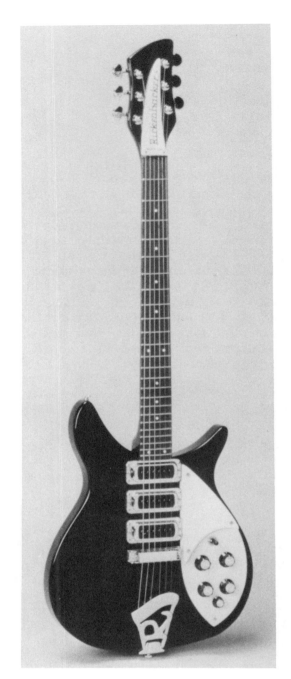

Model 350.

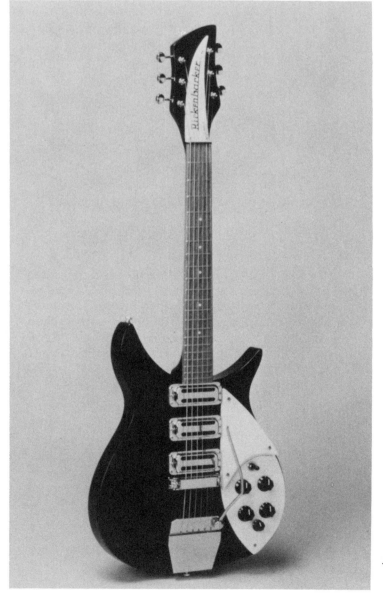

Model 350--The Model 350 is a full scale version of the modern Model 320. Introduced in 1985, this guitar has the same body, pickups, and electronics as its three-quarter scale little brother.

Vintage Series Model 325V63 with a Jetglo finish.

166

Models 330-345--This set consisted of full size guitars with an extreme cutaway to the last fret:

Model 330 (two pickups, no vibrato).
Model 335 (two pickups, vibrato).
Model 340 (three pickups, no vibrato).
Model 345 (three pickups, vibrato).

The full sized Thin Hollow Body Standard Models 330-345, along with the Deluxe Models 360-375, were the quintessential Rickenbacker Capris. There were at least two experimental version of these styles made in 1957. One experimental model had standard features with a long, narrow shaped body which was never put into full production. The other experimental model was essentially a Model 365 as it appeared in production a year later. The factory and Mr. Hall decided to use this same 365 body shape on the 330-345 guitars.

The factory delivered the first production rendering of the familiar 330-345 shape with standard features on February 14, 1958-- the invoice called it a "long scale acoustic vibrato." There are many pictures in Mr. Hall's collection showing guitars from this group. One fact is clear: there were several variations in the earliest 330-345 Capri guitars. Being Standard models, they had dot fret board inlays and no binding (except where noted). Originally offered in two tone brown sunburst and natural maple, some of the natural maple ones had dark brown wood binding.

Nearly every combination of pick guards, knobs, and switches appeared in 1958. In April the factory delivered the first two production Model 345 guitars, each with different tone circuits. One had a single gold backed lucite pickguard, two chrome knobs, and two switches--the so-called Combo 850 circuit. The other had a single pickguard, two control knobs, and one switch like the first 325. Later examples had single gold pickguards, four T.V. style knobs, and single switches. The factory used double gold pickguards as early as December 1958.

One of the earliest Model 335 guitars.

167

There were some Model 330-345 features singular to 1958. The first tail piece used on the non-vibrato 330 was a generic trapeze style, right out of a wholesale parts catalog. The slash sound holes on the earliest 330-345s were noticeably larger than those produced after mid 1958. One Model 345 with a two tone sunburst finish had a solid top.

Most features on the earliest Capris carried through from late 1958 to the early 1960s. Rickenbacker used the Kauffman Vibrola on all the vibrato models until early 1961. Like later examples, the 1958 Thin Hollow Series guitars had a gold backed logo plate on the headstock and two gold backed lucite pickguards. These features lasted until late 1963. The guitars had four T.V. style knobs, slash sound holes, and one switch. The factory installed a flat tail piece on the non-vibrato models.

In 1961 Rickenbacker introduced the Ac'cent vibrato tailpiece and made the bodies thinner. 1962 examples were 1 1/2 inches thick. In 1963-64 the company introduced white plexiglass pickguards and the R tailpiece.

In 1965 there were experiments with a new Model 330 body style. This was like the 1965 Models 360-375, but with the Standard features: dot inlays and no bindings. The company shipped at least one of these guitars in 1965, perhaps more on special orders. Another rounded top special 330 appeared on a 1968 invoice. Despite the experiments, the body style on the normal production model 330-345 guitars remained the same.

The late sixties and early seventies brought changes to the Rick hollow bodies. The first recorded prototype slanted frets guitar was a Model 340 shipped by the factory on November 11, 1969. On May 13, 1970 the factory shipped a twenty-four fret Burgundyglo Model 330 with the new Hi-Gain pickups. The production of twenty-one fret guitars continued simultaneously with the production of twenty-four guitars. The latter were usually special orders. The company first listed a standard Model 330 with 24 frets in 1981.

The company dropped the Model 345 (three pickups and vibrato) from the catalog and price lists in 1975. In 1978 they deleted the Model 335 (two pickups and vibrato) from the price lists.

Late 1958 or early 1959 Model 335 with a two tone brown sunburst finish.

Early 1970s Model 330 with a bound finger board and twenty-four frets.

This was a late 1958 or early 1959 Model 335 with a natural maple finish.

1980s Mapleglo Model 330.

Model 331--The company first offered the Model 331, nicknamed the light show guitar, in 1970. It was the psychedelic spin-off of the Model 330. Stephen F. Woodman and Marshall Arm created the initial design for the 331 and then licensed Rickenbacker to develop and manufacture it. Rickenbacker dropped the 331 from the price sheets in 1975.

To convey the intent of this guitar an excerpt from the brochure that described it follows:

"The Model 331 combines a fine musical instrument with the thrill of a light show. Internally lighted by a set of frequency modulated lamps, this instrument will shimmer with infinite color and pattern variety. This instrument also features Stereo out put, Hi-gain pickups, and 24 frets. The three modulation channels are variable with a sensitivity control to make this patented instrument a beautiful performer in the stage situations professionals encounter."

What did it do? The top of the instrument was translucent and the body had lamps built into it. Red lamps lit on for treble notes played, yellow (or green) lamps lit for middle range notes played, and blue lamps lit for bass notes played. You can imagine how cool it looked. A Rickenbacker factory employee remembers that Buck Owens played the Model 331 frequently on the Hee Haw television show.

Rickenbacker built the light show guitar with two different light circuits. The first version relied on clear light bulbs with colored filters--the factory invoice called it the "Xmas Tree Special." They delivered a prototype on January 20, 1970, while actual production began after June 22, 1970. The factory hand wired the first versions. The second version of the Model 331 was a superior design; it had colored lamps and a better circuit the company mounted on a P.C. board. The second 331 also had a larger outboard transformer.

The factory built both versions of the Model 331 guitar around the body and neck of a Model 330. Some had binding on the body and on the headstock. The factory also made some three pickup light show guitars, the Model 341. (See also Model 331/12 and Model 4005L.)

Today, at the factory, there are parts for a rounded, plastic top guitar. Presumably this was a light show Model 360 prototype (Model 361?).

Model 331 light show guitar from 1970.

170

Models 360-375--The third division of the 1958 Thin Hollow Body Series consisted of full sized guitars with the Deluxe features. The body shape was the same as Models 330-345 from 1958 to the summer of 1964; then it changed.

Model 360 (two pickups, no vibrato).
Model 365 (two pickups, vibrato).
Model 370 (three pickups, no vibrato).
Model 375 (three pickups, vibrato).

The evolution of features in this group approximated the pattern set up to mid 1964 by the 330-345 group. Changes in the 360-375 group usually happened slightly earlier, but not necessarily. The biggest divergence between these two groups was the mid 1964 change in the 360-375 body design.

The guitars from this group were the finest and most expensive of the Thin Body Capri guitars. They had neck binding, triangle finger board inlays, and body binding. The two tone brown sunburst guitars had white body binding while the natural maple guitars had brown wood binding which was later changed to white.

The factory produced the first commercially sold Deluxe Thin Body guitars in May and June of 1958. (They produced the forerunner prototype at least a year earlier according to a dated photo in the Rickenbacker archive.) The guitars had single gold backed lucite pickguards with matching gold peghead logos plates. The first Model 365 had two control knobs and two selector switches. The first slash or cat's eye shape sound holes were larger than later examples. The first vibrato unit used was the **Kauffman Vibrola**.

Two gold pickguards, four T.V. style knobs, and one switch became standard for the Models 360 and 365 before the end of 1958. The non-vibrato model had the flat tailpiece. Mr. Hall did not have photographs of Deluxe 1958 three pickup models; the factory made only one and delivered it the last day of the year.

Natural Maple Model 365 circa 1959.

A single pickguard 1958 Model 365.

In 1959 Autumnglo, sunburst with a slight amount of red, was standard on most examples produced after the middle of the year. These guitars had white trim. Gold backed pickguards and gold backed logo plates were standard. The factory produced some incredibly flamed maple, natural finish guitars around this time. They were among the most stunning electric guitars produced by anyone during any period.

The factory introduced the genuine Fireglo finish in 1960. At first, some dealers and some salesmen preferred the Autumnglo sunburst finish over Fireglo. One comment from a salesman was that Fireglo had too much pink in it. However, after the initial shock of its stunning effect, Fireglo became a universal favorite and the trademark color for Rickenbacker guitars. The factory continued to use Autumnglo on the 360 style guitars occasionally. Another highlight that became part of the Deluxe package featured on the 360-370 models was the Rick-O-Sound stereo jack. This feature appeared in June 1960. Guitars with Rick-O-Sound had two output jacks.

There are interesting photos of a Model 360 at the trade shows in 1961. They show a guitar with a single gold pickguard and an embossed metal logo plate. It was not necessarily made in 1961, but it is a curiosity. Examples such as this illustrate the difficulty of pinpointing precise cutoff points for the dates of Rickenbacker features.

By early 1961, the Ac'cent vibrato unit replaced the Kauffman Vibrola. (1961 invoices from the factory and letters from Mr. Hall to customers state when the new units were available.) The factory also refitted many older guitars with the Ac'cent. The guitars pictured at summer trade shows, probably samples produced earlier, had the old accessory. Often, the original Ac'cent manufacturer delivered the accessory late, delaying production.

1958 Model 365 with a double pickguard.

Again, 1963 was a another year for some uncommon Rickenbackers. One guitar photographed in 1963 had two switches rather than one. Perhaps this was the Model 360 produced in 1963 with a built-in remote transmitter, one of the first cordless systems. Another mystery guitar was a natural finish 360 with a small body; the factory listed it on inventory sheets, however they gave no other details. Some Deluxe guitars from the early 1960s had bound sound holes, available only by special order.

1964 was a transition year for the Models 360-375. During the first half of 1964, the Deluxe Model Thin Body guitars retained the classic double-bound body. These guitars had two white plexiglas pickguards and white logo plates.

Non-vibrato Model 360 circa 1960.

The features in 1961 and 1962 for the Models 360-375 were a mixed bag of old and new. They still had gold backed pickguards and logos. However, invoices for 1961 indicate that the first thinner Model 360 appeared in April. The new slim bodies on the Models 360-375 were 1 1/2 inches thick. These became standard by late 1961. One invoice from March 1961 describes a 365 guitar with an "extra control knob." This fifth knob created a balance between the different pickups' output and the amplifier. By 1962 it became a standard production feature. The R tailpiece appeared at the trade shows in 1963 when it presumably became standard on the non-vibrato models.

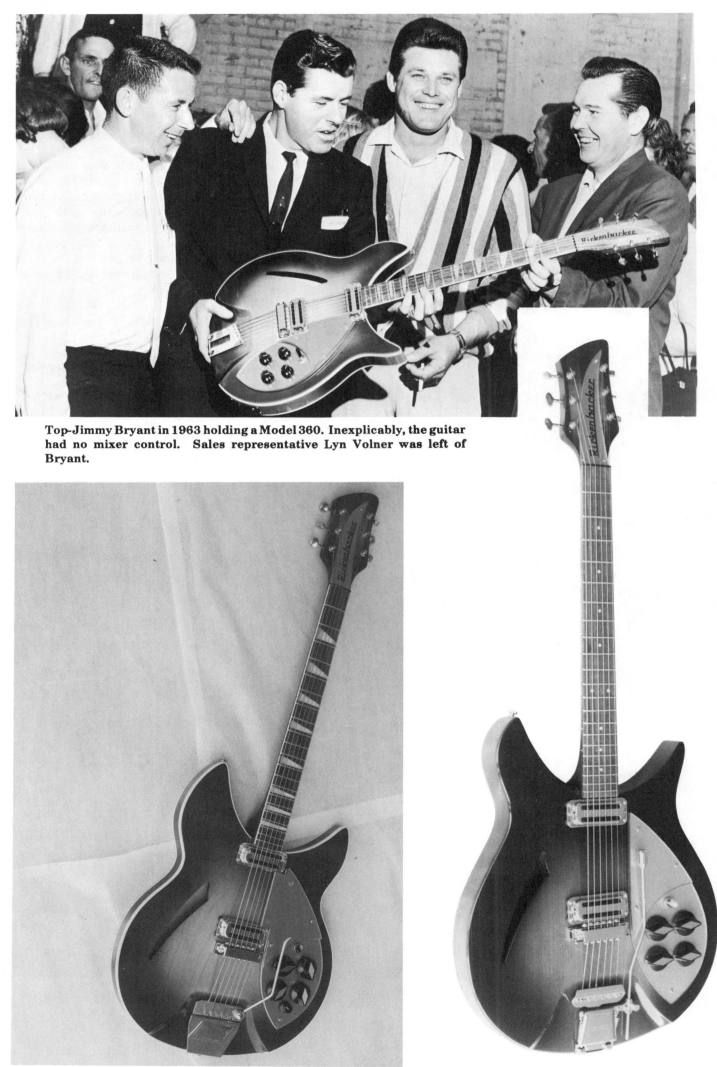

Top-Jimmy Bryant in 1963 holding a Model 360. Inexplicably, the guitar had no mixer control. Sales representative Lyn Volner was left of Bryant.

Compare the Model 365 (circa 1963) on the left with the Model 335 (circa 1959) on the right.

In 1964 Rickenbacker changed the body style of the Models 360-375 significantly. The factory shipped the first known example, a Model 365, on June 1. (A memo from the factory indicated they first contemplated the new body in 1963.) The company achieved the new shape by rounding the top edge on the face of the guitar's body. Mr. Hall described the new look in a press release to the trade papers: "The smooth roundness avoids all that is harsh and yields flowing lines for smooth, easy playing." The new design did not allow for binding on the top front edge of the guitar, however bound tear drop sound holes became standard. The guitar makers kept all other Deluxe features on the new 360 style guitars.

A 1966 Mapleglo Model 370.

A mid 1960s Model 365 with the new body style.

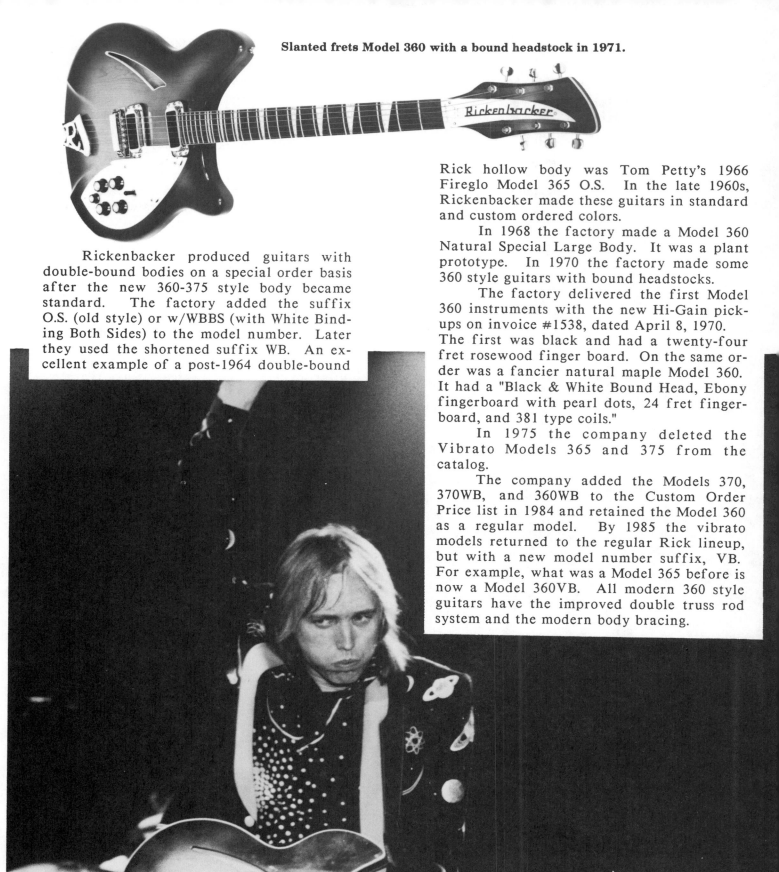

Slanted frets Model 360 with a bound headstock in 1971.

Rickenbacker produced guitars with double-bound bodies on a special order basis after the new 360-375 style body became standard. The factory added the suffix O.S. (old style) or w/WBBS (with White Binding Both Sides) to the model number. Later they used the shortened suffix WB. An excellent example of a post-1964 double-bound

Rick hollow body was Tom Petty's 1966 Fireglo Model 365 O.S. In the late 1960s, Rickenbacker made these guitars in standard and custom ordered colors.

In 1968 the factory made a Model 360 Natural Special Large Body. It was a plant prototype. In 1970 the factory made some 360 style guitars with bound headstocks.

The factory delivered the first Model 360 instruments with the new Hi-Gain pick-ups on invoice #1538, dated April 8, 1970. The first was black and had a twenty-four fret rosewood finger board. On the same order was a fancier natural maple Model 360. It had a "Black & White Bound Head, Ebony fingerboard with pearl dots, 24 fret fingerboard, and 381 type coils."

In 1975 the company deleted the Vibrato Models 365 and 375 from the catalog.

The company added the Models 370, 370WB, and 360WB to the Custom Order Price list in 1984 and retained the Model 360 as a regular model. By 1985 the vibrato models returned to the regular Rick lineup, but with a new model number suffix, VB. For example, what was a Model 365 before is now a Model 360VB. All modern 360 style guitars have the improved double truss rod system and the modern body bracing.

Tom Petty with his old style Model 365 with binding and a missing vibrato handle.

The Thick Body Series
Models 380-394

Introduced in 1958, the Thick Body Series was a catchall group of guitars that included electrics and acoustics. (Originally, Mr. Hall called this the Western Concerto Series, a name that never reached the public.) As the Thick Body Series name implies, each of these guitars had a full length neck scale and a deep body. Each guitar in this category had Deluxe features (except where noted).

Exact documentation of this group of Rickenbackers is difficult. First, the factory invoices often used model numbers different from those used on the price sheets, and there is no way to know what these were without more information. For instance, the factory called some models "large body acoustic" and "acoustic model #1 and acoustic model #2." The second reason it is difficult to document this group is because

This carved top 1958 Model 384 had a traditional style F sound hole.

Roger Rossmeisl ran a virtual custom shop when he worked at Rickenbacker. He made some samples and special order guitars for Mr. Hall that had no corresponding invoices or paper work.

In the late 1960s, there were more unusual Rickenbacker acoustic guitars with ambiguous descriptions. One invoice from January 1969 lists two. The first was a "Deluxe Acoustic, Ebony F Board, Rotomatic Hds, Ebony Bridge--all solid woods, spruce top, rosewood rims and backs." The second was a "Acoustic--Std. Rosewood (ply) rims, maple back, spruce top." The message on the bottom of the invoice was "To be returned-- plant prototypes."

Models 380-384--The body style for this group of guitars had an extreme double cutaway. They also had a carved arch top and a carved back.

Model 380 (Acoustic--no pickup).
Model 381 (two pickups).
Model 382 (two pickups, vibrato unit).
Model 383 (three pickups).
Model 384 (three pickups, vibrato).

This Capris prototype was like a Model 381 with a flat top instead of a carved top.

177

James Burton (left) and James Kirkland field tested Rickenbacker guitars in the late 1950s. Here Burton had a prototype Model 381, and Kirkland had a Model 4000 bass.

The most common model in this group was the 381. In 1957 and 1958 there were two versions of it. One prototype 1957 381 version was similar to a Model 360 with a flat top and back, but it had a much thicker body. The other 381 version had the more characteristic carved top and back. (The factory made a few Model 382 guitars, but called each a Model 381. See below.) The first 381 type guitars had single pickguards and two control knobs. The finger boards had either dot or triangle inlays. They were available in two finishes: brown sunburst and natural maple. At least one 1958 Model 381, the special order prototype played by James Burton, had the traditional F shaped sound hole. In most instances it is assumed that these guitars had the cat's eye slash.

The company abandoned the Model 381 in the early 1960s and reintroduced it in the late 1960s. At that time they made many more--at least twenty-five in 1969. John Kay from the group Steppenwolf used a 381 during this time.

On the new 381s, the factory changed the single pickguards to double split pickguards. They added two additional knobs and the mixer control to the tone and volume circuit. The body was undoubtedly narrower, although it was still beautifully bound and carved on the top and back. One 1969 special order 381 had a carved face and a flat back; the invoice called this a "thin model." Another special 1969 381 had a flat finger board. Some had special order pearl tipped tuning pegs.

The Model 381 was first with the redesigned higher gain Rickenbacker pickups. These first appeared in February 1969 on an experimental Model 381 and later became standard on production models. At first, the factory even called the new Hi-Gain units the "381 type coils."

Rickenbacker dropped Models 382, 383, and 384 from the 1964 price sheet. However, things were not that simple: in the late 1960s the company sold some 381 guitars with vibrato. If they had kept to the original 1958 numbering scheme, they would have called these Model 382 guitars.

The company dropped Model 380 in 1971 and Model 381 in 1974. However, Rickenbacker plans to reissue the 381 as part of the Vintage Series in early 1987.

A 1969 Fireglo Model 381.

179

Models 385-389--The only model out of this group known to exist was the Model 385. There were two versions. One version's body style was a dreadnaught acoustic flat-top with a round sound hole. The other was a Gibson J200 style body. Like the Model 381, the company made few of these guitars. This is how the company listed the different models in the 1958 Technical Data and Price List:

Model 385 (non-electric).
Model 386 (two pickups).
Model 387 (two pickups, vibrato).
Model 388 (three pickups).
Model 389 (vibrato and three pickups).

Rickenbacker booted the vibrato versions and the triple pickup model off the price lists in 1964. They dropped the two pickup Model 386 in 1970 and the acoustic Model 385 after 1971. In the late 1960s there was an acoustic Model 385S with a classical guitar shaped body. The company pictured it in a catalog, but never listed it on the price sheets. Likewise, Mr. Hall displayed a single pickup Model 385 at the 1970 N.A.M.M. show, but never listed it.

The Dreadnaught style version of the Model 385 seems to be the one made after 1958. There are two examples like this in the Rickenbacker museum--each has a fish-tail style headstock. Later 1960s versions had more conventional Rickenbacker style peg heads.

1958 Model 385

Pictured in the center is a single pickup Model 385 acoustic in 1970.

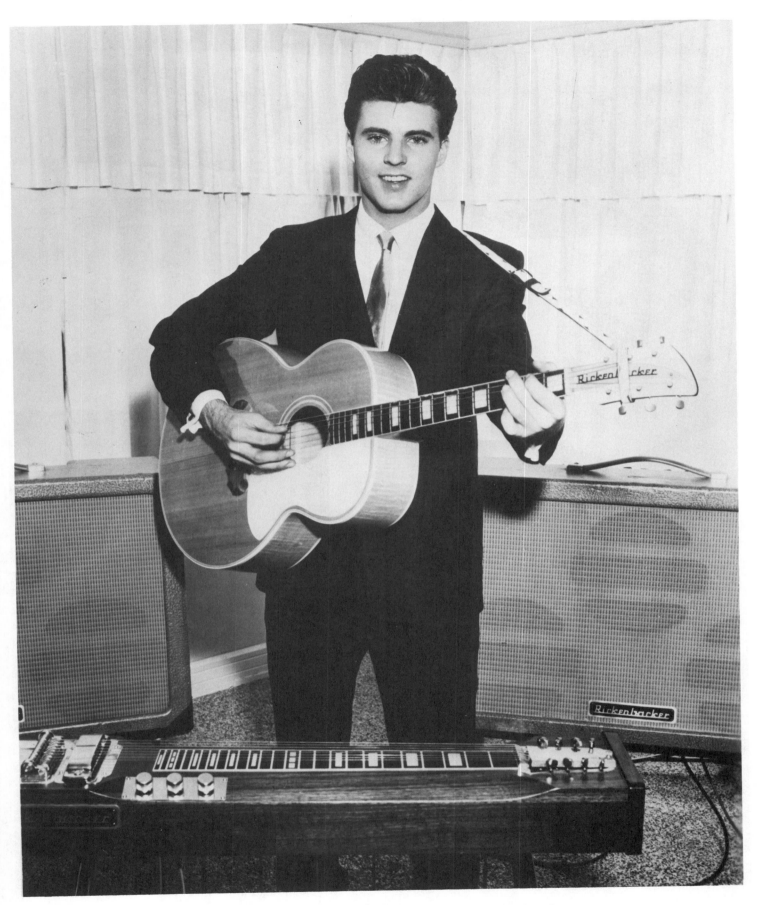

Rick Nelson with a custom-made acoustic in the late 1950s

Jimmy Bryant on guitar and Rex Allen on fiddle in 1963.

Steve Finston, "The Singing Marine," with a Rickenbacker acoustic in 1970.

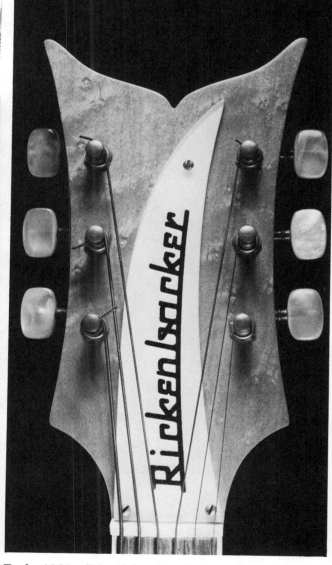

Early 1960s fishtail headstock with simulated pearl tipped tuners on a Rickenbacker acoustic guitar.

Model 390-394--The body for this group had a single cutaway, a carved top, and a carved back:

Model 390 (Acoustic).
Model 391 (two pickups).
Model 392 (vibrato and two pickups).
Model 393 (three pickups).
Model 394 (three pickups and vibrato).

There was only one known model in this set of rare Rickenbackers: the Model 390. The company displayed one early example at the 1957 trade shows. Models 391 through 394 probably never appeared, but the company still offered them. Rickenbacker dropped the three pickup versions after the 1963 price sheet. As with the 385-389 group, the Model 390 body shape did not lend itself to three pickups and vibrato. Rickenbacker deleted the two double pickup models from the price sheets in 1970. This left the arch-top acoustic 390. The company removed the Model 390 from the line in the early 1970s.

Roger Rossmeisl handcrafted this Model 390 acoustic in 1957

The Thin Full-Body Series Models 330F-375F

Model 330F
(Standard features, two pickups, no vibrato).
Model 335F
(Standard features, two pickups, vibrato).
Model 340F
(Standard features, three pickups, no vibrato).
Model 345F
(Standard features, three pickups, vibrato).
Model 360F
(Deluxe features, two pickups, no vibrato).
Model 365F
(Deluxe features, two pickups, vibrato).
Model 370F
(Deluxe features, three pickups, no vibrato).
Model 375F
(Deluxe features, three pickups, vibrato).

One of the first Model 330F guitars, pictured in June 1958.

This was the last group in the Capri Series listed on price sheets (1959). However, Mr. Hall took samples to the late 1958 trade shows. The overall body shape remained essentially unchanged until Rickenbacker dropped these models in the early 1970s. The last guitar with this styling was the Model 360F/12 Deluxe (See electric twelve string section).

The early guitars in this group of Rickenbackers were approximately 2 1/2 inches thick, single cutaway hollow bodies. (The body widths varied as much as 1/4 of an inch.) They came with either Standard or Deluxe features. The neck left the body at the fourteenth fret and the cutaway on the lower bout gave easy access to the seventeenth fret.

Toots Thielemans demonstrated the first known 330F at a 1958 trade show. This guitar had a trapeze tailpiece, a one piece pickguard, slash inlays, and two knobs. Like most subsequent 330Fs, the body was not bound, but the neck was. This inconsistency was a departure from the usual Deluxe/Standard differentiation. Stock finishes were two tone sunburst and natural maple.

Jimmy Bryant with a 360F circa 1960.

Late 1958 style Model 335F with double pickguards, T.V. knobs, and the Kauffman Vibrola.

By late 1958, the features on the 330F-375F guitars were more familiar. The guitars usually had split gold backed pickguards and four T.V. style control knobs. (At least one 365F had a single black pickguard. Another pictured in ads had a combination black and gold double pickguard.) Like the early example, late 1958 Thin Full-Body Ricks had two switches. The vibrato models used the Kauffman style unit.

This Model 365F appeared in several late 1950s magazine ads. It had a split pickguard with a black lower section.

185

A non-vibrato Model 360F circa late 1959. Notice the long flat tailpiece.

A late 1959 365F with a natural maple finish.

In 1959 the non-vibrato models employed the standard flat Rick tailpiece and the instruments had one selector switch. Roger Rossmeisl slimmed these guitars slightly to make them lighter.

In the early sixties, changes in these models followed the pattern set by the 330-375 guitars. The gold logo plate and pickguards changed to white plexiglass. A long R tailpiece replaced the flat one on non-vibrato models after 1963. The factory added the fifth knob mixer control. The Ac'cent became standard in 1961 on the vibrato models. The factory slimmed the width of these guitars down again in the early 1960s. The final narrow version was about 1 11/16 inches thick.

The placement of controls on the late 1960s models was completely different from earlier versions being mounted through the body rather than through the pickguard. Also, on later versions the factory bound the slash sound hole.

The Banjoline and Bantar

Rickenbacker made two types of electric instruments based on the banjo: the five string Bantar and the six string Banjolines.

Model 6000--The company introduced the Bantar in the summer of 1966. The Bantar was an electric five string banjo with two pickups: "Half five string and half the sound of the electric guitar," according to company literature. (Four string models were available on a special order basis.) Bantars were available with a Fireglo finish or with a Mapleglo finish. They came with Deluxe features or with Standard features.

Doug Dillard from the modern bluegrass group called the Dillards and Roger McGuinn of the Byrds used the Model 6000. (A curious note in the Rickenbacker Byrds file says that McGuinn used a Bantar originally given to Bob Dylan.)

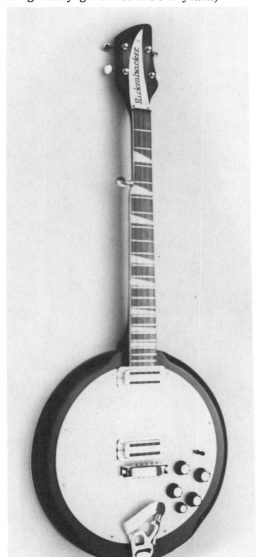

Model 6000 Bantar with Standard features.

Model 6000 Bantar with Deluxe features.

187

Model 6005--Eddie Peabody, a famous plectrum banjoist, helped to design the Banjolines Rickenbacker introduced in early 1968. Eddie had played an electric banjo type instrument made by another manufacturer in the 1950s; he based his suggestions to the Rickenbacker factory for the Rickenbacker Banjolines on his old instrument and his original ideas. The people at the factory made a large contribution to the final product.

The Rickenbacker Model 6005 had a 360 style guitar body with Standard features, a banjo style neck, and an Ac'cent vibrato. Peabody played the instrument using plectrum banjo chords although the Banjolines had six strings. He made plectrum banjo chords possible by tuning two pairs of strings in unison and tuning the two remaining strings normally.

Model 6006--The Deluxe Banjoline had a double-bound carved guitar body and triangle finger board inlays. Both Banjoline models were available in Fireglo, Mapleglo, and Azureglo. Some of the Deluxe model 6006 Banjolines had special order gold hardware. One prototype 360F style Banjoline exists in the company museum.

"King of the Banjo Showmen." Eddie Peabody with his Model 6005 Banjoline.

A 1965 magazine ad for the Rickenbacker twelve string guitars.

Probably no one single guitar typifies mid 1960s rock music better than the Rickenbacker electric twelve string. During that period, major groups like the Beatles, Beach Boys, Jefferson Airplane, and Byrds used Rickenbackers on countless recordings. The twelve string's brilliant tone was the basis for folk rock. The resurgence of a sixties style sound in the late 1970s and the popularity of artists such as Tom Petty brought it back. Far from being obsolete, the Rick twelve string was a potent tool for the 1980s musician.

The idea for electric twelve strings was not new when Rickenbacker put the 360/12 on the drawing board in early 1963. A small company from Springfield, Missouri had made electric twelve strings called Stratospheres in the 1950s. The Stratospheres usually came setup for alternative tunings-- the player had to learn new scales and chord fingerings. The new tunings were an innovative idea, but not accepted. Gibson had made electric twelve strings with the regular tuning before Rickenbacker, but these Gibsons were not widely popular.

In the early 1960s, folk musicians used twelve string guitars extensively, while other stylists found little use for them. However, most of the folk people had a disdain for electric instruments. In mid 1963 no one had a good application in any style for the electric twelve string. Nevertheless, Mr. Hall sensed that the instrument had potential, if designed correctly and played by musicians looking for a new sound.

The company produced three different Rickenbacker electric twelve string guitars in 1963: two 360/12 guitars and one 625/12. An inventory sheet mentioned a back-order for a 360F/12, but there is no evidence that the factory made it. Rickenbacker listed no twelve strings on the 1963 price sheets; the ones made were either samples or special orders. The company displayed the first 360/12 Deluxe at the 1963 summer trade shows.

Heartbreaker guitarist Michael Campbell owns the 1963 625/12. Tom Petty is holding it on the cover of the Damn the Torpedoes record album. It is one serial number away from George Harrison's December 1963 360/12 as Electro String prouced both within days of each other.

Mike Campbell's December 1963 Model 625/12.

The first Rickenbacker twelve string had a conventional setup. By the end of 1963, Mr. Hall devised a novel way to make his new guitar easier to play and to make it sound more distinctive: he intentionally reversed the traditional twelve string stringing. On the new stringing, the twelfth string was the low E instead of the octave above the low E. The eleventh string was the octave string, etc. Strumming down, the lower pitch string was hit before its octave counterpart. George Harrison's double-bound 360/12 was the first Rick strung in this manner. (This is why Mr. Hall always calls George's the first *Rickenbacker* twelve string.)

The Beatles gave the twelve string great exposure on records and in the movie *A Hard Day's Night.* Because of the increased demand created by the Beatles for the instruments, they became regular production items in 1964.

Model 360/12 Deluxe--The 360/12 is the flagship for Rickenbacker electric twelve strings as some of the most noted and acclaimed guitarists in the world have played it. Today it is still the company's most popular twelve string. The earliest ones had a variety of features.

The first 360/12, shown at the 1963 trade shows, had gold backed lucite pickguards, T.V. style control knobs, and a double-bound Fireglo painted body. This guitar had a flat tailpiece used on other non-vibrato Capris. In addition, it had triangle fret board inlays and a non-bound slash shaped sound hole. Like all of the 360 Deluxe models made after June 1960, the twelve string versions normally had Rick-O-Sound stereo.

George Harrison's first 360/12 was similar to the one shown at the 1963 festivals. It had a slash sound hole, triangle inlays on the finger board, and a flat tailpiece. This twelve string had a double-bound body with a Fireglo finish. However, the factory equipped George's guitar with double white pickguards, black control knobs, a mixer control, and the reverse stringing.

The 360/12 displayed at the 1964 N.A.M.M. show was different. This guitar had white guards, a double-bound body, triangle inlays, and an F shape sound hole. Its flat tailpiece and controls were the same as George's earlier model, but it had chrome top knobs.

The production model 360/12 made after the summer of 1964 had a new body style. Like the six string Model 360, the top front edge of the guitar was rounded. The factory bound the back of the body, the slash sound hole, and the neck. The guitar had a cast, chrome plated R style tailpiece. The lack of this single piece delayed the production of new style twelve several weeks, if not a couple of months. The standard finishes were Fireglo and natural maple.

After the introduction of the new style 360/12, the factory still made a significant number of the old style double-bound twelve strings. As with the double-bound 360 style six strings, the factory added the suffix O.S. to the model number. Later they added w/WBBS to the model number. The double-bound instruments came in a variety of colors. Today's nomenclature specifies the old style body with the letters WB, as in 360/12WB.

This 1964 Model 360/12 had a traditional F sound hole while most other 1964 examples had slash shaped sound holes.

Tom Petty with his mid 1960s 360/12.

Australian singer Danny De'Lacy demonstrated the 360/12 at the 1964 summer trade show.

1980s White finish and Black Trim Model 360/12.

Model 625/12 and Model 620/12--The factory made a sample of this guitar in December 1963. They called it the 625/12 at the time. Simply a twelve string version of the solid body Model 625, the first one had Deluxe features, a flat tailpiece, and double white pickguards. Interestingly, the 625/12 was on an 1964-65 Rickenbacker in-house price sheet, but not put into full production that year. Besides the Mike Campbell guitar, the factory made only one more 625/12 during this period, in late 1964.

After the mid 1960s, the company called this model the 620/12. (Usually, non-vibrato guitars did not have a *5* in the last digit.) They were all special orders. The factory delivered a Fireglo three pickup 620/12 on January 27, 1971.

The 620/12 did not appear as a regular on price sheets until 1980. This was after the Tom Petty album cover created a renewed curiosity in solid body Rickenbacker twelve strings.

Model 325/12 and Model 320/12--In February of 1964, Rickenbacker made John Lennon a three-quarter size electric twelve string patterned after his six string Rick 325 guitars. The factory called this guitar a 325/12, although it had no vibrato. John's twelve string was a one of a kind instrument at the time. The factory made another Jetglo Model 320/12 in 1968. A limited production run of these guitars went to Japan in 1985 and a limited number were part of the 1986 Vintage Series.

Model 330S/12--Carl Wilson's first Rickenbacker twelve string had a double-bound body. It had a F shaped sound hole and dot inlays. Like George Harrison's first double-bound 360/12, Wilson's had white pickguards. The factory equipped it with a flat tailpiece and a mixer control. The American model number for this guitar was 330S/12. This style twelve string was the export Model 1993 in England.

1980 Model 620/12.

193

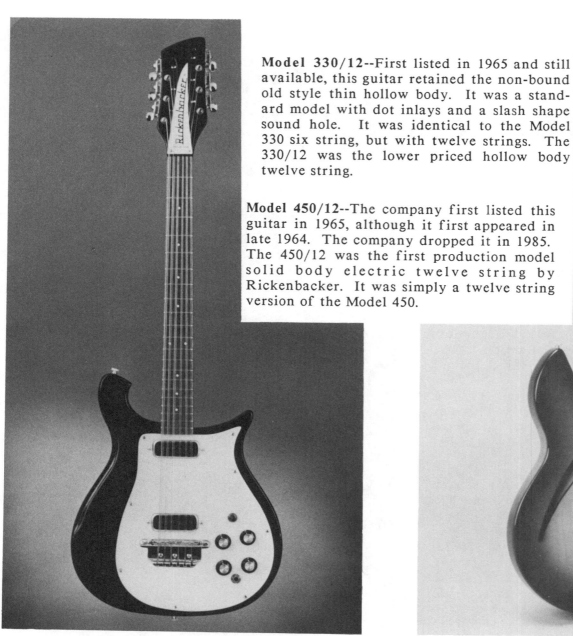

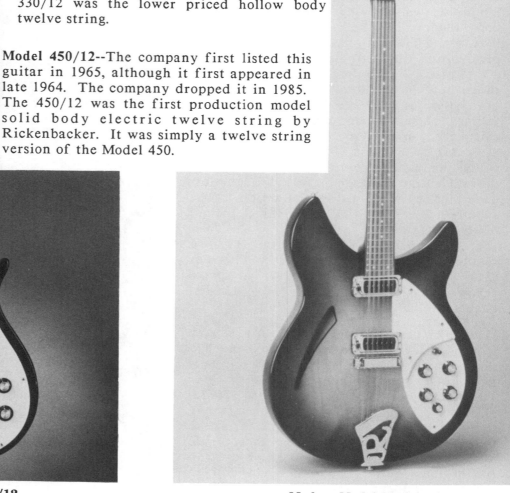

Model 330/12--First listed in 1965 and still available, this guitar retained the non-bound old style thin hollow body. It was a standard model with dot inlays and a slash shape sound hole. It was identical to the Model 330 six string, but with twelve strings. The 330/12 was the lower priced hollow body twelve string.

Model 450/12--The company first listed this guitar in 1965, although it first appeared in late 1964. The company dropped it in 1985. The 450/12 was the first production model solid body electric twelve string by Rickenbacker. It was simply a twelve string version of the Model 450.

Early 1980s Model 450/12.

Modern Model 330/12.

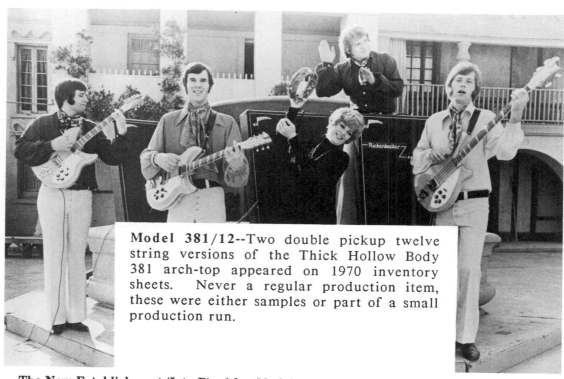

Model 381/12--Two double pickup twelve string versions of the Thick Hollow Body 381 arch-top appeared on 1970 inventory sheets. Never a regular production item, these were either samples or part of a small production run.

The New Establishment (L to R) with a Model 381/12, a Model 381, and a Model 4005.

A 1968 Model 360F/12.

Model 360F/12--Rickenbacker considered making at least one of these guitars in 1963. According to the invoices, they did not deliver it. (Remember that all Rickenbacker guitars produced did not have corresponding invoices.) The first invoice for one was from June 1966. Rickenbacker introduced the 360F/12 as a regular production model in 1973 and offered it until 1980. It was a twelve string version of the single cutaway, Thin Full-Body 360F.

Model 340/12--This guitar was a three pickup version of the Model 330/12. Rickenbacker added it to the price lists on June 1, 1980.

Model 331/12 and Model 341/12--Rickenbacker made a handful of light show electric twelve string guitars. One three pickup Model 341/12, made for Roger McGuinn in late 1970, was just about the zaniest Rickenbacker ever. It had the built-in light show, twenty-two slanted frets, and special Byrd wiring.

Model 370/12--This was the three pickup model played by Roger McGuinn of the Byrds.

Although not listed as a regular production model until June 1980, the factory consistently made 370/12 guitars after the mid 1960s. Some had the special wiring used by McGuinn, the so-called Byrd wiring. The factory did other custom wiring on 370/12 guitars: one made in December 1968 had three volume controls and three tone controls.

Model 370/12WB--This was the double-bound version of the Model 370/12. They also called this model the 370/12 O.S or 370/12 w/WBBS. It had three pickups, Deluxe bindings, and triangle inlays. This model usually remained unlisted, until recently. Still the factory made 370/12WB guitars throughout the late 1960s to the present.

Model 360/12WB--This is the double-bound version of the modern style Model 360/12. In the 1960s they called this model the 360/12 O.S. or 360/12 w/WBBS.

The compact Rickenbacker twelve string headstock made from maple and walnut. This guitar was a mid 1960s Model 456/12.

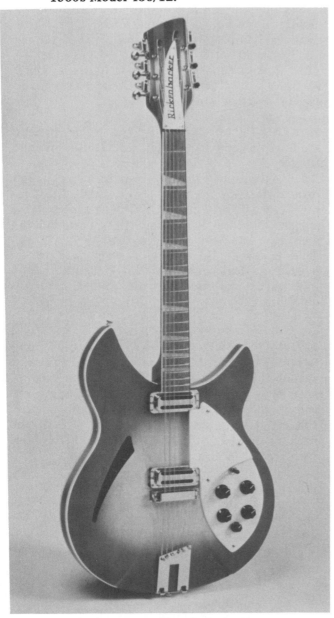

Vintage Series Model 360/12V64.

Model 360/12V64--Introduced in 1984, this is a reissue of the Rickenbacker double-bound twelve string, like George Harrison received in 1964. Finished in Fireglo, it is the same as the original cosmetically, with some structural improvements in the neck rod system and in the body bracing.

Convertible Twelve String Guitars

Rickenbacker introduced a very practical idea to the music world in 1966--the convertible guitar. It changed from six strings to twelve strings (or any number in between) with the flick of a lever device called the converter comb. This is how it worked: When the player did not engaged the comb, the guitar was a standard twelve string. When the player engaged the comb, it pulled any number of strings down and away from the player's pick. Usually, the guitarist played the convertible as a twelve, nine, or six string guitar.

The string converter was the design of James E. Gross of Glenview, Illinois. He installed converters on two Rickenbacker twelve strings for the 1966 music shows. After signing a licensing agreement with Gross in August, the company put the convertibles into full production during the Winter of 1966. Rickenbacker dropped them in 1976.

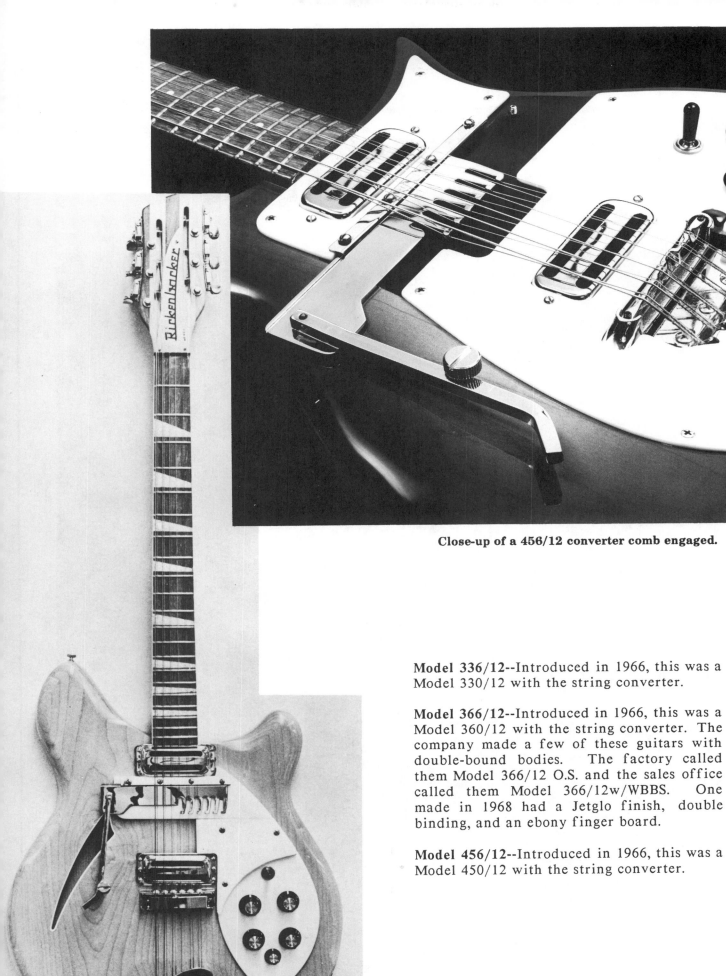

Close-up of a 456/12 converter comb engaged.

Model 336/12--Introduced in 1966, this was a Model 330/12 with the string converter.

Model 366/12--Introduced in 1966, this was a Model 360/12 with the string converter. The company made a few of these guitars with double-bound bodies. The factory called them Model 366/12 O.S. and the sales office called them Model 366/12w/WBBS. One made in 1968 had a Jetglo finish, double binding, and an ebony finger board.

Model 456/12--Introduced in 1966, this was a Model 450/12 with the string converter.

A 1967 Model 366/12 convertible guitar.

Rickenbacker
Electric Basses

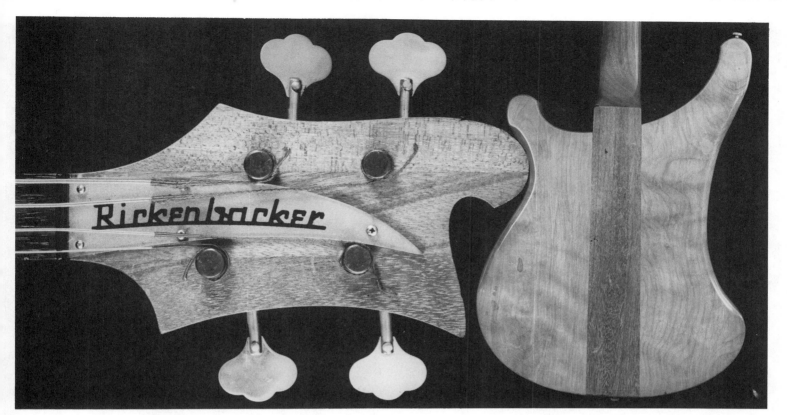

1959 Model 4000 walnut peghead.   Walnut neck-through-body on a 1959 Model 4000.

Rickenbacker Electric Basses

Rickenbacker electric basses are among the most popular electric bass guitars ever produced. They have become well known for their distinctive styling and tone. There is considerable collector interest in the older model Rick basses because of their historical significance and rarity.

Leo Fender invented the fretted electric bass guitar and introduced it through Mr. Hall's company in late 1951. Not only was it a convenient instrument for bass players, its musical potential had a lasting effect on the evolution of modern music. By the mid 1950s, the electric bass was standard. When Mr. Hall took over Electro String, he knew that the development of a bass guitar was essential to Rickenbacker's modernization.

The engineering of the early Rickenbacker and Fender basses reflected two completely different philosophies in instrument construction. There is still a debate in the industry over which design is best as each has its own advantages. Fender's electric bass had an ash body with a detachable maple neck. (The bolt-on neck was an idea first used on electric guitars by Electro String in the 1930s.) Customers were happy because it was easy to service or replace the neck. The manufacturer was happy because the neck was relatively inexpensive to produce.

The first Rickenbacker bass was fundamentally different from the Fender bass. The Rickenbacker's solid, one piece neck extended from the patent head to the end pin of the guitar. Also used on some of the company's standard guitars, they called the Rick bass design neck-through-body construction. The design provided a secure anchor for the strings that enhanced the tone and sustain of the instrument. Today, widespread imitation of this construction confirms its validity.

Modern Rickenbacker basses use both styles of electric bass construction. The Professional Series Basses all have the neck-through-body construction: Rickenbacker still feels this is the best. Despite this philosophy, the company also recognizes that they can make high quality instruments using the more economical approach and introduced new, lower cost basses in the 1970s and 1980s with removable necks.

Geddy Lee of the group Rush with his Model 4001.

Model 4000--The first Rick bass was the single pickup Model 4000. The factory sent the prototype to the sales office to have it photographed in April 1957. They produced the first commercial model in the following June. The Model 4000 remained on price sheets until 1984.

The instrument pictured in the 1957 catalog had a one piece solid mahogany twenty fret neck/body. Two pieces of maple laminated to the mahogany center made up the outer body. The factory mounted the tailpiece, bridge, nut, and tuning keys on the mahogany. (The factory soon switched to walnut for this long body/neck.) The 1957 catalog described double truss rods in the neck and a bridge that was adjustable for individual string height and intonation. There was a single horseshoe style pickup, one volume control, and one tone control.

By late 1957 they equipped the bass with a string mute built into the bridge cover plate which was movable. When it was in normal position, it allowed the strings to ring clearly. When the player moved the cover forward, it muted the strings to create what Mr. Hall called a "bass viol effect." Interestingly, the bridge anchor plate had six holes like the ones on standard guitars.

The first Rickenbacker Model 4000 electric bass guitar.

Model 4000 circa 1958. Notice the sliding cover plate and the walnut neck/body.

Mr. Hall characterized the distinctive Model 4000 body shape in the literature as an extreme cutaway--the fingerboard was clear of the entire body. The pickguard was gold backed lucite. The logo plate on the headstock was either black with white lettering or gold with black lettering. In 1957 and 1958 the finish on the Model 4000 was either natural wood grain or a two tone brown sunburst. By 1960 it was available in Fireglo. The factory turned out solid black and Autumnglo basses in the early sixties too.

The features on the Model 4000 between 1958 and 1965 changed gradually as documented by the company's slide collection and factory memos. The knobs on the earliest bass looked like little black flying saucers; yet, subsequent ones were usually chrome. By 1963 they were the same black knobs as on the standard guitars. The company used white plastic pickguards as early as 1958; they became standard by 1963. The company narrowed the neck width on the basses in 1959.

Rickenbacker made three fundamental changes in the Model 4000 during the early sixties. First, in 1960 a maple neck with walnut pieces laminated onto the peghead replaced the original mahogany (or walnut) one. Second, starting sometime in 1961 the new body was lighter because it was slimmer and more contoured. Third, by the end of 1963 the Rickenbacker tailpiece changed to include under-string mutes.

Although the Model 4000 was a standard model, they produced at least one Deluxe 4000 with a thin body in 1961. It had a Fireglo finish, triangle inlays, and full neck/body bindings. Mr. Hall photographed the Deluxe Model 4000 as Buck Owens' bass player used it at a night club performance.

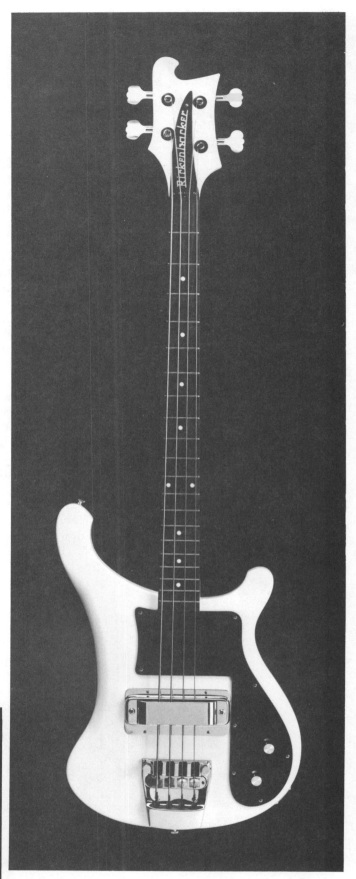

The Model 4000 bass shown in the 1975 catalog.

Left--Neck-through-body construction on a 1963 4001 bass. The Maple neck was an improvement over the mahogany and walnut necks used on earlier Rickenbacker basses.
Right--1963 Model 4001 bass headstock with maple sandwiched between walnut.

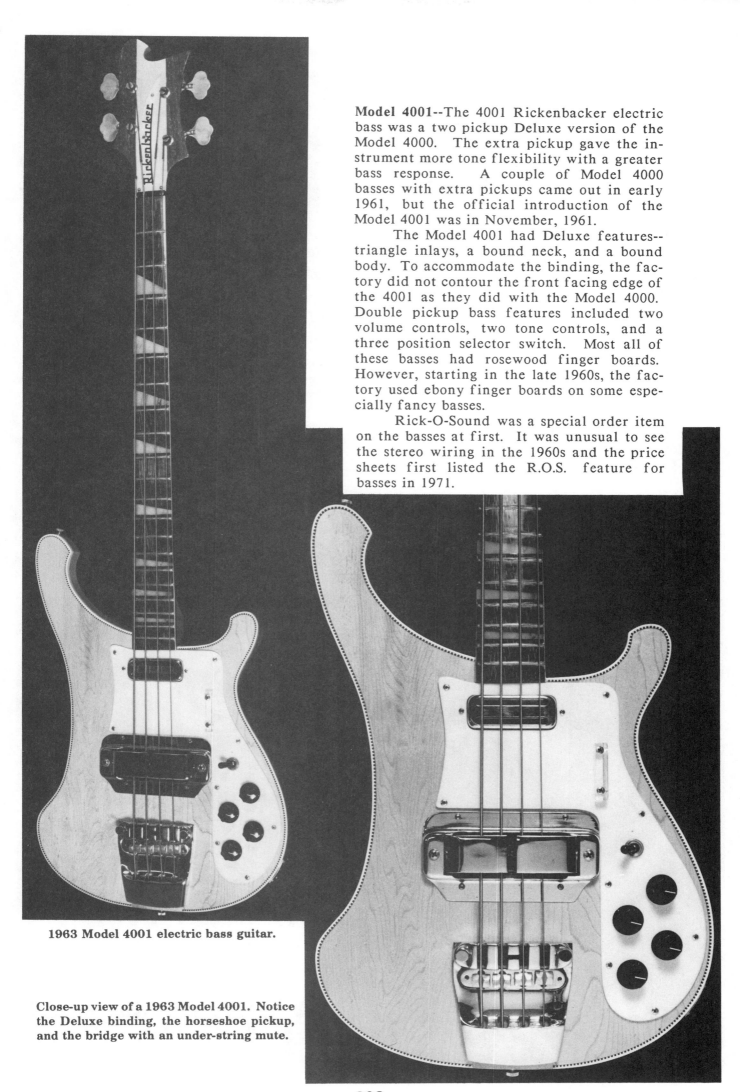

Model 4001--The 4001 Rickenbacker electric bass was a two pickup Deluxe version of the Model 4000. The extra pickup gave the instrument more tone flexibility with a greater bass response. A couple of Model 4000 basses with extra pickups came out in early 1961, but the official introduction of the Model 4001 was in November, 1961.

The Model 4001 had Deluxe features-- triangle inlays, a bound neck, and a bound body. To accommodate the binding, the factory did not contour the front facing edge of the 4001 as they did with the Model 4000. Double pickup bass features included two volume controls, two tone controls, and a three position selector switch. Most all of these basses had rosewood finger boards. However, starting in the late 1960s, the factory used ebony finger boards on some especially fancy basses.

Rick-O-Sound was a special order item on the basses at first. It was unusual to see the stereo wiring in the 1960s and the price sheets first listed the R.O.S. feature for basses in 1971.

1963 Model 4001 electric bass guitar.

Close-up view of a 1963 Model 4001. Notice the Deluxe binding, the horseshoe pickup, and the bridge with an under-string mute.

203

There are some special Rick basses collectors should know about. The factory made three six string Model 4001 basses in 1965. They produced at least three 30 inch scale Model 4001 style basses in the early 1970s. One 1971 special order bass had a white finish, a bound head, and a special pickguard. To contrast with its white finish, the factory installed a black nameplate with white letters. Of interest to instrument photo collectors, the February 1977 issue of Playboy Magazine featured centerfold Playmate Star Stowe holding an Azureglo Model 4001.

Eventually, Rickenbacker dropped the horseshoe pickup on the basses in favor of a redesigned under-string pickup. John Hall believes that the factory used both pickups simultaneously in the early seventies before a complete change to the newer style. The 1975 catalog shows only the under-string pickup. It had a chrome cover that looked like the old pickup's horseshoe magnets. Many players preferred to remove the cover.

Rickenbacker discontinued the regular production Model 4001 in early 1986.

Rickenbacker's double truss rod adjustment nuts on a mid 1970s bass. The factory updated the design in the 1980s.

A mid 1970s under-string style bass pickup with a removable cover.

Uriah Heep bassist Trevor Bolder in 1978 with a 1970s style 4001 bass.

Model 4001S--The factory manufactured the Model 4001 basses with standard features (dot inlays and no bindings). This was the Model 4001S in America and the export solid body bass, Model 1999, in Britain.[30] Rickenbacker's two most famous bass artists--Paul McCartney and Chris Squire--played the 4001S.

The 1960s American price sheets or catalogs did not advertise the plain wrap 4001S. It was available on a special order basis, but the factory made few other than the ones exported. Rickenbacker received more orders for the 4001S in the early 1970s when fans saw McCartney and Squire playing them. The company added the 4001S to the June 1980 price list as a regular model, but replaced it in 1986 with the 4003S.

Paul McCartney with his original Rickenbacker in the 1970s.

Experimental 4001S from 1967 with two under-string pickups.

205

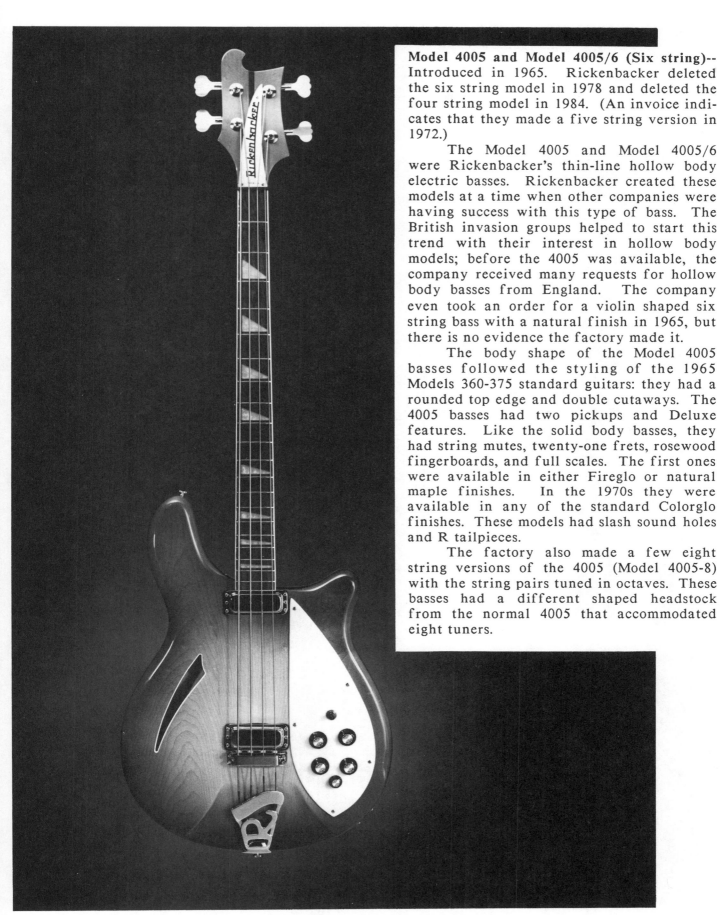

Model 4005 and Model 4005/6 (Six string)--
Introduced in 1965. Rickenbacker deleted
the six string model in 1978 and deleted the
four string model in 1984. (An invoice indicates that they made a five string version in
1972.)

The Model 4005 and Model 4005/6
were Rickenbacker's thin-line hollow body
electric basses. Rickenbacker created these
models at a time when other companies were
having success with this type of bass. The
British invasion groups helped to start this
trend with their interest in hollow body
models; before the 4005 was available, the
company received many requests for hollow
body basses from England. The company
even took an order for a violin shaped six
string bass with a natural finish in 1965, but
there is no evidence the factory made it.

The body shape of the Model 4005
basses followed the styling of the 1965
Models 360-375 standard guitars: they had a
rounded top edge and double cutaways. The
4005 basses had two pickups and Deluxe
features. Like the solid body basses, they
had string mutes, twenty-one frets, rosewood
fingerboards, and full scales. The first ones
were available in either Fireglo or natural
maple finishes. In the 1970s they were
available in any of the standard Colorglo
finishes. These models had slash sound holes
and R tailpieces.

The factory also made a few eight
string versions of the 4005 (Model 4005-8)
with the string pairs tuned in octaves. These
basses had a different shaped headstock
from the normal 4005 that accommodated
eight tuners.

Early 1970s Model 4005 hollow body bass guitar.

Model 4005L--This was the light show bass, a companion to the Model 331 light show guitar. The instruments had the same features as the standard guitar versions, but on a 4005 bass body without a beveled top. The factory made a few 4005L basses in the early 1970s on a special order basis.

Model 4005WB--Rickenbacker produced some 4005 basses in the 1960s with white binding on both sides of the body. At that time factory called these models 4005 O.S. There were six string examples too (4005-6 O.S.).

Double-bound basses were readily available as a production items in the early 1980s. They were in the catalog, but not on the price sheets.

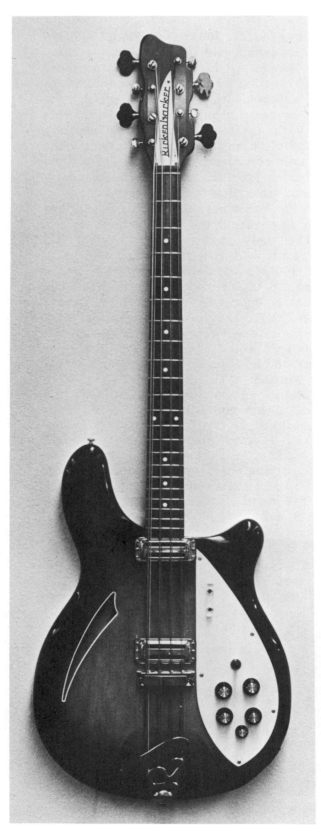

A very rare 1960s 8 string Model 4005-8.

MODELS 4000-4005

Rickenbacker bass models 4000-4005 comprise an extremely complete bass series. The three basic designs offer a wide selection of bass models. Models 4000 and 4001 are Solid Body instruments, allowing a wide bass-tonal variation. String tension is sustained entirely by the neck, as the neck runs the entire length of the instrument. Bridge-tailpiece, pickups, and strap button are actually mounted on the body portion of the neck, assuring perfect structural alignment. Model 4001 is hand-bound with black and white "block" binding. The 4005 series is based on Rickenbacker's famous thin-line semi-acoustic design. This Deluxe series is hand-bound on neck and back, in specially matched binding. Model 4005-6 is a full-scale six string bass, providing the bassist with extra versatility. Body design is identical to Model 4005. All instruments feature special Rickenbacker electronics, combining wide-range variable controls with instantaneous tone switching. All models are available in natural grain Fireglo and Mapleglo.

Model	Hollow Body	Solid Body	No. of Pickups	Deluxe	Neck Binding	No. of Strings	Body Binding	Fret Markers	No. of Frets	No. of Neck Rods	Volume Controls	Tone Controls	Master Mixer	Tone Switch	String Saddles	Mute	Rosewood Fretboard	Maple Body	Thin Neck	Laminated Neck
4000		●	1			4		●	21	2	1	1			●	●	●	●		●
4001		●	2	●	●	4	●	●	21	2	2	2			●	●	●	●		●
4005	●		2	●	●	4	●	●	21	2	2	2			●	●	●	●	●	●
4005-6	●		2	●	●	6	●	●	21	2	2	2			●	●	●	●	●	●

1968 Catalog

Bass virtuoso Chris Squire of the group Yes further enhanced Rickenbacker's reputation for quality bass guitars.

Model 3000 short scale bass from the 1975 catalog.

Model 3001--Although first listed in 1971, the 3001 in its first incarnation was abruptly dropped. In fact, the company made only one prototype of the early design. The factory reintroduced a new version of this bass in 1975, and they made it until 1984.

The factory bound the body and neck on the first Model 3001 bass prototype. This bass had an oblong finger rest on the pickguard and a thirty inch scale with twenty frets.

The second rendition of the Model 3001 was like a full 33 1/2 inch scale Model 3000. The standard finishes were either black or brown stained natural maple. Colorglo finishes were optional. The neck was detachable with twenty frets. The factory made the neck from laminated maple with a walnut stringer and installed a rosewood finger board. Unlike the Model 3000, this bass had three controls (a volume, a bass boost, and a treble boost) instead of two. The single humbucking pickup on the second 3001 was the same as the 3000's.

Model 3000--Rickenbacker first listed the Model 3000 in 1971 and then abruptly dropped it because the original prototype was unsatisfactory. The company introduced a much improved Model 3000 in 1975 and made it until 1984 with its intended role as a low price, economical instrument.

The first Model 3000 was a single pickup bass with Standard features. Its design was the first departure from the traditional Rick bass styling and construction as it had a detachable neck. Also, the body had a totally different shape when compared to the 4000 series, and the neck had a shorter thirty inch scale with twenty frets. The company did not commercially produce this bass as it appeared in 1971.

The second Model 3000 was similar in shape to the first design, but it had a different bridge, a different pickguard, and different electronics. It was available in natural maple and in the Colorglo satin finishes. This Model 3000 bass had a thirty inch scale with twenty-one frets, standard dot inlays, and one humbucking pickup. The combination bridge/tailpiece had individual saddles, adjustments for intonation, and an adjustable mute. The factory contoured the maple body.

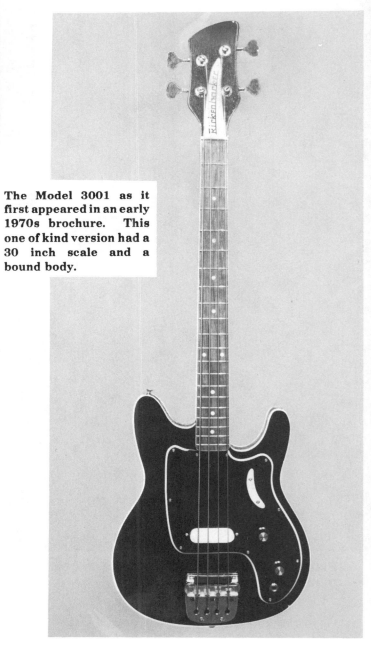

The Model 3001 as it first appeared in an early 1970s brochure. This one of kind version had a 30 inch scale and a bound body.

The Model 3001 from the mid 1970s had a full scale and no binding.

Model 4002 prototype on display at the Rickenbacker museum.

Model 4002--Introduced in 1981 as a limited edition, the Model 4002, in terms of features, was the fanciest bass instrument Rickenbacker ever produced. These were some of the features listed for it in the 1981 catalog:

Body: Selected seasoned Birdseye and Curly Maple finished in Mapleglo or Walnut.
Deluxe Block Binding.
Laminated custom pickguard.
4001 double cutaway body styling for full fret access.
Neck: Laminated, fully bound Maple neck and head.
Dual double truss rods for four-way adjustability Twenty-one frets on a 33 1/2 inch scale.
Imported Ebony fingerboard with pearl style inlays.
Pickups: Two super high gain humbucking pickups

Special effects and controls: Individual tone and volume controls   for each pickup.
Triple position pickup selector.
Separate Rick-O-Sound stereo and mono output jack.
Special low impedance output jack for direct connection with   recording studio control board.

211

Model 4002 from the 1980s.

Left-Model 4003. The company designed this bass to use round-wound strings.

Model 4003--Introduced in 1979, the Model 4003 started as a Model 4001 redesigned for use with round wound strings. The current 4003, much further refined, represents the state of the art Rickenbacker bass. It has an improved neck rod system and different wood lamination so it can use any type string. The body and neck have features that help eliminate dead spots on the finger board, thus improving the instrument harmonically. In 1986 the versatile 4003 replaced the 4001 entirely.

Model 4003S--Introduced in 1980, this is the unbound, Standard features version of the 4003.

Model 4001FL--This was the fretless version of the 4001. The last catalog version pictured had pearloid dot inlays, but otherwise was the same as the fretted version. Although first listed in 1984, the fretless basses have been available on special order since the late 1960s.

Model 4001V63--Introduced in 1984, the Model 4001V63 is a faithful reissue of the early 1960s Model 4001S. The company offers it with the Vintage Series guitars. The 4001V63 is currently available in the original Fireglo and natural maple finishes. The only concession to modern technology is a redesigned truss rod system that allows round wound strings. Cosmetically it is the same as the original 1960s version.

**Vintage Series Model 4001V63
in Mapleglo.**

Paul's bass when it was Fireglo.

Model 4008--This is Rickenbacker's solid body eight string bass, a special order item introduced in the 1970s.

Headstock on a solid body eight string bass Model 4008 from the 1980s.

Model 2030--Introduced in 1984, the Model 2030 in the current catalog is also called the Hamburg Bass. It has a double cutaway body with a contour on the top edge while the rosewood finger board neck is removable. It has two pickups with four control knobs and active circuitry.

Model 2030 Hamburg Bass.

Model 2050--Introduced in 1984, this model also currently appears as the El Dorado Bass in the catalogs. It has gold tuning keys, bridge, and hardware on a double cutaway bound body. The fingerboard is bound rosewood with dot inlays. The electronics include two pickups and an active tone circuit. The factory equips the Model 2050 with round wound strings.

Model 2050 El Dorado Bass.

Rickenbacker Doubleneck Instruments

The Kenny Blackwell Doubleneck--In 1961, amateur musician Kenny Blackwell ordered an unfinished doubleneck body with a batch of un-assembled Rickenbacker hardware. (Kenny was also a friend of the Brook Twins, Rickenbacker artist/promoters.)

The Blackwell doubleneck was the first of its kind produced by Rickenbacker and recorded by an invoice. Electro String sent it to Rickenbacker's sales office on November 30, 1961. Made to Blackwell's specifications, the double-bound hollow body instrument had a bass neck on the bottom. This neck had an extremely short scale by bass guitar standards (26 inches); it had only sixteen frets. The Spanish neck on top was a full scale 360 style with twenty-one frets. Both necks had Deluxe bindings and triangle inlays with two chrome bar pickups for the standard neck, one horseshoe pickup for the bass neck, and a Rick-O-Sound jack.

Blackwell finished the slim 1 1/2 inch thick body with a cherry stain and put the guitar together. The bulk of the guitar had original Rickenbacker parts. However, he bought a few electronic components, like the stacked tone and volume controls, elsewhere. Blackwell made the pickguards out of clear plastic and later mounted a fuzz-tone in a clear plastic box onto the face of the guitar. This personalized guitar definitely had its own character.

Rickenbacker's first known doubleneck bass/Spanish guitar, made for Kenny Blackwell in late 1961. Both necks had sliding bridge covers with mutes.

The Tommy Page Doubleneck--Tommy Page was the leader of a group called the Page Boys. In June 1962 he ordered a doubleneck six string guitar/bass with a Fireglo finish. Delivered by the factory in April 1963, like Blackwell's, it was one of Rickenbacker's most unusual instruments.

The bound body followed the pattern of the 625 solid body, but it was hollow. The bass neck was above the guitar neck. A note by factory manager Ward Deaton indicated that one finger board had four less frets than normal. Undoubtedly, this was a sixteen fret bass neck like Blackwell's. The factory's original plans called for completely separate controls for each neck with a switch to change between the two.

Model 4080--Introduced in 1975, this was Rickenbacker's production model doubleneck guitar and bass. (Earlier doublenecks were always special order items.) The guitar half had Model 480 features and the bass half had Model 4001 features. The instrument had Deluxe bindings, stereo output, and triangle finger board inlays.

1980 Model 4080.

216

Roger McGuinn owns a Rickenbacker doubleneck similar to this mid 1970s Model 362/12.

Model 362/12--Introduced in 1975, this instrument was a hollow body doubleneck guitar with one six string neck and one twelve string neck. It had the double-bound 360 style features. In other words, the body had binding on the top and back. The necks had binding and triangle inlays. The factory installed Rick-O-Sound stereo/mono wiring.

Model 4080/12--This model was a doubleneck combination electric bass and electric twelve string. Each neck had two pickups. A solid body with the styling of the original Rick basses, this instrument had Deluxe features and was a highly specialized item available in the 1970s.

The Rickenbacker Export Guitars

The mid 1960s British Invasion groups had a new look and a new sound that intrigued many young American guitarists. Unlike other U.S. guitar manufacturers selling instruments in England, Rickenbacker inadvertantly added to the unique British image: many Rick guitars played by the Invasion groups were export models with their own characteristic features. Rickenbacker created these export models for an English distributor which sold them primarily in the U.K. and in Europe from 1964 to 1969.

Rickenbacker had sold musical instruments internationally since 1935. Throughout the late 1930s they sent guitars to England, Australia, New Zealand, and Japan. Most of the company's early exports were Hawaiian guitars, although they sent some Bakelite Spanish guitars to England. In the 1950s and early 1960s, Rickenbacker guitars and steels went to such diverse countries as Canada, India, West Germany, and Mexico. In the 1970s and 1980s Rickenbacker guitars and basses were available through their distribution chain to the entire Western world.

Rose, Morris newspaper ad from April 18, 1964.

In the 1960s the Beatles were responsible for a sudden upsurge in demand for Rickenbacker standard guitars. John Lennon played a Rickenbacker in Hamburg and in Liverpool long before he was famous; the American guitar was one of his earliest trademarks. As the Beatles became increasingly popular, more guitarists noticed John's distinctive Rickenbacker. The free promotion for the company was ironic: Rickenbacker had no regular distributor outside of North America and could not easily take advantage of the situation.

Several British music distributors contacted F.C. Hall during the early days of Beatlemania. Rose, Morris & Co. Ltd. was the first, in the summer of 1962 even before the Beatles' first EMI single *Love Me Do*. Despite the different requests, Hall selected Rose, Morris as Rickenbacker's exclusive distributor for the U.K. However, it took about eighteen months to complete the agreement.

With previous export plans, Rickenbacker's sales office had sold instruments to foreign companies. The new arrangement with the British was different; the Electro String factory sold instruments directly to Rose, Morris. The factory prepared to make the first orders for England in December of 1963. They shipped the first sample guitars in January 1964.

Initially, there were five Rose, Morris models--four standard guitars and a bass. Soon they added a twelve string. (In contrast, the 1964 American price list had forty different models.) Eventually, many of these same export models went to Italy,

Sweden, Canada, and Australia. In 1967 Rose, Morris expanded their line further with a hollow body bass and a convertible twelve string.

The export instruments were thoroughly Rickenbacker; the company manufactured them in California with the same quality as the domestic guitars. Although built to the specifications of the export company, they had no exclusive features. Each model had a domestic counterpart--if not exactly the same, then only superficially different. (Please note that small differences in features can make a big difference to guitar collectors.)

In the United States there were Deluxe and Standard versions for most of the different Rickenbacker body styles. The sixties export models had Standard features. The odd exception to this was the export twelve string, which had a bound body and an unbound neck.

The stock export finish was Rickenbacker's trademark Fireglo. After 1964, the English requested black and Autumnglo too. According to factory invoices, Rickenbacker shipped no black guitars, but sent Autumnglo instruments in 1966. Rose, Morris ordered Fiesta Red, the color of popular English guitarist Hank B. Marvin's Fender Stratocaster. Fiesta Red was not a Rickenbacker color.

The export guitar models all had white plexiglass double pickguards adjustable for height, while the bass had a single white pickguard. The company equipped the standard guitar models with Ac'cent vibratos. None of the exports had the Rick-O-Sound stereo jack as used on the Deluxe American models like the Model 360. Knobs on the export models were almost always plain black plastic with a small white line on the top, like early 1960s U.S. versions. After 1963, the U.S. guitars also used the so-called chrome top knobs. These were black plastic with a flat metal insert pressed into the top.

The British ordered the hollow body guitar models with traditional F sound holes. According to distributor Roy B. Morris, there was a great demand in England for a "more traditional and elaborate design like Gibson and Gretsch." After May 1966, Rose, Morris did not require the F hole. They believed that dropping the special request would help Ricken-backer hasten delivery of guitars. Neverthe-less, Rickenbacker still shipped many guitars to Europe featuring the F sound hole.

The export company obviously did not carry the complete line of Rickenbacker guitars available in the U.S., because the fac-tory usually required quantities of at least twenty-five instruments for each model ordered. Despite this requirement, the British possibly received some left-handed models and other special orders priced with a different discount. Rose, Morris wanted to sell Rickenbacker steel guitars, but thought they were too expensive for the 1960s English market.

The British faced Rickenbacker's back order situation (as long as six months in the mid 1960s) and the shipping distance from California. They had problems getting spare parts for repairs, especially for the fragile Ac'cent vibrato. The vibrato tailpiece gave the British real problems.

The export models all had two model numbers: the one used by the American fac-tory and the one used by Rose, Morris. The factory considered export models special orders; so, they added an *S* to the model number they used. For example, the factory called the U.S double pickup bass the 4001; they called the double pickup bass ordered by Rose, Morris the 4001S. Without explana-tion, Rose, Morris created their own model numbering system for the English catalog. Below are descriptions of the export models with their British model numbers.

Model 1995--A solid body with two pickups and Ac'cent vibrato, this model was the same as the mid 1960s Model 615. While every other Rickenbacker export model was a success, the solid body six string sold poorly in England. Rose, Morris shipped forty-five back to America after they sat unsold in England for nearly two years. Obviously, hollow body guitars were more in vogue in the U.K. at the time. The British price with a hard case was 135gns. (One Guinea equalled twenty-one shillings or about $2.52. All prices were for 1964.)

Model 1996--This was the export version of the 3/4 size U.S Model 325, the guitar Beatle fans unofficially called the John Lennon Model. Rose, Morris ordered all 1996 models with F holes. In contrast, some American examples of the Model 325--like two of John Lennon's--featured solid tops. The 1996 and its contemporary Model 325 had three chrome bar pickups and the Ac'cent vibrato. The British price with case was 159gns.

Model 1997 (two pickups) and Model 1998 (three pickups)--The 1997 and 1998 were the two most popular export models. Their American counterparts were the Model 335 and the Model 345, respectively. The F sound hole distinguished both full sized ex-port models from the American editions; the U.S. versions rarely had F holes. Rose, Mor-ris offered only the vibrato versions of the six string hollow body models.

The British called the 1997 and 1998 "slim-line guitars." The British price for the 1997 with a case was 159gns and the price for the 1998 with a case was 170gns.

Model 1999--This was the solid body electric bass export. It had two pickups and Stand-ard features: dot inlays and no bindings. Depending on your point of view, the Model 1999 was either a double pickup American Model 4000 or a dressed down version of the American Model 4001. The 1964 British price with case was 166gns.

Model 1993--The export twelve string landed in England in the summer of 1964. The Model 1993 had a double-bound style body like the original 1964 Model 360/12. However, unlike most of these, the 1993 had an F hole rather than a slash shaped hole. No Rickenbacker twelve string guitars had vibrato; the early export twelve strings had a flat tailpiece and the later 1965 ones had the more stylish R tailpiece.

The body binding and the F hole on the export twelve string differentiated it from the domestic Model 330/12. The latter had no binding and a slash sound hole. Both the 1993 and the U.S. 330/12 had dot finger board inlays. In the Electro String factory numbering scheme the export twelve string was a Model 330S/12; the company sold a few of these in the U.S. and Canada.

Model 3261 and Model 3262--Rose, Morris added two additional models to the export line in 1967: the 4005 hollow body electric bass and the 336/12 convertible twelve string. The export hollow body basses had Deluxe features and slash shaped sound holes like the American versions. Their Rose, Morris designation was Model 3261. The convertible twelve string's export model number was 3262.

Unlike most fads started by the Beatles, the Rickenbacker guitar craze had musical substance. The young musicians following the Beatles' lead found that they achieved a new, unique sound using Rickenbackers. The export line was successful and ironically, helped the company find a whole new market in the United States. The British bands introduced Rickenbackers to many young Americans. In fact, during the British invasion some American guitarists actually thought Ricks came from England or Germany.

In 1969 the relationship between Rose, Morris and Rickenbacker ended because the guitar company found it advantageous to change distributors. Nevertheless, the Rose, Morris connection had fused the Rickenbacker name to the sound of the British invasion groups. This British sound, still widely imitated, had a profound effect on popular music as we know it.

Illustration from the 1960s Rose, Morris catalog.

221

Unusual and Custom Rickenbackers

The Rickenbacker company built custom guitars throughout the 1950s and 1960s. They even advertised their willingness to do so on the inside page of the 1957 catalog: "Custom built guitars may be made to your own specifications, including design, layout, and colors." Unfortunately, the factory maintained no written records for custom instruments other than the regular invoices. And many of these guitars had no invoices. Even if there were an invoice, sometimes it was more tantalizing than informative: One dated June 15, 1962 had the description, "Custom Acoustic, verbal FCH. Pickup by Hall on way to Vegas. To be priced later." This guitar was probably for one of the Western bands Mr. Hall knew in Nevada. A Rickenbacker collector can only imagine what the instrument might have been since *acoustic* often meant thick hollow body, with or without pickups.

Even though all custom instruments did not have invoices, the company preserved their history in other ways. One reliable repository for information about the custom guitars was Mr. Hall's photo and slide collection. Another reliable warehouse for information about other original one of a kind Rickenbackers was the company's museum.

Custom built and one of a kind instruments fell into two categories. The first consisted of instruments custom ordered by either artists, dealers, or customers. These included many regular models with individualized features. This book describes many of these guitars in other sections. The second category consisted of those instruments built as either prototypes or samples to test the feasibility of a design or style. Below are descriptions of some unusual Rickenbacker instruments.

The Custom-Built--Roger Rossmeisl built this guitar on a special order from Mr. Hall in 1956 and the company displayed it at subsequent trade shows. The Custom-Built was a single cutaway, carved top solid body guitar with two pickups. The bound rosewood neck joined the body at the fifteenth fret. This Rickenbacker was one of the first with checkered binding on the body and an Autumnglo finish.

The factory never commercially produced guitars like this 1980 solid body prototype of the Model 320.

The El Toro--The El Toro was a prototype solid body model designed for the otherwise hollow body Western Concerto Series. It was never put into production. Delivered by the factory on June 12, 1958, this unusual Rickenbacker appeared at the summer trade shows with a $700 price tag. One photograph clearly shows that the factory hastily attached the pickguard with Scotch Tape for one of these trade shows. Tommy Sand's rockabilly backup band, the Raiders, used the El Toro for some performances in 1958.

The El Toro prototype had a carved top and natural finish. The body, neck, and headstock had double layered binding and the finger board had small rectangular inlays. The guitar had Grover tuners. The asymmetrical body cutaways and headstock shapes were unlike any Rickenbacker seen before or since.

Like the Custom-Built above, this guitar had two pickups. The El Toro units, placed in a slanted position, had white covers.

Rick Nelson's Custom Acoustic--The factory modeled this round hole, flat top body Rickenbacker after the Gibson J-200. Mr. Hall knew that Rick Nelson had a Gibson. He had seen a picture of it in <u>Look</u> magazine before the factory made Nelson's Rickenbacker in April 1958.

Jim Reeves and the Blue Boys' Guitars--In early 1961 the Rickenbacker factory made three custom ordered instruments for the late Jim Reeves' band. (Reeves was a popular country singer and RCA Victor recording artist.) The Blue Boy lead guitar player received a powder blue Model 360F while the bass player got a powder blue Model 4000 bass.

The truly original and one of a kind Rickenbacker in this order was a powder blue acoustic flat-top Spanish guitar. Interestingly, the factory invoice for this guitar called it a "Blue Boy Martin." (Note its body shape and construction.) The neck was thoroughly Rickenbacker with Deluxe inlays and a gold color logo plate. On the face of the body was a gold lucite pickguard and the letters JR.

Tom Petty's and Michael Campbell's Mystery Guitar--Mike Campbell of the Heartbreakers owns a 1960s three pickup guitar with an unusual top cutaway. Petty usually plays this guitar. A careful search of factory invoices indicated that it was originally a 1965 Fireglo Model 615.

Somewhere along the line someone professionally reshaped the top cutaway and refinished this guitar black. Someone also added a pickup. No Rick solid bodies came standard with three pickups, but it was possible to order an extra pickup on most. It is unlikely the factory modified this guitar because the original Fireglo finish remains under the black over-spray. The factory would have stripped this off before refinishing.

Early 1969 prototype solid body with Hi-Gain pickups. The body on this guitar was thicker than any other Rickenbacker solid body.

Dating Rickenbacker Guitars

Undoubtedly the question arises, how can you determine the age of a vintage Rickenbacker? Players and collectors want to answer this question for several reasons. The most important to some is that the date of an old guitar affects its resale value. For others, the date is interesting just to know and appreciate.

Since determining a guitar's date is both art and science, to do it without help you must have good intuition about the subject, much experience, or both. In any case, there is no substitute for having a sharp eye for detail.

If you are confident about its originality, can you date a Rickenbacker by its features? The answer to this question is a qualified yes. Certainly you can date the guitar to a definite period, but not to its exact year and month. The other sections in this book should help. Though I did not attempt to delineate all the unrecorded changes in Rickenbacker features, I pointed out the obvious ones.

If a guitar is not totally original, you cannot date it accurately by its features. How do you determine originality? This is where the sharp eye for detail comes to play. Examine a lot of guitars and be suspicious. Learn to notice the signatures of the original finishes, tooling marks, and features. Look at a lot of pictures of guitars, especially old pictures. You can find these in books about guitars and entertainers. Collect old guitar catalogs and advertising; though they often had dated pictures, catalogs presented a good overall impression of the instruments available during certain periods.

Early Rickenbackers

Rickenbacker guitars from the 1930s and 1940s present some special problems in dating because there were no serial number and date correlations. The first step should be to identify the model and determine from facts in the book the period the company produced it. The dates of the newspaper stuffed into some metal body steels can be the most reliable way to approximate their age.

Compare clues such as the number of knobs, pickup dimensions, etc., to dated photographs in the book. There were conspicuous differences between prewar and postwar Rick steels; the most notable difference was the size of the pickup magnets. (Prewar pickup magnets were 1 1/2 inches wide while most postwar pickup magnets were narrower.) Look for patent numbers or patent pending stamps and compare these with the patent dates in the book. If an instrument had a patent number, Electro String produced it after the date the patent office assigned the number.

Rickenbackers After 1953

To maintain an inventory, the Rickenbacker company under Mr. Hall made guitars in anticipation of orders from dealers. The Rickenbacker sales people stored the finished instruments at Radio-Tel. When orders came--perhaps on the day the factory delivered the guitar or perhaps months later--they shipped the guitars. So, on any one day the company could have shipped a guitar finished that week or one finished months earlier.

Understandably, to the Rickenbacker sales office a guitar was new on the day its original owner bought it, regardless. The company has always had this policy, even in the most extreme scenario: The factory made a guitar, and it sat unsold for months in Rickenbacker's inventory. Then the company shipped the instrument to a dealer who displayed it for months before a customer finally bought it.

Whatever the company's policy, to collectors a guitar was new the day it left the factory rather than the day a retail customer bought it.

Rickenbacker instruments made after 1953 usually had a serial number date code. Nevertheless, the Rickenbacker factory date codes were only totally reliable when used with inventory/sales records kept at the Rickenbacker office. Since the factory intended to use the numbering schemes inside the company, they used what served their immediate purposes. There were many inconsistencies, both intentional and unintentional, in the different schemes they used. Surely the Rickenbacker factory personnel had no idea that what they did would interest collectors years later.

Original factory records revealed the most frequent inconsistency in the Rickenbacker date codes: many guitars manufactured ended up with numbers from previous months. The date code numbers and the actual delivery date from the factory were out of sync when the factory stamped serial numbers faster than they completed instruments. There was another problem: sometimes, the factory made mistakes stamping the codes, or they intentionally skipped letters and/or numbers in the code.

Another problem in dating Rickenbackers with serial numbers concerns the numbers' integrity. Serial numbers usually appeared on the jack plates or on bridges. On most Ricks these were interchangeable. And yes, today there is a jack plate black market among some unscrupulous vintage guitar dealers as dealers have an incentive to change serial numbers on some models, even on instruments not stolen. Older dates can raise the price for some models while not significantly affecting the price of others. By switching number plates on certain instruments, a dealer can derive the maximum profit from two instruments. Of course, only unscrupulous dealers engage in this practice.

The 1950s Serial Number Codes

You can either date or estimate a date for most Rickenbacker guitars made in the 1950s using the factory serial number codes for that time. However, like the haphazard model numbering system, the factory date code system was a crazy quilt until late 1960.

1950s Solid Bodies and Basses

The code for 1950s solid bodies and basses was simple when the factory used it consistently.

Model Designation for Full Size Solid Bodies--A close examination of the examples below reveals that the first number before the letter in the serial number was an abbreviation for the model number. The letter following the first numbers was an abbreviation for the instrument style.

These are examples of complete serial numbers as they appeared on the full size standard guitars, basses, and mandolins:

> #4C6231 was a 1956 Combo 400. (4C=Combo 400 or Model 425).

> #6C444 was a 1954 Combo 600. (6C=Combo 600).

> #8C410 was 1954 Combo 800. (8C=Combo 800).

> #65C7110 was a 1957 Combo 650. (65C=Combo 650).

> #85C7121 was a 1957 Combo 850. (85C=Combo 850).

> #B7105 was a 1957 bass. (B=Bass).

> #M101 was a 1958 mandolin. (M=Mandolin).

The Model 450 usually had a 4 rather than a 45 in the first space of the serial number. Its last figure was the letter A, e.g., #4C7414A was a 1957 Model 450.

Date Code Numbers on the 1950s Solid Bodies--On solid body guitars made before September 1959, the number after the letter was the year of manufacture in the 1950s. For example, #6C7139 was a 1957 Combo 600. (See the other examples above.)

The last digits in the serial number were the identifying number for the individual instrument. So, the guitar serial #6C7139 was a 1957 Combo 600, #139.

Exceptions to the 1950s Solid Body Date Code--The factory mislabeled some guitars, like the Model 1000 #V8537. It had a 1958 date in its serial number, but the company produced the guitar in 1959 according to its factory invoice. The factory omitted the date on a few 1955 guitars. These guitars had two digit numbers after the C, e.g., #6C75 was a 1955 Combo 600.

On full sized solid body guitars made between September 1959 and October 1960, the code did not reveal the date of manufacture. The factory had used all the possible three digit numbers up to 999 following the date number. Inexplicably, when the factory started the three digit sequence over, they omitted the date code number.

However, you can date the full size solid body guitars produced between September 1959 and October 1960 because their serial numbers ran in approximate sequence. For example: #4C100 was a September 1959 Model 425. The first 1960 Model 450 was #4C216A. One of the last 1960 Model 425 guitars coded with this system was #4C570. (You know this was not a 1955 guitar because the factory introduced the 425 in 1958.)

Date Codes on the Bass Guitars--The number following the letter B in the bass guitar code revealed the date of manufacture. The last three numbers revealed the approximate order of manufacture. The #B7100 was for the first Rickenbacker bass guitar; the factory built it in 1957. #B8113 was a 1958 bass and the fourteenth in the series that started in 1957.

1960 basses continued the numbers started in 1959. The first bass number in 1960 was #B9144. #B9172, made in October of 1960, was one of the last 1960 basses labeled with the 1950s code.

3/4 Size Guitar Serial Numbers--The factory usually numbered the three quarter size guitars like these examples:

> #V7379 was a 1957 Model 1000
>
> #V7255 was a 1957 Model 900.
>
> #V0139 was a 1960 Model 900.
>
> #V014 was a 1960 Model 950.

V usually stood for Model 900 or Model 1000 and sometimes for Model 950; the code on these guitars revealed no specific model number, but it did tell you that the instrument was one of the three smaller student models.

Date Code on 3/4 Size Guitars--The date code for these instruments was the same as the other models. There was one exception: The code continued without change for the three quarter size guitars in 1960. For example, A *0* in the first position after the letter, as in the #V014, meant 1960 on Models 900, 950, and 1000.

Exception to the 3/4 Size Number Scheme--The factory marked some Model 950 guitars with an A in the last position like #7384A, a 1957 Model 950.

1950s Hollow Body Guitars

The code for Rickenbacker hollow bodies made from 1958 through December 1959 revealed model information, but not the exact date of manufacture. The first digit in the serial number usually equaled the number of pickups on the guitar. The factory marked the hollow body guitars like these examples:

#2V165 was a September 1958 Model 365.

#2V166 was a September 1958 Model 335.

#2T388 was a May 1959 Model 330.

#2T417 was an August 1959 Model 360.

#3V701 was an October 1959 Model 345.

#3V254 was a December 1958 Model 375.

Exceptions to the Hollow Body Code--The first Capris, like early 1958 Model 325 #V85, did not have a pickup designation number before the letter. On other guitars, the number was incorrect. For example, #2T344 was a three pickup 1959 Model 370 instead of the two pickup model the 2 indicated.

The letter in the serial number on hollow bodies, either a V or a T, indicated the tailpiece style. V stood for vibrato model and T stood for tailpiece (non-vibrato) model. However, there were exceptions to this: #2V172 was a non-vibrato Model 330 produced in October 1958 instead of a vibrato model the V indicated.

Approximate Dating of the 1950 Hollow Bodies--The factory made guitars with the code described above from 1958 through the end of October 1960. On these guitars, the number that followed the letter indicated an approximate sequential order of production, a sequence that started in 1958 with #V80. The last Capri number in 1958 was 3V254, a three pickup vibrato Model 375. So, the factory made hollow body guitars with numbers between 80 and 254 in 1958.

By the end of 1959 the numbers were considerably out of sequence: The highest number in 1959 was 2T835, a dark Model 330. The last 1959 Capri, delivered by the factory four days after #2T835, was a dark Model 365, #2V823. The first Capri delivered in January 1960 was #3V706.

1960 Hollow Bodies--The hollow body code numbers started over in January 1960. #2T001 was a dark finish 1960 Model 330F. 1960 numbers below 100 had three digits with a 0 in the first position, like #2T001; 1958 numbers below 100, like #V85, had only two digits after the letter. (Despite the new sequence of numbers, as late as March 1960, some guitars slipped through with old 1959 numbers in the range of 820 through 838.)

In June of 1960 the factory started a new sequence of numbers for Deluxe model hollow bodies. They replaced the T or V with an R. The R stood for Deluxe models with Rick-O-Sound. For example, #2R022 was a Deluxe Model 360F made in July 1960.

There were 1960 numbers between 100 and 155 that duplicated 1958 numbers. For example, #3V121 was a 1958 Model 345 and #2V121 was a 1960 Model 335. The 1960 hollow bodies with these duplicate numbers invariably were models with Standard features: Models 310-325, Models 330-345, and Models 330F-345F. The highest repeat number used in 1960 was #3V154, a Fireglo Model 325 delivered on November 4, 1960.

Post-1960 Date Code

All Rickenbacker instruments manufactured after October 1960 had a seemingly simple serial number code, usually found stamped on the jack plate or bridge. These are examples of numbers found on instruments made after October 1960:

#JK20 was a November 1960 Model 425.

#AA47 was a January 1961 Model 4000.

#AB112 was February 1961 Model 950.

#DJ416 was an October 1964 Model 360/12.

#HL1746 was a December 1968 Model 4005.

This is how the post-1960 Rickenbacker date code worked. The first letter of the code represented the year and the second letter in the code represented the month. The first month and year of the scheme was November 1960, e.g., #JK20 was a number from November 1960. J, the tenth letter in the alphabet, stood for the zero in 1960. K, the eleventh letter in the alphabet, stood for the eleventh month of the year, November. (Dating Chart A lists these letter/date correlations from November 1960 to 1970.)

The pattern started afresh in January 1961. The first letter in the serial number stood for the year; an A, the first letter in the alphabet, represented 1961. An A in the second position of the serial number represented January, the first month. So, January 1961 was AA. February 1961 was AB; the A stood for 1961 and the B stood for February. AC was March 1961.

The letter B, the second letter in the alphabet, stood for 1962, the second year in the scheme. So January 1962 was BA. February 1962 was BB.

Before 1966, numbers in the code started with 01 and ran to 999, in rough sequence. Then they started over. After 1965, it was normal to find four digit numbers after the code letters. For example, #GD2042 was a 1967 Model 615.

Exceptions to the Post-1960 Date Code--The cutoff date for the institution of the new system, November 1, 1960, was not precise; some guitars delivered after it had old numbers. Obviously, since the factory used the letter J during two months of 1960 and the entire year of 1970, some 1960 numbers were possibly the same as 1970 numbers.

Some instruments, like #CM105 made in December 1963, had date codes that made no sense in the context of the defined system. (Unless 1963 had thirteen months.) Some instruments simply left the factory later than their date indicated: #JL182 was a January 1961 Model 360, though the code said it was a December 1960. #CG727 was an August 1963 Model 365, although the date code indicated the factory made it in July 1963.

Getting Help--This book is a guideline only. If your are serious about accurately dating your guitar or confirming a date, the Rickenbacker company can help. Guitar dating is a free service to customers, and they would like to hear from you. You must supply your complete name, your complete address, and your guitar's complete serial number. The complete serial number includes all its letters and numbers. (A snapshot sent to the company will help it identify your guitar's model number.)

Dating Chart A

Here is a helpful chart that shows the letter/date correlations in the post-1960 serial number code.

First Letter--------Year	Second Letter------Month
J.................1960 (November and December only.)	A.................January
A.................1961	B.................February
B.................1962	C.................March
C.................1963	D.................April
D.................1964	E.................May
E.................1965	F.................June
F.................1966	G.................July
G.................1967	H.................August
H.................1968	I.................September
I.................1969	J.................October
J.................1970, etc.	K.................November
	L.................December

Production Totals 1932-1942

I gathered the totals listed below from several different sources in the Rickenbacker files. No complete records from the 1930s remain; some year's records were comprehensive and some years records were incomplete. Years with incomplete totals are marked with an asterisk (*). For some years, the totals reflected the number of instruments sold as opposed to the number actually produced. The actual number produced was more than likely slightly higher.

Totals for the years 1932 to July 1936 were for a complete unit (instrument and amplifier), except where noted.

```
1932-28
    Break down      17 complete Haw. sets
                     4 Spanish sets
                     5 Spanish guitars
                     2 amps
1933-95
1934-275
1935-1288

    Break down      140 seven string steels
                    1136 six string steels  (probably includes Spanish guitars,
         though not stated.)
                     12 violins

1936*  First six months--707 (plus 112 from July to August 10)
    Break down      606 six string steels (Spanish Guitars?)
                     71 seven string steels
                     28 violins
                      2 bass viols
    July-Aug. 10     95 six string steels
                     13 seven string steels
                      3 violins
                      1 bass viol
```

Hand Vibrolas for May 15, 1936 to Jan. 15, 1937--161 (Hand Vibrolas were standard issue on the Spanish guitars, tenor guitars, and mandolins. This number should be used by you to estimate how many of these items the company produced.)

```
1937* Hand Vibrolas--163

1938* Hand Vibrolas--98
    Vibrola Spanish Guitars--46

1939* Hand Vibrolas--37
    Vibrola Spanish Guitars--10
```

1940 Number sold. B=Bakelite
Sil.=Silver Model
59=Model 59 Steel

	B	Sil.	59	Span.& Misc.
Jan.	49	18	54	11
Feb	44	25	46	6
Mar.	28	10	48	22
	121	53	148	39
Apr.	28	15	52	6
May	27	11	62	5
June	23	10	38	12
	78	36	152	23
July	16	12	37	20
Aug.	15	6	12	10
Sept.	64	19	74	9
	95	37	123	39
Oct.	24	8	61	15
Nov.	41	31	49	9
Dec.	47	27	123	13
	112	66	233	37
total	406	192	656	138

Vibrola Spanish Guitars--26
Hand Vibrolas--38

1941* Hand Vibrolas--8
Vibrola Spanish Guitars--8

Electro's New Vibrola Spanish Guitar

An amplified Spanish guitar with a patented, electrically operated mechanism that moves the strings in a perfect vibrato—pulsating, rhythmic, throbbing tones that express emotions characterized in the past only by the human voice. The tonal quality surpasses anything you have ever heard before.

An important new feature of this model is the convenient stand which is part of the amplifier. It holds the guitar in playing position, and may be moved laterally or vertically as the player desires.

The amplifier is the Professional Model described to the left which incorporates the newest ideas in sound amplification and radio construction.

Hear for yourself what wonders can be done with the Electro Vibrola SpanishGuitar—Hawaiian effects with chord combinations (impossible for the Hawaiian guitar)—majestic organ crescendos—novel mimicry effects of reed and percussion . . . ALL are made with very little practice on this sensation new instrument!

No. 198-S—Electro Vibrola Spanish Guitar Outfit, complete with
    Professional Model Amplifier and stand.................... **$198.50**

Patents

A patent is a government grant to an inventor that supposedly gives the exclusive right to make, use, or sell an invention if that patent does not infringe on somebody else's previous patent. The Patent Office, which grants patents, is a division of the United States Department of Commerce with its main headquarters in Washington D.C. In theory a patent is an advantage to an inventor and his company--it should guarantee them the just rewards for their efforts in developing new ideas. Nevertheless, there are many popular misconceptions about what a patent is and what a patent is not.

For the 1930s guitar makers, a patent was more a license to fight in court than it was a right to manufacture. The Patent Office in its patent investigation proceedings did not consider whether an invention infringed on prior patents. That was the role of the United States District Courts. If challenged by holders of prior patents, a patent holder was vulnerable. So, patents were really meaningless until they were adjudicated in court.

In the early music industry, many companies were reluctant to challenge other company's patents: they feared that the courts would examine their own patents and find them infringing on prior art (previous patents). Companies did lose patents in court as the Schireson Bros. did in an infringement case with National over single cone resonator guitars.

The process for obtaining a patent was expensive and time consuming; it deterred many people with original ideas. That is why so many inventors did not patent their novel devices. For those who went through the process and received a patent, defending or challenging claims often took years. Challenging other's claims was frequently more expensive and complicated than it was worth; many dubious patent claims stood because nobody bothered to fight them. Clearly, the ones that always gained from the early patent fights that did take place were the patent attorneys.

The patent office deemed that some patents were only improvements or additions to previous patents. To use these, a manufacturer received permission or a license from the previous patent's holder. Al Frost put together a patent portfolio for Valco and calls the whole process a "legal jungle." Nevertheless, practical businessmen applied for patents in hopes they would get some protection.

According to the Patent Office rules, only the actual inventors could apply for patents. Since the notch on the inventor's six shooter was a patent number, if they could afford it, they applied for patents just for the sake of doing it. However, sometimes the name on a patent did not tell the whole story, especially if that person was an employee of a business where people shared ideas on a daily basis. It was impossible to sort out who did what in those situations; the name on the patent often reflected shop politics as much as individual creativity. The patent laws did not protect a device before the actual issuing of the patent. So the two most famous phrases in guitar collecting, "Patent applied for" and "Patent pending," were meaningless in a legal sense. Al Frost says that any company that wanted to scare competition just stamped these terms into their products. Sometimes these companies had really applied for a patent and sometimes they had not. Many firms that did not bother to apply for a patent went years making believe they had.

Despite its potential flaws, the patent record is one way to prove a point about early accomplishments. It is one of the only ways to establish (or at least begin to establish) when who did what in industry.

Rickenbacker Related Patents

Below is patent information related to the Rickenbacker instruments. Included is the patent number, the application date, the patent date, the inventor's name, and the subject of the patent.

#1,839,395 August 19, 1929--January 5, 1932 C.O. Kauffman-- *hand vibrato tailpiece.*

#1,881,229 August 15, 1928--October 4, 1932 A.P. Young--*molded musical instrument bodies and necks.*

#2,089,171 June 2, 1934--August 10, 1937 George D. Beauchamp--*Frying Pan guitar and horseshoe pickup.*

#2,130,174 January 14, 1936--September 13, 1938 George D. Beauchamp--*headless electric violin class instruments.*

#2,152,783 May 26, 1936--April 4, 1939 George D. Beauchamp--*roller vibrato tailpiece.*

#2,241,911 Septemaber 26, 1939--May 13, 1941 C.O. Kauffman--*Vibrola Spanish Guitar.*

 # 2,310,199 October 14, 1940--February 9, 1943 George D. Beauchamp--*tubular body electric violin class instruments.*

#2,310,606 October 25, 1941--February 9, 1943 Paul M. Barth--*detachable horseshoe pickup.*

#3,091,150 August 30, 1961--May 23, 1963 Peter P. Sceusa--*the Sceusa neck.*

#DES. 208,329 September 26, 1966--August 15, 1967 F.C. Hall--*Bantar.*

Production Totals for Guitars and Basses 1954-1968

These totals reflect information on Rickenbacker factory invoices. Some samples and prototype guitars did not have invoices; so, I did not count these instruments. The factory designated acoustic guitar models with numbers different from those used on the price sheets; rather than guess what acoustic models the factory made, I left them uncounted. Invoices for 1967 and the first two months of 1968 were not found, and I did not consider guitars made after 1968.

The invoices did not always list the same specific colors listed in the catalogs or price sheets. The abbreviations for color represent the invoice description when possible. I combined color categories for some models to make the tables easier to read.

These are the abbreviations used in the tables:

DK - means dark finish, two tone brown, or Autumnglo.

BR - means brown.

FG - means Fireglo.

NT - means natural or Mapleglo.

BLK - means black or Jetglo.

GR - means Cloverfield Green.

BL - means blue, turquoise, or shaded blue.

OT - means other color(s) than those listed.

NC - means no color listed on the invoice.

BL/GR - means blue green (The factory probably meant Cloverfield Green when it stated blue green.)

BLD - means blonde

WHT - means white

GRY - means gray.

Thin Hollow Body Guitars

O.S.- Old Style

Model		58	59	60	61	62	63	64	65	66	67	68
310	DK		1	4								
	NT		1							4		
	FG			2				5		12		
	OT	1										1
315	DK		6									
	NT		4							1		
	FG			3	1			5	1	5		
320										4		1blk
325	DK	20										
	NT	8								6		
	FG			1				23	1	20		5
	BLK							2	1	20		5
330	DK	15	21	1								
	NT	1	19	8			1	5	17	41		27
	FG			13	11	1	4	27	46	216		38
	OT									7blk		18
335	DK	30	26	4								
	NT	19	23	7	1		2		15	86	Not Available	
	FG			13	8	2	6	22	34	329		2
	OT									27		26
340	DK	1					1					
	NT											
	FG					1		2	4	38		3
	OT									5		10
345	DK	22	16	7								
	NT	2	13	12	5					12		16
	FG			25	16	2		2	8	82		13
	OT								1	34		1
360 O.S.	DK	12	83	10								3
	NT	2	13	11	6		2					1
	FG			39	20	1	4		4			11
	OT											6
365 O.S.	DK	33	74	10			4					2
	NT	1	16	15	5	2	7		4	7		7
	FG			50	74	41	26	4	15	62		19
	OT	3				1				1		8

Thin Hollow Body Guitars

Model	58	59	60	61	62	63	64	65	66	67	68
NEW STYLE 360 FG							6	73	180		27
NT							1	23	59		20
BLK									23		7
OT											19
NEW STYLE 365 FG							58	94	459		52
NT							8	31	140		80
BLK							1	1	23		7
OT								1			8
370 O.S. DK		2									2
NT		2									1
FG				3							9
OT											3
375 O.S. DK	1	5								Not Available	
NT		4	5	6	2	3					4
FG			2	3	4	5		1			8
OT											1
NEW STYLE 370 FG									1		17
NT									5		
BLK											3
OT											7
NEW STYLE 375 FG							6	9	43		16
NT							2	7	24		16
BLK							1		7		7
OT							2				3

Solid Body Guitars

Model	54	55	56	57	58	59	60	61	62	63	64	65	66	67	68
400 BLK			122	94											
BR			35	6											
BL/GR			62	54											
OT			1	3											
420 FG												13	13		8
BLK												20	2		5
NT												9			
425 DK					1	70	36								
BLK						15	40	4	4	32	14	19			
NT						44	18	2	11	10	13	17	2		
FG							44	91	89	126	89	73	14		3
OT							1			1		4			
ELECTRO ES17 FG											98	255	27		72
NT											1				
BLK											5				
RYDER 425 FG										14	51	24			6
CONTELLO 425 FG									23						
BL									19						
450 DK				23	11	26	33	1							
BLK				45	32	17	67	32	11	8	6	35	43		12
BL/GR				21											
FG							123	90	9	36	27	79	64		1
NT						7	43	25			1	12	15		6
OT					1										11
460 FG								59	50	30	11	6	15		
NT								4		2	2		12		4
BLK									2	3	12	13	8		1
OT												1			1
600 BLD	13	5	20	8											
OT			9	3	4										
615 FG									4	10	18	23	1		
NT											2	2			
BLK									1*nv		2	6			
625 FG									62	70	35	61			1
NT									2	3	4	28			5
BLK									9	11	6	8			2
OT									1	1					

*Non-Vibrato

Solid Body Guitars

			Year				
Model	54	55	56	57	58	59	60
650 NT				2	2	1	
BL/GR					1		
800 BLD	23	19	30	17		1	
BL/GR			7	8			
850 NT				17	3	1	
BL/GR					6	9	
WHT				1			
DK					2		

3/4 Size Soild Body Guitars

					Year						
Model	57	58	59	60	61	62	63	64	65	66	67
900 FG							22	12	15		
BLK	10			3		1	8	4	2		
NT				4	2	1	5	5	4		
BR				2							
NC	90						°				
950 FG					6		23	20	10		
BLK	5			1	4		2	8	6		
NT					3		6	5	5		
BR			1								
NC	29	4							1		
1000 FG						6	45	18	15		Not Available
BLK	8	2	4	14		2	7	5	3		
NT			26	17			10	2	4		
DK		7	5	5							
GRY	8										
NC	199	59									
ELECTRO ES16 FG								50	37	38	
RYDER 1000 FG							21	28	23	17	
ASTRO KIT							74	104	5		

Bass Guitars

Model	57	58	59	60	61	62	63	64	65	66	67	68
4000 DK		3	7	6								
NT		2	10	11	9		5		2	2		11
FG				15	36	3	40	1	21	3		17
NC/NT	13nc	12nc										2BLK
4001 FG					5	2	29	33	42			83
NT							12	9	3			74
BLK							1	2	4			31
OT							1					11
4005 FG									14	27	Not Available	37
NT									4	8		18
BLK										1		11
OT												6
4005/6 FG									2			2
NT												
BL												
OT												
4001S FG					2			2				3
NT												
4005 O.S. FG										10		
NT										7		

F Series Guitars
Thin Full Body Models

Model		58	59	60	61	62	63	64	65	66	67	68
330F	DK		1	6								
	NT		3	3								
	FG			4								
335F	DK	3		5								
	NT											
	FG			6								
340F	DK											
	NT											
	FG											
345F	DK			2								
	NT			2	3		1			Not Available		
	FG			1	1	*1						
360F	DK	1	2	4	1BL	1						2*
	NT	5	12	16	7							3
	FG			15	4							9
365F	DK			2								
	NT			3								
	FG			5		3						
370F	DK											
	NT											1
	FG											
375F	DK		1									
	NT			3								
	FG			2		1						

*1 Autumnglo
1 Burgandyglo

239

Model	63	64	65	66	67	68
330/12 FG		1	12	275		9
NT			10	87		5
BLK				30		
OT						
330S/12 FG		1	2			
360/12-O.S. FG	2	5	23			1
NT			6			6
BLK						
OT						1
NEW STYLE 360/12 FG		29	346	827		24
NT		6	130	270		28
BLK		1	4	67	Not Available	4
OT						9
370/12 FG				2		
NT				2		1
BLK				1		
OT						
450/12 FG		12	212	278		
NT			117	97		
BLK			7	109		1
OT						
625/12 FG	1	1		2		
NT						
BLK						
456/12 FG						17
NT						10
BLK						
OT				1		2
366/12 FG				3		92
NT				2		13
BLK				1		6
OT				1		14
360/12F FG				1		

Model	68
336/12 FG	15
NT	7
BLK	
OT	
366/12 O.S. FG	
NT	
BLK	4
OT	1
370/12 O.S. FG	
NT	1
BLK	
OT	1

Production Totals for Rose, Morris Exports 1964-1967

		1964	1965	1966	1967
Model	1995	101	0	0	
Model	1996	201	0	0	
Model	1997	101	75	50*	50
Model	1998	126	50	50**	50
Model	1999	101	25	25**	
Model	1993	25	75	0	

Rickenbacker shipped one Model 360S/12 twelve string sample in mid 1964. (This was a double-bound Model 360/12 with a traditional F sound hole.)

Other Exports--1966

Other Rickenbacker exports in 1966 included 25 Model 1998 guitars sent directly to Rose, Morris Australia.

27 Model 345S guitars and 2 Model 335S guitars went to Audrea Buari, & Figli in Italy.

25 Model 335S guitars went to Muskantor & Co. in Sweden.

25 Model 335S guitars went to Barabash Music Corporation in Canada.

*25 of these were Autumnglo.

**All of these were Autumnglo.

241

Chapter Notes

1. John Dopyera's version illustrates the inherent contradictions in the National story that no one can resolve with certainty. To this author's knowledge, the only time Dopyera agreed or acknowledged that George made any contribution to the tri-cone was when he assigned his patent to the National stockholders in 1929. Then he agreed that George, Paul, and Ted had "each contributed his time and efforts and substantial sums of money in and about the development and perfection of the said invention." One point often ignored, and agreed to by everyone, was that Dopyera was making the first tri-cone guitar for Beauchamp. Custom-made instruments usually follow the customer's wishes to some extent. Readers wishing to further explore the National story and its controversies should read <u>American Guitars</u> by Tom Wheeler, published by Harper & Row, 1982.

2. The Patent Office granted this patent, #1,762,617 on June 10, 1930.

3. Patent #1,741,453, granted December 31, 1929. The tri-cone was also covered by Design Patent # 76,382, **granted September 25, 1928.**

4. Al Frost's records, which include minutes taken at the National corporate meetings, start in 1928.

5. To illustrate how enthusiastic Beauchamp was about his experiments, the phonograph he tore apart and sacrificed to the cause was a new present from Ted Kleinmeyer to George's brother Al.

6. Beauchamp, and probably others, had the correct analysis of the electric guitar problem. However, inventors such as Lloyd Loar were trying to amplify the guitar strings and the full guitar tone itself. See August 1936 <u>Music Trades.</u> Beauchamp's conceptualization of the electric guitar allowed him to make a successful one.

7. The first Electro String factory was a one story brick structure owned by Lazard Bernstein. Later, Adolph bought the building. Before it was a guitar factory the building housed a restaurant.

8. Original documents show there were 1500 corporate shares divided between six individuals. Each stockholder advanced the cash amount shown below.

George D. Beauchamp	600 shares	$100.00
Adolph Rickenbacker	360 shares	$250.00
Charlotte Rickenbacker	360 shares	
Paul M. Barth	300 shares	$100.00
C.W. Lane	225 shares	$ 50.00
C.L. Farr	15 shares	

At one time all the stockholders in Ro-Pat-In except Billie Lane either worked for National or owned National stock.

9. Adolph's wife Charlotte was wealthy by inheritance and Adolph's manufacturing company was successful--money was not a burning issue for the Rickenbackers. Rick advanced Ro-Pat-In Corp. $1,330.28 in addition to the initial $250.00 in 1932.

10. From a company document, the "History of Rickenbacker" written by Adolph Rickenbacker in July 1960.

11. Adolph never actually changed the spelling of his name; his last business card in the 1970s had the old spelling. The company used both spelling inconsistently until the late 1950s. Most of Adolph's Swiss-American relatives Americanized the spelling of their name because the war hero Eddie Rickenbacker did.

12. A December 1934 factory inventory sheet listed a "violin mold--in progress." The letter to the Bakelite Corp. is on file in the Rickenbacker archive.

13. Patent #1,881,229.

14.   Kauffman is better known for his association with Leo Fender and their short-lived quasi-partnership called K&F. His work with Electro String and Fender was a vital link in the history and development of the electric guitar in Southern California.

15.   Patent #1,808,756 was for the single resonator type National produced. National sold many thousands of these in the 1930s, and many acoustic blues guitarists still prefer them. Patent #1,808,757 was for George's other single resonator design that National did not produce. Patent #1,787,136 was for the National finger picks. About the inspiration for the finger pick design, Nolan Beauchamp says, "I think he must have had sweaty fingers."

16.   Among Electro String's competitors with new electric guitars in the 1933-37 period were Epiphone, Vol-U-Tone, Gibson, Vega, Vivi-tone, Kay-Kraft, Fretted Instrument Mfrs., National, Dobro, and National-Dobro. Dobro was the first in 1933.

17.   Estoppel meant that the court stopped Miessner from asserting its claim against the electric guitar makers because it was inconsistent with a position Miessner had previously taken.

18.   Nolan Beauchamp says that Harry Watson used Douglas fir for the first Frying Pan.

19.   Adolph said they solved this problem by stuffing the necks with newspaper. If they used this remedy, they used it infrequently on Frying Pans.

20.   The Rickenbacker files and the National corporate minutes confirm this fact beyond a doubt.

21.   Lloyd Loar's solid Vivi-Tone is another contender. However, it did not have a modern electric pickup.

22.   Harold Kinney died on July 21, 1952. Adolph apparently bought his widow's interest in the company. Paul Barth was a corporate officer until he left.

23.   Rickenbacker used distributors such as Coast Wholesale Music Co., Grossman Music Co., the Progressive Musical Instrument Corporation, and many others.

24.   Musician, August 1980, p. 98.

25.   The Who--Maximum R&B, Richard Barnes, published by Eel Pie Publishing, Ltd. London, England. 1982.

26.   Bud Scoppa, The Byrds, Scholastic Book Service, New York, 1971. p. 16.

27.   Bob Rissi has his own company today called Norcraft, which manufactures Risson amplifiers.

28.   Because of their rarity, the Transonic amps are quite collectible.

29.   The mixer control was called the compensator control too.   This is how Mr. Hall described the feature in letter dated July 26, 1966:
      "The small fifth knob, located on the pick guard panel, controls the balance between the instrument and the amplifier you are using. The best position for the setting of this knob is determined by placing the tone control switch in the center position and rotating all of the tone and volume controls to their maximum position except the bass tone control which is rotated in the maximum counter-clockwise position. Adjust the volume on your amplifier to the loudest volume you will be using during the time the instrument is played. Rotate the small knob to the position that produces the tone you will be using the majority of the time. After these adjustments have been made, do not turn the small knob, but use the other knobs to get additional sound effects." It panned from the front pickups to the rear pickup.

30.   There was some confusion about the model design bass. At one point the company referred to it as "the Rickenbacker 4000 solid body bass guitar with extra pickup." The factory called it the 4000S/2 and the 4001S/2 in correspondence to England.

Richard R. Smith, a professional guitarist and freelance writer, was born in Fullerton, California. He attended the University of California, Santa Barbara and California State University, Fullerton earning a bachelor's degree in sociology and a teaching credential. Internationally recognized as an expert in vintage guitar collecting, Richard R. Smith writes the Rare Bird column for Guitar Player magazine. Smith has also contributed several articles about guitar history to Guitar Player and Guitar World magazines.

For more information about Rickenbacker Guitars
Contact:
RICKENBACKER INT'L. CORP.
P.O.Box 2275
Santa Ana, CA 92707 U.S.A.

Bass books from Centerstream Publishing

P.O. Box 17878 - Anaheim Hills, CA 92807 - P/F (714) - 779-9390
Email: Centerstrm@AOL.com

SCALES AND MODES FOR THE 5-STRING BASS

by Brian Emmel
foreword by Mark Egan
Centerstream Publications
The most comprehensive and complete scale book written especially for the 5-string-bass. Divided into 4 main sections: 1) Scale Terminology 2) Scales 3) Fingerboard chart and diatonic triads 4) Scale to Chord Guide – tying it all together and showing what scale to use over various chords.
_____00000146...........................$9.95

ROCKIN' CHRISTMAS FOR 5-STRING BASS

by Brian Emmel
Centerstream Publications
12 of the most popular Christmas songs arranged for rock guitar, including sweep picking and two-hand tapping, and cool string bending. Songs include: What Child Is This? • Joy To The World • Silent Night • We Wish You A Merry Christmas • and more. Correlates with *Rockin' Christmas For Guitar.*
_____00000172...........................$9.95

BASS GUITAR CHORDS

Centerstream Publications
84 of the most popular chords for bass guitar, including: finger placement, note construction, chromatic charts and most commonly used bass scales. Also has helpful explanation of common 2-5-1 progression, and the chords in all keys.
_____00000073...........................$2.95

Art of the Slap

by Brian Emmel
Centerstream Publishing
This slap bass method book, designed for advanced beginning to intermediate bassists, is based on the understanding and application of modes. The focus is on the concept of groove sculpting from modes, and not on the actual right and left hand techniques. The CD features recordings of all the examples, plus a split-channel option to let you practice your playing. Includes 13 songs.
00000229 Book/CD Pack $16.95 (1-57424-053-6)

BLUES GROOVES

NEW! **INCLUDES TAB**

Traditional Concepts Playing 4 & 5 String Blues Bass
by Brian Emmel
Centerstream Publishing
This book/CD pack has been designed to educate bass enthusiasts about the development of different styles and traditions throughout the history of the blues, from the 1920s to the early 1970s. Players will learn blues scales, rhythm variations, turnarounds, endings and grooves, and styles such as Chicago blues, jazz, Texas blues, rockabilly, R&B and more. The CD includes 36 helpful example tracks.
_____00000269 Book/CD Pack.....................$17.95

5-STRING BASSIC FUNDAMENTALS – THE FUN APPROACH TO BASS IMPROVISATION

by Brian Emmel
Centerstream Publications
This fun new bass method will help you improve your solos, grooves, and bass lines, no matter what style you play. Accompanying CD includes recorded examples.
_____00000086 Book/CD Pack $17.95

CREATING RHYTHM STYLES FOR 5-STRING BASS WITH DRUM ACCOMPANIMENT

by Brian Emmel
Centerstream Publications
This book is designed for bassists to program the written drum grooves into a drum machine and develop a working knowledge over the rhythms and various styles. Drummers can play the written patterns along with a bassist and both can elaborate their playing skills over each examples. The accompaniment CD allows you to fade out the bass guitar part on the left channel or the drums on the right channel.
_____00000162 Book/CD Pack $17.95

PURRFECT 4-STRING BASS METHOD

by Brian Emmel
Centerstream Publishing
This book will teach students how to sight read and to acquire a musical vocabulary. Includes progressive exercises on rhythm notation, 1st to 4th string studies, enharmonic studies, chords and arpeggios, blues progressions and chord charts.
_____00000201...........................$9.95

...I'm here to proclaim that this is one of the best books ANY beginner, regardless of age will find today. . .I recommend this book to teachers who have sought but not found a great book to start their beginners off with. . .--Jim Hyatt, BASS Frontiers Magazine

Video

Beginning 5-String Bass
by Brian Emmel
This hour-long video is all you'll need to build a lasting foundation on the 5-string bass! Brian will take you through all the basic techniques, with exercises to help you develop familiarity on the 5-string. Includes information on scale patterns, how to practice, chords and chord substitution, slap technique, and rhythm patterns such as rock, R&B, shuffle, country, soul, funk, and blues. All exercises and patterns are shown in standard notation and tablature in the 18-page booklet that comes with the video. 60 minutes.
00000199 . . . . **$19.95**